THE FRAMEWORK OF ANGLO-SAXON
HISTORY TO A.D. 900

THE FRAMEWORK OF
ANGLO-SAXON HISTORY
TO A.D. 900

KENNETH HARRISON

formerly Fellow of King's College, Cambridge

CAMBRIDGE UNIVERSITY PRESS

CAMBRIDGE

LONDON · NEW YORK · MELBOURNE

Published by the Syndics of the Cambridge University Press
The Pitt Building, Trumpington Street, Cambridge CB2 1RP
Bentley House, 200 Euston Road, London NW1 2DB
32 East 57th Street, New York, NY 10022, USA
296 Beaconsfield Parade, Middle Park, Melbourne 3206, Australia

First published 1976

Printed in Great Britain
by W & J Mackay Limited, Chatham

Library of Congress Cataloguing in Publication Data
Harrison, Kenneth.
    The framework of Anglo-Saxon history, to A.D. 900.
    Bibliography: p.
    Includes index.
    1. Great Britain—History—Anglo-Saxon period, 449-1066—
Historiography. 2. Calendar, Anglo-Saxon. 3. Beda, Venerabilis,
673-735. Historia ecclesiastica gentis Anglorum. I. Title.
DA129.5.H37   941.01'07'2   75-13450
ISBN 0 521 20935 8

CONTENTS

Preface   *page* vii

1 The moon and the Anglo-Saxon calendar   1

2 Raiding and settlement   15

3 The Easter tables of Dionysius   30

4 The Christian era in Britain   52

5 Bede's History   76

6 Annals and charters   99

7 The Anglo-Saxon Chronicle   120

Appendix 1: Succession among Kentish kings   142

Appendix 2: Numerology   147

Bibliography   151

Index   163

v

PREFACE

This book is concerned with the historical framework provided by dates – for which, like most other people, I have a poor head. But to anyone with a scientific training the chief interest of dates may well be found in how they were arrived at and whether we have reason for believing them. Here science and history begin to overlap, because reckonings of time are based on calendars which in turn are based on astronomy. Although the historian is in pursuit of larger quarry he must sometimes stop to ask whether something did happen when somebody says it did. In modern history, days or even hours can be important to our understanding of events; at the pleasant pace of Anglo-Saxon life we tend to deal, on the whole, with months or years, even if these longer measures are not free from doubt or difficulty. Thus an enquiry into particular dates will not lose sight of the chief end: to discover, if possible, the systems of dating which were employed during the various stages of early English history.

A good deal of space is devoted to the development of a concept which now extends far beyond the island then called *Britannia*. Although the Anglo-Saxons did not invent the Christian era, still less the Julian calendar on which it is founded, they promoted it to become a standard reckoning for historians, and in everyday use, over many parts of the world. As often happens when changes of outlook take place, the process is slow and the first steps are obscure; at several points I must confess to being guided only by what is simple and probable. The Christian era, with its years A.D., arose from attempts to calculate the festival of Easter by means of a luni-solar calendar; the same type of calendar was also employed by the Anglo-Saxons in their heathen days, a reckoning which only looks difficult because it is unfamiliar.

PREFACE

From the time of Kemble, Plummer, Birch and Stevenson to Sir Frank Stenton in our own day the documents have been edited and criticised to a point where the chronologer can step in. It is to a continuator of this tradition, Professor Dorothy Whitelock, that I owe my greatest debt – and not only because she has persevered in reading through the whole book, as well as the papers on which it is largely based. Without her friendly and acute remarks, backed by a memory for inconvenient fact, there would have been altogether too many loose ends and errors of judgement; and without her rare knowledge of diplomatic an enquiry into several problems could not even have been started. For their comments on particular sections I am also grateful to Professor L. Alcock, Professor B. W. Cunliffe, Dr D. N. Dumville, Dr D. C. Heggie, Dr Kathleen Hughes, Dr D. P. Kirby and Dr J. M. Wallace-Hadrill; but they, and Professor Whitelock, are not responsible for the opinions put forward here.

I should like to thank the Editors of *Anglo-Saxon England*, *Antiquity*, the *English Historical Review*, the *Journal of the Society of Archivists*, and the *Yorkshire Archaeological Journal* for giving me their permission to quote from previously published material.

From the beginning I have enjoyed advice from the staff of the Cambridge University Press, who have carefully drawn attention to lapses of various kinds; the rest are mine. I also wish to thank Barbara Coysh and Julia Mankowitz for their patience in typing so accurately a manuscript full of figures and unusual names, and the librarian to the Society of Antiquaries, Mr J. H. Hopkins, for help in many directions.

November 1974   KENNETH HARRISON

To

MICHAEL and FORTUNE

sans changer

There is no appeal from the verdict of a date.

G. M. TREVELYAN
English Social History, chapter 4

CHAPTER I

THE MOON AND THE ANGLO-SAXON CALENDAR

❦

Battle, murder and sudden death – these are among the obvious ingredients of our early records, mixed with tales of courage and loyalty, and the fact or fancy in remarkable lives. From biography and history, from the pages of Asser and Bede, we expect to find shining examples and dramatic incident; we seldom get a glimpse of the ordinary Anglo-Saxon, who spent most of his time as a peaceful farmer. He worked, and must have worked hard, to clear and culti-vate; his trademark is printed in many of the place-names on a modern map. Even now, when economic histories of England before the Conquest can be written, and the broad pattern of trade and agriculture is understood (Loyn 1962; Finberg 1972), the thoughts and beliefs of a pagan society are still far from clear. Until about A.D. 600, when the people of Kent began to change from heathenism to Christianity, there is no reason for supposing that the Anglo-Saxon invaders of Britain had adopted the reckoning of imperial Rome, the Julian calendar which is founded on a solar year and, in a modified form, is still in use today. From about the middle of the fifth century, when the massive settlements began to take place, until the end of the sixth, this island was largely cut off from con-tinental influence, except in the western areas; and the people whose time-reckoning we shall study were illiterate. Yet of one thing we can be sure: for the farmer and stockbreeder, as for king and thegn, a calendar of some sort is indispensable, whether as a guide to the seasons or, on occasion, when men must gather to talk or to fight. The Anglo-Saxons were at first guided by the moon.

People who live in cities nowadays can forget about the moon, though sailors will keep an eye on the cause of tides. Long before men set foot on it the moon had ceased to be of much use after dark, except in remote places, or of any use as a clock. Yet in a primitive

I

society the waxing and waning of moonlight represent a simple and practical measure of time (because lunar months of 29.5 days each are more easily remembered than the long revolution of a solar year. A single nation in the ancient world had reason to differ from the rest: the annual flooding of the Nile, on which their livelihood depended, seems to have led the Egyptians, before 2000 B.C., to their determination of the length of a year.[1] They arrived at a figure of 365 days, which the neighbouring countries brought close to the modern value 365.24 days. In a year made up of lunar months the nearest approximation is $12 \times 29.5 = 354$ days, and a calendar of this kind would quickly run out of step with the seasons. There was thus every inducement to find a relation between the phases of the moon and the solar year to which the ripening of crops and breeding of animals are tied.

In a very distant past the length of the lunar circuit must have been known, running from new moon to new moon, or rather, the very thin crescent to be seen when the moon is a day old; and equally, with the advantage of counting by whole numbers, that two circuits occupy 59 nights. A year of 12 lunar months is about 11 days shorter, but of 13 months about 19 days longer, than the solar year. With a proper arrangement, therefore, the short and the long can be brought into balance over a series of years, to form a cycle, a luni-solar calendar. By about 430 B.C. the Greek astronomer Meton had arrived at a cycle of 19 years, his capital discovery being that 235 lunar (synodic) months = 6939.7 days and 19 solar (tropical) years = 6939.6 days. Expressed in another way, the new moons recur on the same solar days or nights as 19 years before – with a small margin of error. The Metonic cycle passed from Athens to Alexandria and Rome, where it took on a new and enduring life in the Easter calculations of the Church (Chapter 3).

Yet it is only a refinement of the 8-year cycle, the *octaëteris*, usually linked with the name of Cleostratus, a few generations earlier, though the connexion is perhaps doubtful (Thomson 1943: 59; Dicks 1970: 87). As this shorter cycle is the more convenient to describe – and will be described in due course – so it may have been the more convenient in practice, though less accurate than the

[1] For a brief summary of the Egyptian reckoning see Bickerman (1968: 40–43).

version due to Meton. Without bothering for the moment over the origin of these ideas, or how they became diffused among the barbarous or civilised nations, we can examine the Anglo-Saxon calendar which has been preserved by Bede. In his *De Temporum Ratione*, written in 725, after dealing with the Hebrew, Egyptian, Roman and Greek practice he very fortunately devotes a chapter to the Anglo-Saxon months (*DTR*, c. xv).[2] He does not enter into all the details of the calendar, which he was well equipped to do; but anything heathen was distasteful to him and the audience he wrote for. Besides, the monastic training at that time included a thorough study of the computation of Easter and the relation between planets, moon and stars. To people with that type of upbringing, pre-Copernican though it was, most of the details were a trifle, easily filled in.

Bede makes three points: the reckoning was by lunar months; the solar year began on 25 December, then perhaps and certainly later known as Midwinter; and an ordinary year was of 12 lunar months but provision was made for an extra, 13th, month in certain years. Here, then, is the pattern of a luni-solar calendar, where the day-to-day reckoning can be checked by observation of the moon itself. Bede begins by saying that *antiqui autem Anglorum populi...iuxta cursum lunae suos menses computauere*. In an ordinary year there were 12 months, with names that he explains as well as he can:

1. Giuli: meaning uncertain
2. Solmonath: month of the offering of cakes
3. Hrethmonath: goddess Hretha
4. Eosturmonath: goddess Eostre
5. Thrimilchi: cows milked thrice a day
6. Litha⎫
7. Litha⎭: meaning uncertain, perhaps 'calm' or 'moon'
8. Weodmonath: month of weeds
9. Halegmonath: holy month, or month of offerings[3]
10. Wintirfyllith: appearance of (first) full moon of winter
11. Blodmonath: month of sacrifice

[2] For abbreviations in italic capitals, and for spelling, see p. 151.
[3] An alternative name in Kent is Rugern, rye harvest (*EHD*: 361–2). See further Nilsson (1920: 292–7), Bonser (1963: 140–45) and Stenton (*ASE*: 97–8).

12. Giuli: repeat of 1.

In passing we may note that several of these names are related to seasonal events; for others no satisfactory explanation has been found, and there is some doubt whether Bede derived them correctly – though we may feel sure that he would not have invented the heathen divinities Hretha and Eostre, and at the end of the chapter is thankful to have been delivered from such deplorable affairs: *gratias tibi, bone Iesu, qui nos ab his uanis auertens tibi sacrificia laudis offerre donasti.*

The year began at Midwinter, 25 December: *incipiebant autem annum ab octauo Kalendarum Ianuariarum die, ubi nunc natalem Domini celebramus.* And the next piece of information shows that a feature of the calendar was an embolismic or intercalary year, Thrilithi, of 13 months, differing from an ordinary year because three, and not two, summer months were called Litha.[4] Disregarding peculiarities for the time being, such as double months, we can now settle down to the arithmetic. For convenience an 8-year cycle will be chosen. If the figures are to be presented in a convincing way, they must be shown with a degree of precision which the Anglo-Saxons could never have attained to; they demonstrate only the principle of a lunar-solar calendar (Harrison 1973c).

The solar (tropical) year is taken to be 365.24(31) days.[5] Thus 8 solar years = 2921.94 days, and 99 lunar (synodic) months of 29.53(06) days = 2923.53 days, the cycle being made up of 5 ordinary years of 12 lunar months each and 3 embolismic (intercalary) years of 13 lunar months. In the calculations that follow the lunar excess of 1.6 days will approximately be taken care of by 3 negative intercalations of 0.5 days each; in practice, however, an 8-year cycle could also be operated by subtracting two days from one cycle and only one from the next. Then, for single years of each kind:

---

[4] *et quotiescumque communis esset annos ternos menses lunares singulis anni temporibus dabant: cum uero embolismus, hoc est xiii mensium lunarium, annus occurreret, superfluum mensem aestate opponebant, ita ut tunc tres menses simul lida nomine uocarentur, et ob id annus ille thrilidi cognominabatur habens quattour menses aestatis ternos ut semper temporum caeterorum.*

[5] Owing to long-term (secular) changes, in the course of 15 centuries the solar year has shortened to its present value of 365.24(22) days; the figure in the text, calculated by Dr D. C. Heggie, is correct for the fifth century A.D. For details of the calculation see *The Astronomical Ephemeris* for 1975: 536–7 (H. M. Stationery Office, London 1973), or adjacent issues.

		Difference
12 lunar months = 354.37 days		−10.87 days
1 solar year = 365.24 days		+18.66 days
13 lunar months = 383.90 days		

TABLE I

Year	A	B	C
1.O	−10.87	−10.87	−11
2.O	−10.87	−21.74	−22
3.E	+18.66	−3.58 (−3.08 −0.50)	− 4
4.O	−10.87	−14.45	−14
5.O	−10.87	−25.32	−25
6.E	+18.66	−7.16 (−6.66 −0.50)	− 7
7.O	−10.87	−18.03	−18
8.E	+18.66	+0.13 (+0.63 −0.50)	0

In Table 1 an ordinary year is represented by O and an embolismic year by E; and the pattern is that of the first 8 years of the Metonic cycle, known as the *ogdoas*. In column A the yearly difference is given, with a running total in column B – which also includes the 3 intercalary fractions of a day, here assigned to the 13-month embolismic years.[6] Column C, which alone is of any practical importance, represents the corrected differences in Column B brought to the nearest whole number; in other words, (minus) the number of days to be reckoned forward, from the last new moon of the solar year that has nearly expired, in order to arrive at Midwinter. Over the whole period of the cycle, with embolismic months added, the purely solar reckoning of days in the year runs behind the lunar. In any one year the lunar count of days is completed earlier, as in Column B; hence the yearly differences appear with a negative sign.

Calendars look more complicated on paper than they are to live with. The Romans, reckoning by so many days before the Kalends,

---

[6] Dr Heggie has worked out an alternative scheme of ordinary and embolismic years, OEOEOOEO, where columns B and C become

B −10.87 +7.29 −3.58 +14.58 +3.71 −7.16 +11.00 +0.13
C −11 +7 −4 +15 +4 −7 +11 0

No explanation can be offered for this pattern. The first 8 years of the Metonic cycle, as in Table 1, were used in more than one Easter table during the third century A.D. (MacCarthy 1901: xxxii–xliv).

Nones and Ides of each month, had for centuries employed a far more elaborate system than that outlined in Table 1, where the counting of days is only needed to ascertain the turn of the solar year at Midwinter; and the addition to embolismic years of a lunar month – an observable quantity – is in practice no harder than the addition of a day to leap years, a day easily overlooked. To a people living at night under conditions of blackout the advantage of seeing their timepiece was very considerable, apart from those occasions when the moon is visible by day. A trained eye can form a close estimate of the age of the moon: thus in the twelfth century, when the circumstances of workaday life were much the same as in the sixth, an entry in the Anglo-Saxon Chronicle (*ASC*: year 1135) describes a solar eclipse during which 'the sun became like a moon three nights old'.[7] The comparison may sound forced and artificial to our ears, but it was reasonable enough then. In bad weather, or with a thin persistent covering of cloud, the reckoning of time and especially of Midwinter will not always have been quite accurate, within a day or two; and if other primitive societies are anything to go by, there may sometimes have been disputes about which month it really was (Nilsson 1920: 198 and 241–2). Another drawback of luni-solar calendars is that the months do not occupy precisely the same position in each solar year, as judged by a calendar of the Julian type; but the farmer had a workable guide to the seasons, and in any case would sow and reap according to the state of the weather and the crops, as he does now.

From disadvantages it is an easy step to what seems to be a difficulty. Nilsson states that the beginning of the year was not sharply defined: 'when a fixed series of twelve months exists, with a fixed intercalary month, it lies in the nature of things that the month which is doubled in the intercalation should be the beginning of the year, since this month is regulated by a fixed point or season of the year; the month in question is in this case Litha, in summer' (1920: 296–7). He also points out that the beginning of the year does not

---

[7] And the same form of words, 'five or six days' or 'five days' old, is employed by the Spanish chronicler Hydatius, who died about 468, when describing the eclipses of 458 and 464 (Newton 1972: 509–10); another example is quoted by Whitelock (1952a: 56).

necessarily coincide with the beginning of the series of months.[8] Yet arguments from 'the nature of things' are suspicious. Perhaps Nilsson was unduly influenced by the type of calendar where intercalation is performed only as it is needed, in other words, with lunar months being added at random intervals to fit them into a solar year whose length is uncertain or not measured between two definite days (1920: 360–61); and he seems to have extended these considerations to a calendar of different type. Bede's evidence, the value of which will be discussed presently, would suggest that the Anglo-Saxon reckoning was not a random affair. The names of the months are partly seasonal and partly religious, if these elements can properly be separated in a pagan society. We do not know for certain whether Halegmonath, holy month, was connected with a harvest festival, but if it was, a lunar month of that name should not be allowed to occur too early in the solar year; when crops are still standing in the fields no sensible person will think that all is safely gathered in. Again, among northern peoples 'the summer is the good season, when supplies for the winter must be collected; it is therefore a very busy time, when each family has to work for itself and has no leisure for festivals' (Nilsson 1920: 339). An intercalation in summer could arise from motives of this kind, to keep an autumn festival in its place, but the calculations now to be made will suggest that summer was convenient for another reason also.

Suppose that a new moon coincides with 25 December in a particular year. Then, referring to Table 1 and the material on which it is based, the average length of a solar month is 30.43(7) days and of a lunar 29.53(1) days; so at the end of each solar month the sun has gained on the moon by 0.90(6) of a day.[9] In year 3 of the cycle, approximately towards the end of August (in the Julian reckoning) when 32 solar months have elapsed, the sun will be ahead by almost

[8] Also that 'the beginning of the year in this case, however, is on Bede's own testimony the beginning of winter, as among Scandinavian countries'. It is not; Bede says that the (first) full moon of winter occurs in Wintirfyllith, whereas the year began at 25 December, Midwinter.

[9] Only the average lunar month is here considered, whereas lunations, from new moon to new moon, can vary from 29.26 to 29.80 days; and the disappearance of the old moon (conjunction) may occur, depending on latitude and other circumstances, rather more or less than a day before the crescent can be seen. Spread over the length of a year the effect of these factors is not disturbing.

7

exactly 29 days; that is, towards the end of the second Litha in that year it will be ahead by nearly a lunar month. At this appropriate moment the third Litha is added, delaying the onset of Weodmonath, Halegmonath and the rest.[10] Year 6 of the cycle, inheriting a solar excess of 25 days from the previous year (Table 1, column C), will need intercalation rather sooner: 65 solar months after the beginning of the cycle, towards the end of May (Julian style) the solar gain is almost exactly 59 days, two lunar months; but since a lunar month has already been added to year 3, the corrected solar gain is only one lunar month. Thus intercalation of another Litha could take place here. During the last year of the cycle a third Litha automatically falls into place, rounding off the figures. Among an illiterate people the adjustments would be made, presumably, from observation of the new moons, and to that extent can be called empirical. But the name Thrilithi, and Bede's statement that intercalation took place in the summer, seem to show that the calendar was operated under fixed rules. Although the scheme of ordinary and embolismic years, with the arrangement OOEOOEOE, as in the *ogdoas*, is not unique – and an alternative scheme is given above (p. 5, n. 6) – if the pagan year began when Bede says it did, and the pattern of the *ogdoas* is followed, an intercalation during the summer months does become reasonable and probable.

Nevertheless, the value of Bede's information must be treated as a separate issue. His statements are not only precise but derive from a period when heathen ideas had not yet been eliminated. He was born a little after 670, perhaps 673 (Plummer 1896: I, xi). Northumbria did not begin to become a Christian kingdom until 626–7, and its rulers had relapsed into heathenism during the year 633–4 (*HE*, II. 9 and 14; III. 1); we may not readily suppose that in his own day everyone had forgotten the habits and tradition of their ancestors.[11]

---

10 Whether an intercalary half-day was taken into account at this point or some other does not affect the principle of the argument. As already indicated (above, p. 4) the system could be operated by subtracting two days from one 8-year cycle, and only one from the next; but inserting the third Litha at the appropriate new moon is perhaps a more natural procedure.

11 On the contrary, punishment for a variety of heathen customs is defined in c. VIII of the Penitential of Archbishop Egbert of York, who died in 766 (Haddan and Stubbs 1873: III, 424). The Penitential ascribed to Bede is probably not his (Plummer 1896: I, clvi). Writing in 797 to Bishop Higbald of Lindisfarne, Alcuin

And it is very unlikely that a monk in his cloister would deliberately, and of his own accord, identify a pagan ceremony at Midwinter with the feast of the Nativity, if they did not coincide: *ipsam noctem nunc nobis sacrosanctam, tunc gentili uocabulo* Modranecht, *id est matrum noctem, appelabant.* Bede knew that the Church had sometimes adapted heathen festivals to its own use; elsewhere he mentions the *Lupercalia* of 15 February, changed to the Purification of St Mary on 2 February (*DTR*, c. XII), a change which seems to have been required by the forty-day ordinance of Leviticus 12. 2–4. Situated as he was, the chance of his being mistaken over the beginning of the pagan year is rather remote.

Spaced half a year apart, the double months Litha and Giuli may once have been related to the summer and winter solstices. The former, occurring usually between 21 and 23 June, has been celebrated all over Europe by midsummer fires (Frazer 1913: 160–219), and the Church appropriated 24 June to St John Baptist. The Romans had distinguished 25 December, a few days after the winter solstice, when the sun was regaining its strength, under the name *sol inuictus*; by the middle of the fourth century this day had become Christmas (Lietzmann 1903). In the Mediterranean world a knowledge of the solstices can be traced at least as far back as Hesiod, who flourished probably in the eighth century B.C. (Dicks 1970: 37). Julius Caesar, some fifty years before the Christian era, had observed of the Gaulish tribes that *spatia omnis temporis non numero dierum sed noctium finiunt; dies natalis et annorum initia obseruunt, ut noctem dies subsequatur* (*De Bello Gallico*, VI. 18, ed. Edwards 1917). It is understandable, and unfortunate, that he does not say more about how the beginnings of the years were arrived at. Towards the end of the first century A.D., Tacitus also, with eyes directed beyond the Rhine, observes that *nec dierum, ut nos, sed noctium computant*; and again, that except in emergency the tribal assemblies were held on

has this rebuke: 'let God's words be read in the refectory. There it is proper to listen to a lector, not a harpist, to the sermons of the Fathers, not the songs of the Heathen. For what has Ingeld [one of the heroes of vernacular poetry] to do with Christ?' (*Epistolae*, ed. Dümmler 1895: 183; quoted by Page 1970: 160). If this sort of canticle was still attractive to the inmates of a religious house, what of the countryfolk outside?

fixed days, either at new moon or full moon (*Germania*, c. XI, ed. Hutton 1946). These scattered hints, though they point to the moon being used as a clock, do not enable even the outline of a calendar to be constructed.

In the most important respect, lunar reckoning, the Anglo-Saxons had not exchanged the invariable month of 29.5 days for the variable length of Roman months. Referring back to Table 1, it will be seen that the new moon heralding Midwinter fell within the first month of the Giuli pair – though that by itself affords no proper reason for doubling. In the matter of intercalation a Roman influence can also be discounted, since even in the pre-Julian calendar the 'month' of *Mercedonius*, added every other year as a balance, was only 22 or 23 days long (Gjerstad 1961: 209–10). The ancestry of the Anglo-Saxon reckoning is to all appearances remote from the practice of republican or imperial Rome, and may have to be sought among the principles laid down in Babylonia and Greece.[12] Ideas from this quarter could have arrived at a late stage, in the refined form of the 19-year cycle, even after the time of Caesar or Tacitus. They could have arrived earlier, and it is fortunate that archaeology has already given more than a hint of the pathways along which a luni-solar type of calendar might have travelled to northern Europe; or from it, if the views of Renfrew are adopted, and the Mediterranean is seen as a pool fed by several streams of thought (1973).

Three routes can broadly be distinguished – western, eastern and central; separating them for discussion will not exclude their having combined together in practice. The western, wholly or in part by sea, and operating around the first millenium B.C., is well suited to heavy cargo; but perhaps speculative thought – we are now considering the notion of an intercalary month at fixed intervals – would be transmitted more securely by an overland route, with contact between tribes helping to forge the chain. The rivers Danube and Elbe (or Oder), Dniestr and Vistula, indicate stretches

---

[12] The 8-year cycle, with a *regular* intercalation of months, may have been known in Babylonia and Greece independently; in the former, an empirical *irregular* system was in use by 1700 B.C. (Labat 1963: 111–13; Bickerman 1968: 22–3). Whether the Babylonians derived the 19-year cycle from Meton, or by their own devices, is disputable (Neugebauer 1957: 140; van de Vyver 1957). But progress in astronomy was not confined to Mediterranean countries (Thom 1971; Heggie 1972).

of open country, separated by the Carpathian mass, and form eastern channels from the Black Sea to the Baltic. Animal ornament and polychrome jewelry, of Sarmatian type, could have begun to reach Scandinavia along this path during the first two centuries A.D. or thereafter (Talbot Rice 1957: 185–6); the spread of tamga-signs may also be significant (Sulimirski 1970: 143 and 151–5). The central route, long identified by the trade in amber, has recently been considered and mapped by Strong (1966).[13] Of both the western and central routes it may be observed that the Gallic wars of Caesar, and his invigorating effect on the solar calendar already established in republican Rome, together with further expansion to the Danube, will not have been favourable to the spread of a luni-solar principle after about 50 B.C., or a little earlier. At present it would be unsafe to regard the 8-year cycle with regular intercalation as originating either in Greece or Babylonia much before about 700 or 800 B.C., though the Metonic cycle can be more precisely dated. Even so, in time and space there is ample room for a traffic of ideas.

Archaeology may be expected to throw more light on this problem, and on another: did the Anglo-Saxons choose a cycle of eight years or nineteen? The literary sources do not seem to be helpful. For instance, a collection of leechdoms edited by Cockayne (1864), with frequent allusion to various kinds of lunar folklore, seems to be devoid of any clear hint about the primitive calendar. There is a reference in the *Historia Brittonum* ascribed to Nennius, c. XVI (ed. Mommsen 1898b: 159), to an event dated *duo anni in ogdoade usque in hunc annum in quo sumus*; but *ogdoas* we have already seen to be a technical term for the first eight years of the Metonic cycle, and in any case the evidence of a Welsh compiler who flourished about the year 830 can hardly be a useful guide to pagan English practice.[14] The theories of Lappenberg (1845: I, 77–8), which were advanced before a critical examination of the texts had taken place, are best forgotten (see Appendix 2). Already a number of scratches and

---

[13] The hope expressed by Strong (1966: 7) that spectrographic analysis would more closely identify the sources of amber has to some extent been fulfilled, at the cost of a few complications (Beck 1970); but it is unlikely that Jutland and Sammland will lose their position as chief exporters. On the central route see also Malinowsky (1971).

[14] The compilation ascribed to Nennius will be discussed below (p. 136).

symbols, on material like rock or bone, have been interpreted to mean that primitive peoples took an interest in the phases of the moon and the duration of a lunar month (Marshack 1964); yet the unravelling of a cycle may be more troublesome.[15] Besides, a lunisolar calendar is so simple in operation as to be carried without difficulty in the head.

A point of more immediate interest is that the unit of Anglo-Saxon reckoning was a solar year measured from a definite point: progress of time from day to day followed the lunar month, with intercalation to balance the seasons; the fixed point of Midwinter could be ascertained without difficulty, from year to year, by counting forward from the last new moon of the current solar year, as in Table 1 – or by a similar scheme. Running from Midwinter to Midwinter, the Anglo-Saxon year had the same length as the Julian, with a systematic difference of one week. The conversion of England to Christianity did not take place overnight; but the work of Augustine in the south and of Aidan in the north ensured that the Julian reckoning, and the ecclesiastical calendar, had become known throughout all the kingdoms, except Sussex, by about the middle of the seventh century or just after. Apart from other forms of record, the regnal years of kings at different times and in different territories covered the span between a decline of the pagan system and the rise of a new form of solar calendar. It is fortunate, therefore, that for historical purposes the length of the chronological years should be the same in both, and their beginning close together. Consider, for example, a purely lunar calendar of the type which still governs the religious obligation of Islam. Each year the sun gains on the moon by 10.87 days, so that in a little over 33 solar years the observations have fallen apart by 365 days; worse still – when applied to history – after about 16 years the seasons will have become reversed and the battles or campaigns that usually occur in summer will now appear to have taken place in winter. It seems,

15 In the chronicle of Thietmar, I.17, who wrote about the year 1000, there is a reference to a feast at Leire in Denmark, held every nine years (? ninth), where 99 victims were sacrificed (ed. Kurze 1889: 11). This number of victims, perhaps representing the 99 lunar months of the complete 8-year cycle, is also found in Greece (Thomson 1943: 64, n. 98). But the findings of archaeology are needed here.

however, that the Anglo-Saxon concept of 'year' was virtually identical with our own.

At this stage there are reasons for not immediately going on to examine the early annals of the Anglo-Saxon Chronicle, some of which belong to the heathen period and others to the time when the Julian system was being established in England, finally to become the official reckoning in civil and ecclesiastical affairs. The material of this chronicle has been transmitted in five principal Old English versions (A, B, C, D and E), besides fragments, Latin translations and the bilingual version F; after the Conquest, also, several writers drew on lost copies which sometimes differ in small though helpful particulars. Moreover, the dates given in these documents are referred to the Christian era, and in that form cannot be earlier than the seventh century. A record of Anglo-Saxon history which begins in 449 (*recte* 450), but is preserved in no manuscript earlier than the reign of Alfred, can only be examined in a critical way when the forms of chronology that were used in the intervening years have been explored.

The next step, therefore, will be a discussion of Germanic raiding and settlement as they were seen from Britain, Gaul, and the Mediterranean, by people who wrote within a Roman framework of dates, and can now be seen through the eyes of an archaeologist. The chapters then following are devoted to an account of how the Christian era became established in this country, and the ways in which it was employed; so far as we know, the Anglo-Saxons did not think in terms of any era. The reckoning by *Anni Domini* had to make its way gradually. From the sixth century, soon after the time of Justinian, letters and directives from the Papal chancery were dated by the Indiction – not taking 1 January as the start of the administrative year – which remained the official style at Rome until the eleventh century; it plays an important, if sometimes confusing, role in the dating of English charters. But after the end of King Alfred's reign, or thereabouts, when copies of the Anglo-Saxon Chronicle were being distributed to various centres of learning, the more serious and disputable elements in chronology have been sufficiently identified; and with charters also the chief problems are encountered before A.D. 900. When these problems have been studied, our earliest records may emerge in a clearer light, and if historians are not accustomed to working as it were backwards, archaeologists will know that the raw material of history can hardly avoid taking that course.

CHAPTER 2

RAIDING AND SETTLEMENT

When discussing the migration of Germanic peoples into this country, during the fifth century or earlier, we encounter a process – not an episode or a decisive battle which can be tied down to a particular year or two. It will be safe to begin with the secure conviction that no proposals, however cautious, will satisfy historians and archaeologists alike, and that a fortunate run of excavations could modify any judgement which can be made at the present day. Nobody doubts that by the end of the fifth century a considerable body of Germanic invaders had settled in Britain, whereas at the beginning there were relatively few. As a first step, therefore, it is desirable to ask what meanings can be attached to the word 'settlement'.[1]

While the Romans were in control of the country – or a sizeable area of it, up to about the year 410 – they had formed a practice of recruiting mercenaries to help in defence against the Picts and Scots, and the Saxon pirates whose raids were becoming more frequent during the latter part of the fourth century. The phrase 'Saxon shore' is perhaps ambiguous but defines a threatened or threatening quarter (Myres 1956: 37; White 1961). Little is known of these mercenaries at this time.[2] A chieftain, *dux*, by the name of Fraomar, who arrived about 370, will not have been the only man of position and influence from abroad.[3] Such people and their followers, if they died

---

[1] In case the question seems pedantic, compare the following comment on 'tribe': 'anthropologists and social historians use this word in a bewildering variety of senses, ranging from the most primitive units of society to the most advanced' (Binchy 1970: 7).

[2] Technical terms like *laeti, numeri, gentiles* or *foederati* are on the whole better avoided in this kind of discussion, where no attempt is made to determine the conditions of life or employment.

[3] The authority is Ammianus Marcellinus, XXIX. 4 (ed. Rolfe 1939: III, 244); he died shortly after 390, but wrote of events some twenty years earlier. On the status of Fraomar see the remarks of Frere (1967: 220, n. 1).

and were buried in British soil, are 'settlers' in one sense of the word, though even here there are problems (Brown 1974). Again, a considerable quantity of Frankish material, found in graves throughout the south-eastern counties, may represent a similar form of 'settlement' around the middle of the fifth century (Evison 1965: 44). Opinions will differ about its extent and importance for the future, and should be tempered by another thought: 'the more firmly we hold that Kent was in continuous contact with the continent, the likelier it surely becomes that the grave-goods of Frankish provenance were largely the result of trade; their quantity, after all, was not unlimited. This is not to say that some Franks did not accompany the early settlers, or come later' (Wallace-Hadrill 1971: 23). Saxon burials in the Upper Thames valley are too well known to require more than a passing mention.[4] As examples of recent discovery, a Germanic occupation has been detected on the south coast at Portchester (Cunliffe 1970), and two pagan cemeteries in Norfolk, at Caistor-by-Norwich and Markshall, are the subject of a report by Myres and Green (1973).[5]

Yet these discoveries – suggesting the occupation of small areas for several generations, whether continuous or intermittent – can at present throw little light on what these aliens had in mind; that is, whether they resorted to Britain only in search of immediate gain, in the form of pay or plunder, or whether they saw it as a land where their remote posterity might flourish. The presence of mercenaries may also have overshadowed a likelihood that some of the early arrivals were engaged in civilian pursuits. The finds at Caistor, where cremation was being practised from early in the fourth century at least, have suggested that the Germanic people there kept themselves to themselves; and further, 'it is difficult to believe that their settlement in such close proximity [to the Romano-British site] was not deliberate, and that they were not employed in some way that was supposed to improve the security and prosperity of the town and its environs' (Myres and Green

[4] Discussion, with map, by Kirk (1956); they are considered in relation to continental examples by S. C. Hawkes and Dunning (1961).

[5] Additions to a list of places, especially in eastern England, that is already becoming lengthy; see Lethbridge (1956) and the bibliography by Meaney (1964). Late fourth-century burials are now reported from Winchester (Biddle 1972).

1973: 13). A steady trickle of Angles and Saxons throughout the fourth century, part soldiers, part labourers, spying out the land, may have been a necessary prelude to movement on a far larger scale. Although the number of these intruders will appear small when compared with a plausible figure for the British population (Alcock 1973: 291 and 310–11) their knowledge of the countryside may have proved very useful to their continental cousins.

In short, 'We know more of the Roman living, more of the Saxon dead' (Loyn 1962: 1–2). We know that by the end of the fourth century the Roman garrisons had been substantially withdrawn from Wales (Jarrett 1963), and that in 410 the emperor Honorius resigned the government of Britain to native hands. It is less easy to determine the next change in the nature of settlement during the fifth century, from the casual to the deliberate, or, as Myres puts it, from the controlled to the uncontrolled (1969: 100–102), but customary to think of a gradual acquisition of small parcels of land, whether by grant or through force, followed by the carving out of Anglo-Saxon kingdoms in face of armed resistance. 'Settlement' has therefore been used to describe more than one kind of process, spread over more than one generation, with differences of scale and purpose; and since an extended account of these times must fail for want of enough written evidence, our judgement will lean heavily on the consequences that clearly emerge from a period of twilight.

The first connected story, couched in the language of history, is due to Bede (*HE*, I. 15); he in turn drew upon material derived from Canterbury, on the British writer Gildas, who probably lived in Wales, and on a few continental sources. His narrative is brief, so brief as to invite misunderstanding; although sketched in general terms, the detail is confined to the eastern part of Kent, and not unreasonably. As a Benedictine monk, with no taste for political or worldly affairs, he had been encouraged by his friend Abbot Albinus of Canterbury to compose an ecclesiastical history of the English nation.[6] In terms of the Roman section of the Church, as distinct from the Celtic, which is how contemporaries would see the matter,

---

[6] *Denique hortatu praecipue ipsius Albini, ut hoc opus adgredi auderem, prouocatus sum* (Preface to *HE*). See also his letter to Albinus prefixed to Plummer's text of 1896. The ecclesiastical nature of Bede's work has again been emphasised by Bonner (1973: 85–6).

a history of this kind ought to start in Kent. The first twenty-two chapters of the *Historia*, for all that they contain a description of Britain, the landings of Caesar and Claudius, the martyrdom of Alban, Romano-British affairs, the Pelagian heresy and so forth, are handled only as a prelude to the efforts of Pope Gregory and the arrival, in 597, of Augustine in Kent (*HE*, I. 25; Plummer 1896: II, 36). The king's wife was already a Christian; her husband was soon converted; and from his reign the continuous history of the Roman Church could begin.

No estimate of Bede's work should neglect the limits he imposed upon himself. For instance, *Hwicciorum prouincia*, the territory of the Hwicce and a sub-kingdom of Mercia, comes into the story partly because a future queen of the South Saxons had been baptised there and partly because Worcester became the seat of a bishop; and on the boundary with Wessex two memorable consultations had taken place (*HE*, II. 2; IV. 13 and 21). Nothing is said about where the Hwicce came from – Stenton (*ASE*: 43) thinks they were a mixture of Angles and Saxons – or when they settled, or the descent of their Mercian overlords. On all these topics Bede could very likely have informed himself and posterity, but did not. In the same way, his account of the *Aduentus Saxonum* will not satisfy modern curiosity, for his eyes were chiefly fixed on what led to the foundation of Kent, the first of the historic kingdoms, where the only archbishopric of the seventh century was situated. Even so, there are indications that the brief sketch of pagan history, which describes events in the middle of the fifth century and then is nearly but not quite blank until the Augustinian mission arrived, owes something to Bede's amplification or afterthought. No historian can put down all that he is aware of; and Bede was writing a history of the Church, not addressing a concourse of antiquaries.

Bede opens his account of Kentish history by stating, or revealing, that he did not know exactly when it began. In 449, he says, Marcian began to share the imperial throne with Valentinian, and held it for seven years (*HE*, I. 15).[7] In their time, *tunc*, the Angles and Saxons arrived. Again, in the Recapitulation we have *quorum tempore Angli . . . Brittaniam adierunt* (*HE*, V. 24). Bede knew that the

[7] Marcian's reign began in 450, not 449.

worthless Valentinian had been killed in Marcian's fifth year (*HE*, I. 21); perhaps this knowledge is of smaller consequence than occasional references to the *Aduentus*, where the dates are always qualified by *circiter* or *plus minus*, and could show Bede as thinking that the events took place not long after 449, *recte* 450 (Whitelock, *EHD*: 7, n. 1). The nature of Bede's information will be discussed in its proper place (below, pp. 123–5); what matters for the moment is his statement that the origin of the Kentish kingdom could be traced to the years between 450 and 457, or perhaps 455 if the death of Valentinian is taken as a limit.

There are reasons for supposing that early material now in the Anglo-Saxon Chronicle was under compilation during the latter half of the seventh century (Stenton 1926: 163–6; *PASE*: 119–22); reasons, too, for thinking that although Bede wrote the *Historia* in 731 he had never seen this material or been able to draw information from it (below, p. 135). Before taking sources like Gildas into account, a short summary of what Bede has to say will be desirable. By various writers he has been accused of oversimplification, and the more quickly we forget that he was not writing a political history the truer this estimate will seem to be. Yet it is not far from correct if we think of a tidy and scholarly mind working over material that could not all be of equal value for the purpose he had in mind; and the most interesting sidelight on his story is the degree of confirmation it has received from the study of place-names, more especially in Kent and Hampshire (*PASE*: 266–74), and from archaeology – though not on all points. Bede has perhaps not been forgiven for failing to describe the pattern of settlement, in central England particularly, with the amount of detail that modern interests will naturally call for. His own interest, however, was in the movement of peoples. For the rest, it is hard to draw the line between ignorance and restraint. Although Dorchester-on-Thames became the seat of a bishopric in the seventh century, neither Bede nor anyone else may have been aware of pagan burials in the neighbourhood, dating back to the late fourth century or early fifth; they may have been unaware also of similar material outside the gates of York. The phase of tribal migration, on a large scale, was of more significance to Bede than its prehistory, of which he gives no hint except for an alliance between Saxons and Picts (*HE*, I. 20). He contented himself with demonstrating the existence of a pagan society, ready for Augustine to convert; he must have known more than he set down, but there will have been limits to what he knew.

Presently we shall see in more detail what information can be derived from Gildas. From this writer Bede got a picture of Britain ruled by a *superbus tyrannus*; and if Gildas is correct it was this man who invited a group of continental peoples to help defend the country against its northern enemies, the Picts and Scots, and secured their allegiance by grants of land in the eastern parts of the island. The ruler was identified by Bede as Vortigern (on whom see Kirby 1968). At first, then, this mixture of Angles and Saxons, and the people called Jutes, came as *foederati*, trained fighting men bound by treaty (Hodgkin 1952: I, 57). But after defeating the Picts they sent back news of a fertile country and timid inhabitants; the first proposition was true, and perhaps fairly well known, the second they would regret. Reinforcements followed; then, deserting their paymasters, they formed an alliance with the Picts. The alarm and devastation that ensued should not entirely be judged by the intemperate language of Gildas – here paraphrased by Bede (*HE*, I. 15), who now intervenes with a description of the continental force and its components.

He was certainly right in thinking that in his time people of Jutish descent lived in Kent, Hampshire and the Isle of Wight; on the evidence of pottery he may well have been right in supposing a remote ancestry in Jutland (Myres 1969: 95–7; 1970: 169–73), although several lines of evidence would converge to suggest that a number of these Jutes had arrived by way of Frisia, pausing there in the course of migration (*ASE*: 14–15).[8] The home of the Saxons he places in Old Saxony, roughly an area drained by the lower Elbe and Weser, with perhaps a northern boundary near the Eider. The Angles – from whom were descended the East and Middle Angles, the Mercians, and his own people of Northumbria – came from *Angulus*, the modern Angeln in Schleswig; Bede says that the terri-

[8] A passage in *HE*, V. 9. might indicate that Bede was aware of Frisians and others among the early settlers (Myres 1970: 151, n. 2); Gibbon had not overlooked this passage (ed. Bury 1898: IV, 146–7). For further observations on Frisia as a halting-place see Hunter Blair (1956: 10 and 14–15).

tory then became deserted, and if on this point he was not so nearly right as at one time was thought (Jankuhn 1952), the evidence can be derived more convincingly from the neighbouring island of Fünen (Myres 1970: 159). As to the command of the newcomers Bede is a little cautious: *duces fuisse perhibent eorum duo fratres Hengest et Horsa*, their leaders are said to have been Hengest and Horsa. He adds that a monument to Horsa was still shown in Kent, which when coupled with a regnal list given elsewhere (*HE*, II. 5) would seem to show reliance on information from Canterbury. The proposal has been made that Bede revised this passage carelessly (Collingwood and Myres 1937: 337, n. 1), because it now implies that the brothers were in command of only the Anglian tribes, whereas in *HE*, v. 24 we are told that the Anglian kingdom of Northumbria descended from Ida who began to reign in 547.[9]

We can now turn to the *De Excidio Britanniae* of Gildas (ed. Mommsen 1898a; tr. Williams 1901). He unluckily adopted the turgid and overelaborate style in favour with many authors of the sixth century; moreover, he did not write history, or try to write it, in the sense that Gregory of Tours did, a generation later. Certainly he had a purpose in view, his theme being the wickedness of the Britons and some of their kings who are particularly mentioned by name; and to this cause he attributes the horror of foreign occupation and other misfortunes. As to the events before and during the *Aduentus Saxonum* his narrative raises a number of problems for the chronologer; and it is desirable to be clear what they are, because a story cast in an almost timeless mould is bound to invite the following questions:

1. Did Gildas arrange the events in their proper sequence?
2. How far did events that are presented separately, and distinctly, in fact overlap?
3. In what degree is British tradition valid for the whole island, and not just for the western areas?

---

[9] It is a little difficult to follow Myres (1951: 232–4) when he interprets these passages in *HE*, I. 15 to show that the mercenaries came over in two waves, first Angles and Saxons, and then Angles and Saxons and Jutes under the leadership of Hengest and Horsa; in the Recapitulation (*HE*, v. 24) Bede mentions only *Angli*. For the inconsistencies, as they appear, of usage see Hodgkin (1952: I, 157–61) and Whitelock (*EHD*: 7–8). This is not to deny that 'settlement' did take place in areas other than Kent before the time of Vortigern.

These questions will naturally combine into a more general problem of what Gildas knew or can reasonably be expected to have known. An isolated voice from that period must be attended to; yet we should take account of the limits imposed by geography and the barrier of language.[10] He can hardly be thought to possess an equal familiarity with eastern England and with Wales, and without detracting from the value of his information it would be rash to credit him with an all-seeing eye.

The relevant part of his story is as follows. After the Romans had departed – a more gradual affair than is conveyed by the single date 410 (Frere 1967: 262–5) – there followed a period of anarchy, and devastation by the Picts and *Scotti* (Irish), with famine and a decay of town life. Then the Britons sent an appeal for help to the Roman consul Aetius, of whom more presently. Disappointed in their hopes from this quarter, they armed themselves and drove back the Irish pirates, the Picts meanwhile remaining inactive apart from threats and occasional raids. Next followed a time of prosperity and moral corruption; suitably, to the mind of Gildas, there came a plague. The desperate Britons now agreed with their *superbus tyrannus*, whom Bede names Vortigern, to call in the Saxons as allies. After an interval described as *multo tempore* (c. XIX) these Saxons revolted and joined the Picts, with more devastation in consequence. A to-and-fro struggle was then led by Ambrosius Aurelianus, one of the few people whom Gildas identifies; in the end, and perhaps under another leader, the Saxons were defeated at *Mons Badonicus*, a place whose whereabouts is not known for sure. An interval of civil war was followed by a state of peace and calm, during which Gildas wrote – in all probability towards the middle of the sixth century. Reading between the lamentations and the overburden of words, the thread of his story is straightforward enough; but it must now be examined in the light of questions that a scarcity of dates is bound to raise.

A careful and sympathetic study of Gildas is due to Stevens (1941), whose interpretation of the text provides an answer to the first of the questions, the question about sequence. His answer is not reas-

---

[10] He uses, however, the word *kyulis* for the ships of the invading Saxons, which argues an awareness of English tradition, as Whitelock points out (*EHD*: 6).

had been for about twenty years
sion in Gaul and elsewhere, even
sul for the third time in 446 and
To him, says Gildas, the Britons
: 'To Aetius, in his third consul-
s; a little further in their request;
e sea drives us on the barbarians;
s of death we are either killed or
: 47). From the context it might
ere the Picts and Scots of whom
ens, however, is doubtful about
ian' – in its way no more precise
fficult it is to reconcile the des-
and prosperity, famine, plague
t a period as that determined by
450–57 given by Bede. Without
estions, we may turn at once to
ard. He supposes that the appeal
year 446, but at any time until
Aetius became consul again in 454 – was for help against the Saxons.
'Thus Gildas will have quoted a genuine document in an incorrect
context' (Stevens 1941: 362). In other words, he did not arrange this
event in its proper part of the sequence.[11] Yet to take the word
'barbarian' as meaning Picts and Scots on the one hand, or Saxons
on the other, is surely an exercise in black and white, admitting no
shades of grey. We shall presently find, from a writer of earlier date,
that there is evidence of an alliance between Saxons and Picts in
429; Gildas himself is witness to a similar state of affairs after the
revolt against the *superbus tyrannus*. To a Briton of the fifth century
there were at least three kinds of barbarian, with perhaps the Salian
Franks under that heading as well.

Another complication has been introduced by Stevens (1957: 340)
when he suggests that Gildas derived his copy of the letter to

[11] C. F. C. Hawkes (1956: 92–3), who follows Stevens here, would suggest that
Gildas was confusing the appeal to Aetius with a similar appeal in 410 or thereabouts; see also J. Morris (1973: 39). The same view had been advanced by Myres
(1951: 226–7). An incursion by Saxons in 410 is noticed by two Gallic chronicles
(ed. Mommsen 1892b).

Aetius from the historian Renatus Frigeridus, whose work has been lost all but some extracts preserved in the second book, cc. VIII and IX, of the *Historia Francorum* by Gregory of Tours (ed. Krusch and Levison 1951; tr. Dalton 1927). From these extracts, brief though they are, it is clear that Frigeridus was well informed about some of the most influential figures in the first half of the fifth century. A short biography of Aetius tells that for three years he was a hostage to Alaric, who died in 410 (dates from Bury 1923: I, *passim*). The attacks on Rome by the Goths, 408–10, and its fall, are also mentioned, and among others who appear may be noticed the tyrant Constantine III (died 411) and his son Constans (proclaimed Caesar in 409), Jovinus (died 413), Constantius III (died 421), Honorius (died 423) and Valentinian (died 455). Unfortunately we do not know whether Frigeridus dated events by imperial or consular years, then a usual style; but judging by this sample from a history which ran to twelve books it will surely have been apparent to Gildas that a generation, or at least a good length of time, had elapsed between Aetius the hostage, before the fall of Rome, and a veteran commander to whom the Britons could appeal.

There can be no serious doubt that the letter to Aetius comes from an authentic source; and unless Gildas saw only a transcript, divorced from its context, a possibility which only leads to the dead-end problem of how and why, the chance of his making a bad blunder is considerably diminished. He can indeed make historical mistakes: in earlier sections of *De Excidio* (cc. XV–XVIII) he infers that two previous appeals to Rome had been answered by the building of Hadrian's wall and either the turf wall of Antoninus or, if Stevens is followed (1941: 358), the *vallum* of Hadrian's; he confuses building with a period of restoration that took place in the latter half of the fourth century. But the letter to Aetius rests on a different footing, a written source.

At this stage the second of the questions may be asked: did events standing separate from one another in the narrative in reality overlap? If Gildas had supplied a few dates, or had scattered definite intervals of time through his story, this question might be examined in a matter-of-fact way. Since he did not, it becomes possible to think that kings in Wales and the South-west continued to enjoy their prosperity and loose living while fights went on in Kent or elsewhere in the east. Gildas tried to hand down the tradition of his forefathers; perhaps it was ordered and unanimous, perhaps there were several strands mingling to confuse the sequence.[12] To the second question we can now add the third: to what extent was the tradition valid for the whole of the island, as distinct from the western districts? When a modern historian can propose that Gildas has failed in the interpretation of a document, by placing it in the wrong context, the way is open to proposing that some of his traditional matter was more relevant to the west of Britain than to the east. Myres (1951: 223) has observed the preoccupation of Gildas with the Highland Zone.[13] The office of Count of the Saxon Shore had been established no later than 367 (Frere 1967: 348); taking Britain as a whole, it is not very likely that Saxon pirates were any less of a menace than the Irish. Yet if the tradition available to Gildas had preserved more than a faint memory of sea-raiders in the east, while the Romans still occupied part of Britain, it is surprising that he lays so little emphasis on the Saxons at the time, not even mentioning their name, while eloquent enough about the Picts and Scots.[14] Either way, in the writer or his sources, we seem to encounter a limited outlook (see now Miller 1975).

As to the plague mentioned in c. XXII, and placed by Gildas before Vortigern's invitation to the Saxons, the nature of it cannot be determined with certainty: *famosa pestis* lacks the punch of *lues inguinaria*, bubonic plague. In December 442 a comet appeared, followed the next year by a *pestilentia quae fere in toto orbe diffusa est*, as reported by the Spanish chronicler Hydatius (ed. Mommsen

---

[12] Compare the comment by Stevens (1941: 369) on the Anglo-Saxon Chronicle: 'parallel stories of Kentish, Sussex and Wessex settlements have been artificially laid end to end in a continuous narrative...' Even if this remark were true, need the artifice be confined to writers in Old English?

[13] To a historian of the Celtic peoples, 'when Gildas wrote, in the first half of the sixth century, the territory of the *Brittones* was confined to a fringe along the western coast, but for Gildas this restricted area is still *Britannia*' (O'Rahilly 1946: 531). Alcock (1973: 363) considers that Gildas's 'own viewpoint was very circumscribed, if we may judge from the fact that the five kings whom he castigates ruled in a tight arc from Cornwall to Anglesey'.

[14] A sentence in *De Excidio*, c. XVIII, referring to Roman defence against sea-borne barbarians in the south of Britain, may be rather more than a memory of signal-stations, as Myres would read it (1951: 223, n. 1), but he is surely right in thinking that Gildas had no conception of the *problems* of a Saxon Shore.

1893a: 24; Stevens 1941: 363). Unfortunately his work makes no mention of Britain in this or any other context. Marcellinus Comes (ed. Mommsen 1893b: 82) notes a *pestis* at Constantinople in 446, after noting the comet of 442; Attila's withdrawal from Italy in 452 may have been influenced by disease among his troops (Bury 1923: I, 295). A Gallic chronicler, almost certainly living in or close to Marseilles, fails to record either the comet or a plague in this period (ed. Mommsen 1892b: 648).[15] Of all the places likely to be affected by a widespread epidemic the neighbourhood of Marseilles must be ranked pretty high, and if the entries are anywhere near contemporary a medical historian might incline to think that this chronicler had perished in 452, when his work comes to an end and disease was rife in Italy.[16] Certainly there are 'plague years' when the mortality becomes alarming; Hydatius may be describing one such in 443. Yet the phrase *fere in toto orbe diffusa* will invite us to wonder what the limits of this world were. Disagreeable epidemics often start in the east. A plague of any sort – there are several to choose from – which spread along the north coast of Africa to alarm the Spaniards in 443, with bad years in Constantinople and Italy thereafter, is surely no safe pointer to the date of *famosa pestis* in Britain, even if we were certain that one and the same complaint was involved.[17]

More relevant to the state of affairs is another entry in the shorter Gallic chronicle, which is dated 442–3 by Bury (1923: I, 201, n. 2) and by Stevens (1941: 361). It runs: *Britanniae usque ad hoc tempus uariis cladibus euentibusque latae in dicionem Saxonum rediguntur.*[18] These

---

[15] Of the two Gallic chroniclers, the shorter finishes at 452, and the longer, in the same edition by Mommsen, at 511. The shorter is usually followed; for the decade 440–50 both reckon by the imperial years of Theodosius, who died in 450. Since the total of these years is stated at the beginning of his rule, it is not clear whether the entries are contemporary in the strictest sense.

[16] Gregory of Tours, who lived through the pandemic of bubonic plague which lasted during Justinian's reign and after, notes in the *Historia Francorum*, IV. 5, that on one occasion the disease came from Spain and entered Gaul through Marseilles (Dalton 1927: I, 421–2).

[17] The most recent study of bubonic plague in Britain is by Shrewsbury (1970), whose range and variety of learning are spoilt by a tendency to soften the incidence of this type of disease; and the book should be read in the light of a careful review by C. Morris (1971).

[18] Mommsen (1892b: 618) for *latae* would read *late uexatae*; another emendation is *laceratae* (Plummer 1896: II, 28).

words are taken by C. F. C. Hawkes (1956: 91) to mean that the former Roman provinces of Britain 'long troubled by various disasters, are brought under the dominion of the Saxons'. J. Morris (1965: 155) is more economical: 'Britain, which had hitherto suffered various disasters, passed under the control of the Saxons.' Taken at face value this statement hardly looks as if it could be true. Most of Devon remained in British hands until the seventh century, Cornwall until the ninth (Hoskins 1960), and Wales until far later. Nobody will doubt that the island had been troubled for a long while or on a broad front. Yet it is asking a great deal of anybody, to believe that during the 440s a chronicler in the south of France could have known what was going on at the Roman sites of, shall we say, Leicester and Carlisle, or even Winchester. What he could have known, in a natural and probable way, is the condition of trade. If for some years earlier than 442-3 the Saxon pirates had been interfering with the flow of goods – which we may be fairly sure they had – and then were able to deny the east of the Channel to shipping altogether, the circumstance would quickly be felt by dealers in leather and slaves. Occupation of a few strategic sites on either side of the water might easily be magnified by a distant observer into conquest on a scale beyond all likelihood. These records do not form themselves into a convincing pattern: neither the comet of 442 in the skies above him, nor the Spanish epidemic nearby, are to be found in the Gallic chronicler, whose picture of Britain could well have confused control of access with territorial dominion; and a relationship with the events described by Gildas is faraway and indistinct.

The only date at this period, which everyone can agree to, has been furnished by Prosper (ed. Mommsen 1892a: 472), who notes that in 429 Bishop Germanus of Auxerre travelled to Britain in order to combat the Pelagian heresy. Germanus died perhaps in 448, perhaps in 445 (Thompson 1957), and his life was written about 480 by Constantius of Lyon (ed. Levison 1919; ed. Borius 1965). Like many others of its kind, the story is more concerned to exalt the bishop than to provide historical fact; but at this time the Saxons, whether raiders or 'settled' in some sense of the word, are found in alliance with the Picts – information known to Bede (*HE*, I.20) who quotes freely from Constantius. Their threat need not have been tied down to any particular area. Mention of the relics of Alban the Martyr, if it does not implicate the Roman city of Verulamium beyond doubt (Borius 1965: 86), leaves the impression that Germanus spent some part of his time in south-east Britain; and Levison (1941) has argued cautiously for Verulamium. It is, however, the second visit which has led to conflicting opinions. A majority of critics would favour 445-7 (Borius 1965: 84, n. 3). On the other hand Grosjean (1957a, b), putting a case for 444, suggests that Germanus may have landed in south-western Britain, because from about 432 the heathen Franks were on the move through northern Gaul in the direction of ports like Étaples (Quentawic in later times) and might be powerful enough to discourage travel through the territory adjacent to them; but the chronology of this period may need revision (Verlinden 1954). The possibility that the eastern part of the Channel could have been controlled by pirates in 442-3 has already been alluded to. Whatever date may come to be accepted, unless it can be shown that Germanus went to the east of Britain his second visit becomes of greater interest for ecclesiastical than political conditions.[19] Taken as a whole, the continental sources appear to fall short of secure guidance; and allowing that the native traditions embedded in Gildas are historical, there is bound to be some hesitation over the accuracy of their arrangement, whether the fault lies in him or the material he drew on.

Chronology apart, what Bede called the *Aduentus Saxonum* surely marks a change of opportunity or purpose. Like the Vikings four centuries later, the Anglo-Saxons first made their appearances for a short while or in small groups, but then massively and for good.[20] A time arrived when the Britons failed to dislodge such invaders as they wanted to. Territory was occupied which could never be won

---

19 There do not seem to be sound reasons for thinking that Germanus reached Wales (Kirby 1968: 49–54).

20 Although historical analogies are often misleading, it is of interest that before 811 and up to 822 the Vikings had been building fortresses in Kent (Brooks 1971: 79–80); yet the final settlement of part of Healfdene's army in Yorkshire did not occur until fifty years later (*ASC*: year 876). From the evidence of place-names Stenton could say that this process, and what followed on it, 'had the dimensions of a migration' (*PASE*: 312; Loyn 1962: 54–6), although the armies themselves were probably not large (Sawyer 1962: 120–6).

back; and the Anglo-Saxons, no longer content to work under British rule, were determined to acquire land and to direct their own affairs. Adopting the theory of foreign control in 442–3, a recent writer can say: 'of course that mastery did not literally extend to the whole island, but it did extend to most of the civilised lowlands that faced Gaul. In the event, it was not to prove permanent but in 452 [when the shorter Gallic chronicle ends] that was not yet evident' (J. Morris 1965: 155). If mastery of the civilised lowlands did not become permanent in 442–3, we need to know how it bears on the Saxon mastery of Kent, which did. Stevens (1941: 371) would appear to admit that the date 488, given by the Anglo-Saxon Chronicle for the accession of Oisc (Aesc) to the Kentish throne, may have some authority. Yet the particular year is one matter, the throne another. A temptation to reject any English source of information appears to have left an uncomfortable gap, not so much in time as in the circumstance that a kingdom did exist; and it would be an injustice to the Britons, not borne out by any other evidence, to think that they abandoned one of their richest holdings without a struggle. Whether this gap is suitably filled by the Anglo-Saxon Chronicle, and by the writings of Bede and others, can only be determined by examining both the material and the framework within which that material has been presented. No gap seems to be filled by the incoherent annals of southern Europe.

We now take leave for a while of events fixed by the Julian calendar, and return to luni-solar reckoning. The same principles that governed the Anglo-Saxon calendar, applied in another way, led to the development of the Christian era – with only so much of the story being told here as is needed to understand the small print of history.

CHAPTER 3

THE EASTER TABLES OF DIONYSIUS

One of the first and more reasonable hopes of the early Church was to secure a uniform observance of Easter – an expectation not realised until a great amount of disagreement and ill-feeling had been lived through, lasting for hundreds of years. The 'Paschal controversy' was rooted in a type of luni-solar calendar employed by the Jews, in turn an offshoot of the 19-year Babylonian cycle (Schwarz 1905; Bickerman 1968: 24–6). The Jewish year began in spring, with the month Nisan; at the full moon of this month, 14 Nisan, the feast of the Passover was celebrated. In consequence of luni-solar reckoning, 14 Nisan is not a fixed day in the purely solar, Julian, calendar; and because the Crucifixion took place at the time of Passover, Easter could occur in successive years on any day of the week. With the Gospel story in mind, however, it came to be thought that Easter should always be observed on a Sunday, the first day of the week, *feria i* or *dies dominica* (the latter term sometimes meaning any Sunday, sometimes Easter itself). The difficulty, and the debates, turned on the question – which Sunday?

At the Council of Nicaea in 325, when the answer might have been given once and for all, no formal definition was proclaimed: members of the Church were only enjoined to keep Easter on the same day, and to avoid Jewish customs. Considering that 318 bishops were present, from almost every part of the empire and backed by Constantine in person, their answer will seem vague and unworldly. By inference, the Christian feast must never fall on a Passover; and the vernal equinox, the beginning of spring, was then widely accepted as occurring on 21 March. If, therefore, the fourteenth day of the moon fell on a Sunday, the observance of Easter must be deferred for a week; hence *luna xv* and not *luna xiv* is taken as the lower limit. Under the Mosaic law, celebration of the Passover was restricted to the third week of the first Jewish month (Exodus

30

12. 15–19), so the permissible limits for Easter in a solar calendar lie between *luna xv* and *luna xxi*, counted inclusively, with 22 March as the earliest date for that festival. These are the figures adopted by the Greeks of Alexandria, which in the long run prevailed.[1] But the Roman (Latin) church, long before the Council of Nicaea, had adopted the limits *luna xvi–xxii* for reasons that are obscure (Schwarz 1905: 33), and stubbornly maintained them.[2]

Side by side with the problem of ascertaining the date of Easter, in any one year, there arose the separate problem of how to convey the information from a mother church to its daughters, in the interests of uniformity, and of obedience. It seems that these responsibilities were first taken on by the bishops of Alexandria, whose clergy retained a knowledge of Greek mathematics; from them the date of the coming Easter was announced in the form of Paschal epistles (Scudamore 1880: 1562–4). With the expansion of Christendom, more particularly on this side of the Alps – there were bishops in Gaul during the second century – the obstacle of communication began to be felt. Moreover, since Easter is a movable feast, and the Lenten fast begins forty days ahead, in effect the day must be known by January – the earliest date for Ash Wednesday being 4 February, though it can occur as late as 10 March. With storms at sea, and ice or snow on land, a long journey in the winter months could be perilous; if a messenger were lost, the delay in replacing him was at best considerable. By degrees, therefore, the bishops of Alexandria, Rome and others with far-flung jurisdiction were constrained to fix Eastertide during the previous summer. Thus the calculation of tables predicting the date for years ahead solved a couple of problems at once. Or rather, would have solved them, but for two considerations: the disagreement over lunar

---

[1] Among the earliest Christians a few observed Easter on any day that the fourteenth moon happened to occur. They were known as 'quartodecimanians'; as time passed their numbers became negligible, and the word formed itself into a clumsy term of abuse. The practice was even imputed to the Celtic Church, as by Eddius (ed. Colgrave 1927: cc. X and XV). Bede, whose goodwill to the Irish is more than once apparent, except in the matter of Easter reckoning, knew better (*HE*, III. 17).

[2] A priest at Rome, Hippolytus, had composed an Easter table based on the *octaëteris*, already mentioned in Chapter 1; it ran from A.D. 222–333, in modern reckoning, with the lunar limits *xvi–xxii* (Mac Carthy 1901: xxxii–xl), but other considerations are perhaps involved.

limits; and the aspiration of Rome to primacy in every field, which was thwarted by the superior mathematics of Alexandria. The former we shall chiefly be concerned with, because it troubled the British Isles down to the latter half of the eighth century.

The development of Easter tables has been set out at length by Jones (1943), a tale of tedious quarrelling, where the rivalry of particular churches allowed hardly any room for sense or moderation. For the present purpose only three types of table need to be considered, and briefly. All derive from the Metonic cycle, which can be adapted to the Julian calendar in the following way. In lunar terms, 228 months of 29.5 days each = 6726 days, to which must be added 7 embolismic months of 30 days and 4.75 leap-year days, bringing the total to 6940.75 days. But in 19 Julian (solar) years there are 6939.56 days. Thus the moon has gained over the sun by one day, near enough. By a convenient fiction the moon was supposed to skip a day; and this form of (negative) intercalation, known as the *saltus lunae*, can be appreciated from the first of the Easter reckonings we need to look at, the 'Celtic-84'.

This 84-year cycle was employed by the Celtic Church in Ireland, by its influential colony at Iona, and at the time of the Augustinian mission by the Britons of Wales, Cornwall and Cumbria-Strathclyde (*HE*, II. 2 and 4). The 84 years represent 4 Metonic cycles of 19 years with another 8 years added, the *ogdoas*. For the calculation of Easter, 84 is a useful number because it is divisible by 7, and hence the new moons recur on the same days of the week in the Julian calendar. Disregarding small fractions, 84 Julian (solar) years = 30,681 days. In lunar terms 12 × 84 months of 29.5 days = 29,736 days, to which must be added 31 embolismic months of 30 days and 21 leap-year days; in all 30,687 days. By skipping 6 days at intervals – each jump being a *saltus lunae* – the figures are in harmony (details modified from O'Connell 1936). More generally, the Celtic-84 was based on the lunar limits *xiv–xx* and on a vernal equinox at 25 March, a day favoured by the writers of classical antiquity and also the traditional day of the Crucifixion. There is reason to think that these rules were of very long standing, perhaps from the third century, and quite probably derived from Asia Minor (Schwarz 1905: 103). In the Irish reckoning, as exemplified by the Annals of

Ulster (ed. Hennessy 1887), each year opens, and is distinguished by, the day of the week on which 1 January fell, together with the age of the moon: for instance, the year 456 is headed *i feria luna ix*. Thus the years conform to the pattern of the Julian calendar.

At Rome, as we have seen, the prevailing limits were *luna xvi–xxii*. The Latins appear to have employed an 84-year cycle during the fourth century and the first half of the fifth (van de Vyver 1957), but collisions with Alexandria, followed by occasional compromise, became serious in 444 and again in 455 (MacCarthy 1901: cix–cxv; Jones 1943: 62). Pope Leo I then encouraged Victorius of Aquitaine to produce a new set of tables (ed. Mommsen 1892c; Krusch 1938). Victorius on the whole followed Alexandrian principles while also retaining the traditional *luna xvi–xxii*; at some points he gives the Greek Easter, based on *luna xv–xxi*, as well as the Latin. His tables were issued in 457 and, unlike any of the known 84-year cycles, began from a definite and easily recognised era. He chose the *Annus Mundi* 5229, reckoned from the Creation – then supposed to be an event occupying six days – to the first year of his new era, the *Annus Passionis*. In modern terms, A.P. 1 is equal to A.D. 28, or, A.P. plus 27 gives the year A.D. The tables also contained a list of consuls down to the year of issue, which were valuable when records of past events came to be written down in the margin or when such events had to be defined by consular years; but they did not include a column for Indictions – a matter to which we shall return (below, p. 38). The chief improvement which he brought forward appears to have been due more to accident than design (Jones 1943: 63–4): the formula $4 \times 7 \times 19$ gives what is called the Great Paschal cycle of 532 years, after which the lunar and solar data will recur for the next 532 years and so on (for details see Newton 1972: 38–40). These Victorian tables were widely used in Gaul, being officially adopted by the Council of Orleans in 541 (Mansi 1763: col. 113); there can be little doubt that they were also employed in southern Ireland, alongside the 84-year cycle, or at least known, during the latter half of the sixth century (O'Connell 1936: 84–8).

Nevertheless, two factors may have combined to upset the conservative attitude of Rome over the limits *luna xvi–xxii*. First of all, the Victorian system occasionally allowed a choice of Easter dates,

Latin or Greek, which could only be a source of confusion. Secondly, as the theological definitions of the Council of Nicaea became more and more influential, so its attitude to the earliest Easter moon – though implied and not clearly stated – seems to have gathered weight. A new set of tables, in 19-year cycles, was propounded early in the sixth century by Dionysius Exiguus.[3] He followed Alexandrian principles, with the lunar limits *xv–xxi* and a vernal equinox on 21 March.[4] The first of his tables reproduces part of a scheme which is ascribed to Cyril of Alexandria (patriarch 412–44). In it the calendar years were reckoned by an era that started with the reign of Diocletian, equal to A.D. 284, sometimes called 'the era of the martyrs'. A calculation stemming from one of the leading persecutors of the Church did not recommend itself to Dionysius, who instead adopted a specifically Christian era: *sed magis eligimus ab incarnatione domini nostri Iesu Christi annorum tempora praenotare* (Krusch 1938: 64). For obvious reasons the names usually attached to this new era are *Annus Domini*, 'the Year of the Lord' or 'Year of Grace', and *anno ab incarnatione*, 'from the Incarnation'.[5]

We may now inspect the first 19-year cycle of the Christian era, as issued by Dionysius, running from 532 to 550 inclusive; Table 2 only contains the details that are needed for an understanding of method and principles (ed. Migne 1865: cols. 483–98; Krusch 1938: 70). The fourth column of this table, *lunae circulus*, sets out the nineteen years of the lunar cycle, and it will be observed that they are out of step with the years A.D. in the left-hand column, the first year of the lunar cycle corresponding with the fourth Year of Grace in this section (535). But the circumstance arises from the need of

3 *Exiguus* means *humilis, indignus*, a lowly and humble man of heart. The French call him Denys le Petit, as if he were a dwarf. He is not to be confused with Dionysius of Alexandria (bishop 248–66), who applied the *octaëteris* to an Easter table in one of his Paschal epistles (MacCarthy 1901: xliv).

4 It is desirable to notice that Easter calculations are based on an 'ecclesiastical moon' and an 'ecclesiastical equinox', neither of which correspond exactly with what astronomers can observe (Newton 1972: 22–33). But almost without exception the differences are not important for Anglo-Saxon chronology.

5 In a theological sense, *anno ab incarnatione* should be reckoned from the Annunciation, 25 March. In the later Anglo-Saxon period, and for a long while afterwards, 25 March was sometimes taken as the beginning of the year; then it became a quarter day; and ended up in England, after the calendar reform when eleven days were abolished, as the start of the financial year, 5 April.

TABLE 2. *Cyclus decennovenalis primus*

	Anni Domini	Indict- iones	Epactae	Lunae circulus	Dies dominicae festivitatis		
B	DXXXII	X	NULLA	XVII	III	id.	Apr.
	DXXXIII	XI	XI	XVIII	VI	kl.	Apr.
	DXXXIIII	XII	XXII	XVIIII	XVI	kl.	Mai.
	DXXXV	XIII	III	I	VI	id.	Apr.
B	DXXXVI	XIIII	XIIII	II	X	kl.	Apr.
	DXXXVII	XV	XXV	III	II	id.	Apr.
	DXXXVIII	I	VI	IIII	II	non.	Apr.
	DXXXVIIII	II	XVII	V	VIII	kl.	Mai.
B	DXXXX	III	XXVIII	VI	VI	id.	Apr.
	DXXXXI	IIII	VIIII	VII	II	kl.	Apr.
	DXXXXII	V	XX	VIII	XII	kl.	Mai.
	DXXXXIII	VI	I	VIIII	non.	Apr.	
B	DXXXXIIII	VII	XII	X	VI	kl.	Apr.
	DXXXXV	VIII	XXIII	XI	XVI	kl.	Apr.
	DXXXXVI	VIIII	IIII	XII	VI	id.	Apr.
	DXXXXVII	X	XV	XIII	IX	kl.	Apr.
B	DXXXXVIII	XI	XXVI	XIIII	II	id.	Apr.
	DXXXXVIIII	XII	VII	XV	II	non.	Apr.
	DL	XIII	XVIII	XVI	VIII	kl.	Mai.

B = bissextile, or leap, year

adjusting the Alexandrian mode of reckoning to Roman tradition as well as to the Julian year. Neither Dionysius nor anyone else in the Church could escape the imperial calendar, sanctified by long usage from the time of Caesar himself and already the framework of Christian festivals. To be intelligible, the date of Easter must emerge in the form of *x* Kalends, Nones or Ides of April or May. The position can be made clearer by referring to the column for *epactae*. The epact is usually defined as the age of the new moon on the first day of a particular year.[6] If a new moon occurs on 1 January, new moons will also occur on 31 January, 1 March and 31 March, the last being

---

[6] The definition of 'epact' has changed at various times, but we are here concerned only with early practice.

35

helpful in Easter calculations. Taking the equinox as 21 March and supposing a table to be constructed to start from the next day, 22 March (earlier than which, incidentally, Easter should not be allowed to fall), then the difference 31 March minus 22 March is 9, which can be taken as the initial epact of a cycle. Since the lunar year is shorter than the solar by 11 days, neglecting fractions, in the next year the epact will be 20, and in the year after 31. But since the age of the moon cannot exceed 30 days, this last number becomes 1. The epact of the following year will be increased to 12, and so through the cycle. This brief outline of older practice, sometimes called Roman, will serve to introduce the next point.

Although the Roman pattern of epacts is built round 1 January, the equivalent of 31 March in lunar terms, the Alexandrian pattern changed about 1 September; and there comes a year in the cycle when the Alexandrian epact in March is 30, that is, 0, *epacta nulla*.[7] Bede curiously defines the epact in this way (*DTR*, c. L). The reason why the Roman cycle never gave 0 for the epact is that the *saltus lunae* occurred in the sixteenth year, whereas the Alexandrians put their *saltus* in the nineteenth. These relationships are set out in Table 3, which is an adaptation from Mac Carthy (1901:

TABLE 3. Epacts

Roman cycle years	XV	XVI	XVII	XVIII	XVIIII	I	II	III
Roman	16	27[a]	9	20	1	12	23	4
Alexandrian	7	18[a]	30	11	22	3	14	25
Dionysius	7	18[a]	0	11	22	3	14	25
Alexandrian cycle years	XVIII	XVIIII	I	II	III	IIII	V	VI

[a] *saltus lunae* here, that is, 12 now
to be added to the epact instead of 11.

l–li) and includes only the years of most importance. In effect, therefore, Dionysius retained the order of years in the Roman cycle as they appear in Table 2, *lunae circulus*, but combined them with

[7] The great convenience of *epacta nulla*, in saving arithmetic, has been emphasised by Jones (1943: 32). For some interesting comments on its mathematical significance see Newton (1972: 17–22), though the concept is not due to Bede, who only followed Dionysius and the Alexandrians.

Alexandrian epacts. In the course of this diplomatic shuffle, where Roman face was saved by not interrupting its cycle of years, the Alexandrian *luna xv* was allowed to prevail over the *luna xvi* admitted by Victorius. And thus the wrangling of centuries was brought to an end, in principle though not by any means immediately in practice.

By way of filling in another point of detail, Table 4 is intended to

TABLE 4

Years of era beginning 1 Jan	I B.C.	A.D. I	A.D. 2
Roman cycle	XVII	XVIII	XVIIII
Years in Table 2	A.D. 532	A.D. 533	A.D. 534

show the relation between the modern reckoning of years A.D. and B.C. on the one hand, and the figures of Table 2 on the other. It will be evident that according to Dionysius, who seems here to be influenced by the 'History' of Eusebius, I. 5 (tr. Lake 1926: 46–7), or by his 'Chronicle' (ed. Fotheringham 1923), the Annunciation and Nativity occurred in what is now called 1 B.C. Bede was aware of the position (*DTR*, c. XLVII), and to him we owe the reckoning Before Christ (*HE*, V. 24), which follows when 28 cycles of 19 years each are subtracted from the first year of the Dionysiac cycle. A year 0 is intolerable in everyday thinking.[8]

We can next examine the structure of the Christian year a little more closely. By the middle of the fourth century Christmas, the feast of the Nativity, had been fixed at 25 December (above, p. 9); the Annunciation was taken to be nine months earlier, 25 March. The Octave of Christmas – counted from 25 December to 1 January inclusive – represents the eight days from birth to circumcision in Luke 2.21. Then the child Jesus made a formal entry into the Jewish faith, and became qualified for the office of a Messiah. At this moment the reckoning by *Anni Domini* began. Although Dionysius

---

[8] The astronomer, however, must work with a regular series; hence 753 B.C., the reputed date for the foundation of Rome, and the start of the era *ab urbe condita*, A.U.C., becomes −752.

started the era on 1 January, two reasons helped to preserve Christmas day as the beginning of the year in popular estimation. In the first place, the pagan Midwinter festival, in England anyhow, was long remembered. English charters of the eighth and ninth centuries, where Christmas is taken as the turning point of the year, are discussed in Chapter 6; and a couple of generations after the Conquest the Anglo-Saxon Chronicle records that King Stephen was crowned 'on midewintre dai' in 1135 (ed. Earle and Plummer 1892: I, 263). In more recent times, historians may have been encouraged to think that the year always started with 25 December by the following remark: 'Bede, in his theoretical work *De Temporum Ratione* states, as a matter which needs no explanation, that it began on Christmas Day' (Poole 1934: 8). Yet the remark is not true; Bede nowhere says anything of the kind (Jones 1947: 210, n. 65; Harrison 1973b: 53). What is often called 'the Church's year' is reckoned from Advent, the fourth Sunday before Christmas when preparations begin for that festival; but this circumstance also has no bearing on the era inaugurated by Dionysius; and the ecclesiastical calendar, with its festivals and saints' days, begins on 1 January.

The second reason for attaching weight to 25 December came about in a different way. Under the Roman empire it had been the rule to celebrate the Kalends of January in high spirits: people dressed up in animal skins, men wore women's clothes, and so on (Nilsson 1916; Swanton 1974). Even in Rome itself the gaieties were a scandal as late as 742, when Boniface of Mainz wrote complaining about them to Pope Zacharias (ed. Dummler 1892: 301); in the following letter the Pope replies that he could not but agree. England at the same time shows lingering traces of the custom; in the Penitential of Archbishop Egbert of York, who died in 766, there are regulations specifically directed against the *Kalendae* (ed. Haddan and Stubbs 1873: III, 434). Thus the Feast of the Circumcision, which by all rights should have been observed in the early Church, did not become widespread until the sixth century (Holweck 1925: 1).

With most of the ground cleared we are now in a position to look at the second column of Table 2, that for Indictions. At first the Indiction was a solemn edict, issued by the Roman emperors and laying down the scale of taxes; in course of time the name was applied simply to a cycle of fifteen years. From the reign of Constantine, and beginning in 312, each year of the cycle started on 1 September. The first Indiction therefore ran from 1 September 312 to 31 August 313; the fifteenth, last of the first cycle, from 1 September 326 to 31 August 327, when the next cycle began. The years of each cycle were numbered *indictio prima, secunda*, etc. By degrees it became usual to date letters and other documents by the Indiction, which in origin is an administrative year, with or without the imperial or consular years which formed an independent system of reference. Under Justinian, in 537, the Indiction became a compulsory feature of the date (Bickerman 1968: 78); its use at Rome can be traced back to Pope Pelagius II in 584 (Jaffé 1885: ix). The arrangement of the Cyrillic Easter tables, with their column of Indictions alongside the 'Diocletian' years, was very sensibly followed by Dionysius (Table 2), and attention will again be drawn to this arrangement in Chapter 6.

As to the subsequent history of Dionysiac tables, the chief of it is soon told. From 532 to 626, inclusive, the five 19-year cycles were calculated by Dionysius himself; another five, 627–721 inclusive, are doubtfully ascribed to Felix Gillitanus (Jones 1943: 73). Before the tables of Felix had expired, the concept of a Great Paschal cycle of 532 years, deriving from Victorius, was being applied to the Dionysiac reckoning. In a letter to Naiton (Nechtan) king of the Picts, written between 706 and 716, Abbot Ceolfrith of Wearmouth–Jarrow states that many people, *plures*, are able to compute cycles of 532 years (*HE*, v. 21). But the transport of Dionysiac tables from Italy to England is a topic reserved to the next chapter. It is only necessary to add that the Alexandrian principles, as expounded by Dionysius, have proved satisfactory down to the present day – with a few trifling adjustments.

By way of introduction to the methods of dating commonly employed in the seventh century, we may now consider a letter from Pope Gregory the Great to King Ethelbert of Kent (*HE*, I. 32) which ends: 'Given the 10th day of the Kalends of July in the 19th year of the reign of our most devout lord Mauricius Tiberius Augustus, in the 18th year after the consulship of the same lord, the 4th

Indiction.' From these details the date cannot be in doubt: 22 June 601. To check the year, a rule for finding the Indiction is given by Bede: to the number of the year A.D. add three and divide by fifteen, the remainder being the Indiction (*DTR*, c. XLIX). The process cannot be applied in reverse, with any certainty; of the earliest charters in England, many are dated by Indiction alone, and the precise year can only be found by considering the names of kings, bishops and thegns who are mentioned, particularly among the witnesses. Thus the letter of Pope Gregory, did we not know from other sources the length of his pontificate, or when Ethelbert of Kent died, or had the imperial years of Mauricius been omitted, could be referred to 586, 601 or 616. This sort of doubt will not satisfy a tidy historical mind.

Easter tables have survived with notes of historical importance written in the margin; and to illustrate the practice a couple of hypothetical examples will be enough. Archbishop Deusdedit of Canterbury died on 14 July 664 (*HE*, IV, I). An event of this kind, more especially because it occurred soon after a total eclipse of the sun, was excellent material for the annalist, who could write down a marginal note in the form *Deusdedit archiep.ob.prid.id.Iul.*, and, once the news was confirmed, it might have been recorded within a few weeks of his death. Information from overseas, however, could easily take several months to reach this country. The death of Pope Gregory II took place on 11 February 731; he is mentioned in Bede's Preface to *HE* in terms which suggest that he was thought to be still alive, so the notice of it will not have arrived in Northumbria before this part of the book was written, or else no correction was made. If we suppose an annalist hearing of a letter from Rome which said *defunctus est Gregorius papa iii id. Feb.*, *Indictione xiv^a*, the information could have been entered into a Dionysiac table against the appropriate Indiction, even without mention of imperial or consular years. It could not have been entered into a Victorian table, with accuracy, unless the year was defined in some other way, as by A.U.C. or *Anno Mundi*, or could be found or calculated from another source. Dionysius, however, provided a 'ready reckoner', or conversion table, listing both the Years of Grace and Indictions, which went far beyond the needs of anyone seeking only the date of

Easter. This variety of style helped to extend the scope of the annalist, if only by saving time and effort.

Returning to the Indictional cycles, their drawback is two-fold: not only are they out of step with the *lunae circulus* but also the year reckoned from 1 September does not correspond with the Julian year. Take, for instance, a Council at Hatfield presided over by Archbishop Theodore, the acts being dated *sub die xv kalendas Octobres, Indictione viii*[a] (*HE*, IV. 15). We may read 17 September 679 in modern reckoning, although Bede in *HE*, V. 24 gives 680 for the year. This last however, is the Julian year into which the greater part of the Indictional year falls, in other words, the year A.D. corresponding to *Indictio VIII* in a Dionysiac table.[9] Here it is assumed that Theodore was following the rule laid down by Justinian, and continued by Gregory the Great, that documents should be dated by the Indiction of 1 September, that is, by no other.[10] When the new archbishop came to England, after consecration by Pope Vitalian, he was accompanied by Abbot Hadrian of Niridano, one of whose duties was to make sure that Theodore, who had been born in Tarsus of Cicilia, did not introduce Greek customs conflicting with the faith (*HE*, IV. 1). As to the beginning of the administrative year, at least, Theodore was not likely to depart from the usage of Constantinople and Rome. So the assumption appears to be justified; it is most probable that he followed the Indiction of 1 September, commonly called the Greek, but sometimes 'of Constantinople.' Any other interpretation must explain why he should wish to upset the concord between Rome and Canterbury.

In spite of these precedents, which had lasted for a long while, another form of Indiction, beginning on 24 September, was defined by Bede in the following terms: *incipiunt autem indictiones ab viii kal. Octobres ibidemque terminantur* (*DTR*, c. XLVIII). This Indiction is

---

[9] Poole's explanation of this date (1934: 44 and 49) was the first to achieve a wide currency, though he acknowledges elsewhere in the same volume (p. 41, n. 4) a debt to the work of A. Anscombe in 1900. For further remarks on this Council see below, p. 83.

[10] Halkin (1972) has pointed to the Byzantine use of 23 September, the birthday of the emperor Augustus, for the start of the year during the fourth and early fifth centuries. It is not easy to think, however, that this archaic style, with its heathen background, should ever be influential in England, in face of Justinian's rule and Papal practice.

often called the 'Bedan', but since it was adopted under the Holy
Roman Empire, at a time later than we are concerned with, the
adjectives 'Imperial' or 'Caesarean' are also applied.[11] Two questions
at once arise: was it ever followed in England; and, why was it
invented? A full answer to the first question must be delayed until
Chapter 6, but one possibility can be explored now, occurring in the
Historia Abbatum written by an anonymous monk (*HAA*). For all
its title, which seems to have been supplied by the editor, this work
is chiefly devoted to the life of Ceolfrith, who in 716 left the
monastery of Wearmouth–Jarrow on a pilgrimage to Rome. The
account of his journey is circumstantial: not only the dates but the
days of the week are given for two points of arrival or departure,
and thus there can be no doubt about the year (Plummer 1896: II,
375–6; Levison 1946: 269). Ceolfrith was never to reach his destina-
tion. He arrived at Langres, near Troyes, *die septimo Kalendarum
Octobrium, sexta sabbati... circa horam diei tertiam...incipiente indictione xv... Contigit autem ut ipso die, quo uenerat, circa horam X migraret ad
Dominum*, that is, arrival about the third hour on 25 September,
which was a Friday in 716 (*sabbatum* can mean a whole week), and
death at about the tenth hour, in the afternoon (*HAA*: 400–403).
The same particulars are found in Bede's *Historia Abbatum* (*HAB*:
386), except that for the Indiction he substituted *anno ab incarnatione
Domini septingentesimo sextodecimo*; either he borrowed from *HAA*, or
drew upon their common source, changing the style of the date. Yet
the phrase *incipiente indictione* is not quite exact whether the Bedan
Indiction of 24 September is meant or no; it is wrong by a day or
just over three weeks, and the same writer (*HAA*: 394) can refer to
12 January as the beginning, *exordium*, of the year. In this particular
context, then, 24 September seems hardly more probable than the
Kalends of that month.

Various explanations of Bede's choice – if it was his own – have
been put forward. The definition is oddly placed in *De Temporum
Ratione*, at the very end of a chapter and with nothing to amplify it
or to give even a hint that 1 September had for long been the official
date at Rome. The argument by Jones (1943: 282–4), that Bede

---

[11] The Roman, otherwise Pontifical, Indiction beginning on 1 January is also a later
development, an admission that the Julian calendar had again prevailed.

42

misread a passage in the *De Noe et Arca* written by Ambrose of Milan, is not very strong; this was the sort of material which Bede well understood, and it seems unlikely that he would think of the Alexandrians as beginning their year on 24 September, because he knew their lunar count started on or near the first of the month. Classical writers such as Pliny had cleared their minds with the formula *viii kal.Apr.* for the vernal equinox and *viii kal.Oct.* for the autumnal, 25 March and 24 September. Constrained by the vernal equinox at 21 March, on which the Easter reckoning was founded, Bede nevertheless stuck to an autumnal equinox on 24 September (*DTR*, c. xxx). There can be no doubt that the ecclesiastical equinox of 21 March was a stumbling block in several ways, and the complications must not be passed over.

Firstly, the true equinox can fall on more than one day, leap years alone causing trouble in the Julian calendar itself; and again, the circumstance of error in calendrical reckoning will bring about a slow backward drift in the calendar dates.[12] Whether the older contemporaries of Bede were aware of this latter fact, as he was, is not clear; but in Ceolfrith's letter to the king of the Picts (*HE*, v. 21) an equinox at 21 March is argued for, *ut etiam ipsi horologica inspectione probamus*, as moreover we can prove by looking at a sundial (or pair of gnomons). The observation is not easy to make, with accuracy, but seems to have satisfied the Northumbrians, without resolving the discrepancy between this equinox and the autumnal equinox on 24 September. By Bede, therefore, or by someone else, a fixed point for the Indiction may have been sought, independent of the unsteady equinox. From a perpetual lunar calendar, or by calculation, it can be seen that when a new moon falls on 1 January in a particular year another new moon will fall on 24 September (Harrison 1973b: 54, n. 3). Thus in the first year of a 19-year luni-solar cycle – so the argument could have run – the Indiction ought properly to occur on 24 September. It was the beginning of an administrative not a calendar year, but would thus occur on a

---

[12] On the reason why the ecclesiastical equinox became fixed at 21 March, and on equinoxes generally, see Newton (1972: 22–7). Approximate dates for the vernal equinox are: in Caesar's time calculated to be about 23 March; at Nicaea about 20 March; and in Bede's time about 17 March. At the Gregorian calendar reform, 1582, theory and observation had fallen apart by about 10 days.

definite and intelligible day, whereas 1 September is an arbitrary choice. Yet a resuscitation of an ancient value for the equinox cannot be ruled out.

The moment may now be appropriate for an enquiry, along very general lines, into the background of chronology in historical writing during the Dark Ages, and more particularly into the extent to which marginal notes in Easter tables could have served as a quarry for historians. These notes are usually called 'Paschal annals', to distinguish them from other types of compilation. Without risking the easy target of definitions, we may think broadly of three types of record. The Paschal annal, like a gloss, will usually be short and to the point. A more extended record, sometimes called 'Annals' and sometimes 'a Chronicle', is still often set out as a sequence of events year by year, but with fuller information and occasionally a more connected narrative. The line between a chronicle and a history is also vague, and drawn more by taste or opinion than by a rigid set of criteria. And there is another aspect of historical writing that calls for attention, not only during this disturbed period but before it and after it: a want of agreement about eras, the fixed points of reference from which an ordered presentation can most safely begin.

Strictly, the annalist who works in isolation does not depend upon an era – or at least an era that is immediately apparent. The Annals of Ulster, whose ferial and lunar notation has already been mentioned, are an example (above, p. 32). There seems to be little doubt that the style was employed from the earliest stages of annalistic writing in Ireland (O'Rahilly 1946: 235–9; Hughes 1972: 104 and 108; Smyth 1972). Long after the 84-year tables had been discarded in favour of Dionysiac reckoning the *Anni Domini* were inserted, not earlier than the tenth century into the Annals of Ulster (Anderson 1973: 5); at a later time still the ferial and lunar notation was restored. To define each year by the day of the week and the epact (age of the moon) on 1 January is to conform to an orthodox practice, for the ecclesiastical calendar had settled into the Julian framework no later than the fourth century. This combination of *feriae* and *lunae* occurs in the Zeitz table, compiled probably in 447 and preserved in a contemporary manuscript (ed. Mommsen 1891b; Lowe 1959: 10). A little while later, columns for these particulars are found in the Victorian Easter tables. The Julian era from 45 B.C. may be the foundation of Irish annals, whether the compilers were aware of it or not, and without denying an influence from chroniclers like Eusebius and Jerome. No 84-year tables written in Ireland have survived, but it is not improbable that they followed continental models of an earlier date than the Zeitz tables (Anderson 1973: 23, n. 96).

Yet annalistic curiosity will seldom have been satisfied by such memorable events as a kingdom or neighbourhood was able to afford. Just as copies of manuscripts travelled from one scriptorium to another, so, on a more lowly plane, did the bits and pieces of contemporary information. In the eighth century, when the writing of entries into Easter tables had become fairly widespread, diffusion of annals among several monastic houses is not beyond discovery: as by Bresslau (1923), who traces the origin of Salzburg annals, and by Lehmann (1925), connecting Corvey, Fulda and other places with distant Northumbria.[13] This kind of transfer was most easy when the systems of reckoning were the same at each monastery; many of the Frankish foundations, inspired largely by the work of Willibrord, Boniface and other Anglo-Saxons, had in common the era invented by Dionysius.[14] On another level, exchanges between the systems A.P. and A.D. were relatively simple, though carelessness could lead to an error of twenty-seven years. Or a striking event like the appearance of a comet, or an eclipse or the death of a king, might be recorded independently in more than one set of annals, to make a bridge between them. Regnal lists gave meaning to statements of the form 'in the xth year of King Y'; a tolerably long reign of itself could represent an era within an era, providing a focus for collection and dispersal.

It is, however, rather more difficult to find out what was going on before the eighth century, and perhaps we should guard against thinking that the writing of chronicles or history was influenced by Paschal annals to a decisive or even a considerable extent. The

13 Exchange of annals in Ireland is treated by Hughes (1972: 99–159) and by Smyth (1972); for the continent see also Hoffmann (1958).
14 Although Pirmin, the founder of Reichenau and Murbach, appears to have been a Visigoth, the latter place can show early annals dated by the Year of Grace (Poole 1934: 89).

following remarks by Jones (1943: 116) surely go a little too far: 'These Easter tables, or lists of movable feasts, were an innovation in the West. Although the Romans had calendars in pagan times and also had historical lists with political records on them, history was not, in the main, forced into annalistic form by a required annual list. The introduction of such a list . . . eventually changed the whole course of historical writing.' Elsewhere he says: 'The reason why we cannot cite direct evidence of composition from English manuscripts written before the eleventh century is that, although there are literally hundreds of continental Easter tables extant, not one Easter table written in England before the year 1000 has survived' (Jones 1947: 32). Statements of this kind give an impression of abundance, of Easter tables crammed with entries of prime importance to the chronicler and historian. Yet a survey of continental manuscripts by Mommsen (1892d) has yielded only a meagre harvest.[15] The most valuable collections of material may indeed have disappeared because their contents were absorbed by later writers, who then discarded them. Still, we may doubt whether many Dionysiac annals were written before the end of the seventh century, in this country or abroad. Appeal to them, as a hypothetical source, has been castigated by Jones (1947: 202, n. 24), and, to judge by what documentary evidence we have, in the analysis of a chronicle or history it would be preferable first to look for sources elsewhere, if only to avoid a false sense of security.

In the matter of destruction, Victorian tables must have fared even worse than the Dionysiac, since the *Annus Passionis* had largely dropped out of use by the ninth century, even in France. A complete Victorian table which survives has only two marginal entries, at A.P. years corresponding to A.D. 490 and 501 (ed. Mommsen 1892c); which, when we consider that the Great Paschal cycle of 532 years repeated itself, is an inconsiderable number. The main section of the annals known as *Paschale Campanum*, edited by Mommsen as part of the *Consularia Italica* (1891a: 305–34 and 745–9), runs from 464 to 585 in A.D. reckoning; it is drawn up as a consular list, with the

---

[15] Victor of Tonnenna, whose chronicle was written in the sixth century (ed. Mommsen 1893c), shows a knowledge of reckoning from the Nativity and from the Passion; but his entries are laid out by consular and imperial years, with no distinct reliance on one or other of these recently-invented eras.

Victorian dates of Easter, and thus can be described as a set of Paschal annals. Up to 512 the records of historical interest are fairly frequent, and include an eclipse and two eruptions of Vesuvius. Yet the quality of these records, the type of information they convey, will invite us to ask whether they were written down with a definite historical purpose in view. No doubt they helped, in Plummer's words, 'to *characterise* the receding series of years, each by a mark or sign of its own, so that the years might not be confused in the retrospect of those who had lived and acted in them' (Earle and Plummer 1899: II, xix). Whatever the motive, we can now glance briefly at the traces which Paschal annals seem to have left in the historical writing of northern continental Europe at this time – with the proviso that perhaps a representative sample has not been chosen.

It will be remembered that Victorius of Aquitaine had published his tables in 457, nearly a century before Dionysius. For this length of time the earlier tables had the advantage; and the period covers the rise of Merovingian power, particularly the dominion and baptism of Clovis which were of more than ordinary interest to Gregory of Tours when he came to write the *Historia Francorum* (ed. Krusch and Levison 1951; tr. Dalton 1927). The greater part of his activity in composition seems to fall within the decade 575–85. As a bishop and historian – in the latter respect a considerable figure – Gregory was less concerned with chronological tidiness than with a delicate blend of piety and homicide among the Merovingian rulers. He did, however, state an aim and fulfil it:

After what manner the years of this world are counted the chronicles of Eusebius, bishop of Caesarea, and of Jerome the priest plainly teach, setting them all forth in their order. And Orosius, also making most diligent enquiry into these things, set down the whole series of years from the beginning of the world to his own day. Which Victorius did once again when he determined the dates of the Paschal feast. Therefore I am fain in my turn to follow the example of the aforesaid writers, and reckon the whole sum of years down to our own time... [*Historia*, introductory note; tr. Dalton 1927: II, 6].

The calculations are given at the end of the fourth and tenth books, where Gregory arrives at *Annus Mundi* 5204 from the creation to the year of the Passion. The Easter tables of Victorius had been adopted by the Council of Orleans in 541 (above, p. 33), when Gregory was still a child; nevertheless he disregards the Victorian A.M. 5229 as the equivalent of *Annus Passionis*. As to material that might have been entered into these tables, in the *Historia*, II. 13 and 14 there are some brief notices which appear to belong to the decade 460–70, and have a contemporary ring (Dalton 1927: II, 495). Although the information they convey is of no little interest, yet taking Gregory's work as a whole, for material earlier than his lifetime he would seem to have relied partly on episcopal lists – the see of Tours itself kept careful records – and on events that could be dated by the regnal years of various kings, with a background of compilers like Jerome and Orosius, and their continuators, not forgetting also Sulpicius Alexander, Renatus Frigeridus and oral sources.

If Paschal annals were a flourishing form of enterprise in the latter half of the fifth century and the start of the sixth, it is rather surprising that the baptism of Clovis should apparently not have been noticed. About the year 500 he was at the height of his power and influence; unlike the Gothic and Vandal rulers he was not an Arian, a heretic, but instead became a champion of Rome. Even in short retrospect the momentous character of his conversion will have been apparent to many people, yet the exact date of it has not been settled to this day (Wallace-Hadrill 1967: 69). Supposing the *Paschale Campanum* to be representative of fifth and sixth century annals, we must observe not only the entries that furnish information but also the numerous blank spaces. By coincidence, almost exactly where this series comes to an end, a set of Burgundian annals has been incorporated into the chronicle which goes under the name of Fredegar; they run from 584 to 603, in modern reckoning, after which the character of the writing changes (ed. Wallace-Hadrill 1960: xiii). As they stand, the annals are rather too lengthy to have been derived from a single Easter table; they could represent the winnowings from several or many. In their context, these entries more probably, from the first, belonged to the next type of writing we shall consider – the chronicle.

During the early part of the Middle Ages, the great exemplar was the 'Chronicle' of Eusebius, who died about 340; he founded his calculations on the Greek Olympiads and on an era dating from

Abraham (ed. Fotheringham 1923). This work was translated into Latin, with revisions, by Jerome, whose fame as a biblical scholar alone would ensure that men of learning were familiar with the form adopted by Eusebius. The author of a new chronicle, or the continuator of an existing text, was able to start with sheets of parchment and a series of years; he had ample room, since the detail of an Easter table was not needed – room both for contemporary events and information from the past. Once fairly set on his way, he might be ambitious enough to attempt a story of mankind, with the Bible as his guide to antiquity and all manner of sources to fill in the rest. Or he might be concerned chiefly with matters interesting to a local audience, perhaps a small kingdom and its neighbours. The affairs of the Papacy, and of kings, bishops and nobles, will figure in such a record, together with celestial events and remarks like 'the teacher Ecgric died' or 'a synod at *Pincanheale*' which seemed important then and are mysterious now. Moreover, a chronicle of any length is usually the work of more than one hand, and will be lucky to have escaped improvement and interpolations.

Material from Paschal annals will quite often have been entered into a chronicle, although it is sometimes difficult, and sometimes impossible, to be at all sure where a particular piece of information came from.[16] Yet these annals enabled a chronicler to take his story further back into the past, and to secure a greater confidence in the order of events. That said, we should be careful not to overrate their contribution, except perhaps in Ireland. Dionysius Exiguus inaugurated the Christian era, which has lasted as a frame of reference to the present day, but estimates of his influence usually need qualification. For example, Poole has said: 'It was the discovery of this era that made the revival of historiography possible, and it was beyond question an English discovery' (1926: 25). Accepting his view (1934: 32–3) that the Dionysiac tables were formally adopted at the Synod of Whitby in 664, there are signs that Englishmen did not always make entries into these tables with the sort of fervour we

---

16 Even a man like Mommsen, whose patience and erudition are not in doubt, was puzzled how to divide some passages in Bede's *Chronica Maiora* between Paschal sources and Marius of Avenches (Levison 1935: 137, n. 1). Marius, whose chronicle ends in 581, adopted a framework of consular years and Indictions (ed. Mommsen 1894c).

might reasonably expect. Bound up with the Calendar of Willibrord, the missionary archbishop of Utrecht, is a series of Dionysiac tables running from 684 to 759 (ed. Wilson 1918: ix). They contain no historical information, yet it is almost certain that they derive from the monastery at Echternach which he founded (Lowe 1950: 26). Such empty spaces should be treated not as negative evidence, but rather, as positive evidence of missed opportunities.[17] And the model of Eusebius and Jerome owes nothing to Dionysius.

If a line between annals and chronicles cannot be clearly drawn, neither can the transition to history. As an extreme case Thucydides in *The Peloponnesian War* arranges his narrative by summers and winters; nobody will mistake him for a chronicler. But, roughly speaking, a historian is not bound to follow a rigid sequence of years; and while colouring his text with delineation of character can deal with a block of events, perhaps covering a generation or two, and allow himself other forms of digression, before going back to resume the main thread – as Herodotus often did, and Bede too. Above all he seeks to develop a theme, to investigate ruling passions and motives, and perhaps to expose the operations of cause and effect. Less obvious is the need, in this present context, to consider two kinds of historical writing which were of equal value, more or less, to a medieval mind.[18] The lives of saints and martyrs are often cast in an otherworldly mould. Such a story as the *Life of Germanus*, already alluded to, could have thrown light on a dark patch of the 430s if Constantius had said how many years there were between the two visits to Britain, or had mentioned the names of a few places; possibly he knew, but they were not to his purpose. He says enough to anchor Germanus in Britain for a while, enough to show the triumph over heresy, but is little concerned with Romano-British society. In the detailed account of Wilfrid's life, by Eddius Stephanus (ed. Colgrave 1927), there are no years referred to an era, or dated letters, and in treating the chronology as an almost casual affair Eddius is

---

[17] An Easter table of Welsh origin, running from 817 to 832, has been published in facsimile by R. W. Hunt (1961: f. 21r); its lack of marginal entries only deserves mention here to underline what has been said.

[18] 'Students of medieval sources are constantly baffled by the way that plausible history and the wildest fantasy are so often set down side by side, as if of equal credibility' (Brooke 1967: 74).

not to be blamed for working to the demands of a convention. The life of Ceolfrith (*HAA*) is altogether more mundane, though compiled only a few years later; we have taken a sample of its precise and factual element (above, p. 42).

Bede certainly, in Stenton's phrase, 'had reached the conception of history' (*ASE*: 17). Even so – when treating for instance of Aidan and Oswald and John of Beverley – the flavour of hagiography breaks in. Among the distinctive features of his work is the adoption of the Christian era, which seems to have attracted the attention of Englishmen about a dozen years before his birth. Like annalists, the chronicler and historian can manage without an era; yet such people, particularly in the sixth and seventh centuries, will more than once have had good reason to ask 'which year is it that I am in now?' – and a regnal year of their own kings will not have taken them very far.[19] They suffered, as their like were to suffer for a long while afterwards, over the greater part of Europe, from the lack of an era that most men could accept.[20] With a bewildering set of fixed points to choose from, it is not to be expected that the recording of past or present events would flourish, except on a narrow front; and the next two chapters will describe how the Anglo-Saxons threaded their way through the muddle.

[19] For instance, a chronicler would have trouble in relating the fiftieth year of Ethelbert of Kent to any year of Aethelfrith of Northumbria, in default of a standard; and we shall find in Chapter 5 that Bede made mistakes in equating imperial years with his *Annus Mundi*.

[20] The Spaniards had an era of their own, and generally relied on it, starting on 1 January 38 B.C. Of their history it has been said: 'We have to do what we can with chronicles that are little better than annals. There is no Spanish Gregory of Tours' (Wallace-Hadrill 1967: 117). Isidore of Seville buttressed the era with imperial years in his *Historia Gothorum* (ed. Mommsen 1894a), but in his chronicle was constrained to rely on *Annus Mundi* (ed. Mommsen 1894b), and to that extent the peninsula was not free from confusion. On Irish problems see MacCarthy (1892: 237–59).

CHAPTER 4

THE CHRISTIAN ERA IN BRITAIN

❦

During the latter half of the fourth century in Europe, and in Africa soon after, illiterate hordes of tribesmen began to disturb the peace and tranquillity that learning and scholarship require, and the economic security, derived from the labours of others, on which they also depend; though it is fair to add that literature was already in decay. Some writers were lucky in their lives, as Jerome managing to survive in Palestine, and Augustine dying in 430 while the Vandals surrounded Hippo. Many were swept off their feet; yet between the death of Prudentius, about 405, and that of Cassiodorus, 585, we know of numerous works produced within the areas near to, or overrun by, the barbarians (Laistner 1957). Constantius could write the *Vita S. Germani*; a more prolific author, Sidonius Apollinaris, flourished as bishop of Clermont in the Auvergne from 430 to 484, in territory that came to be held in turn by Goths, Burgundians and Franks. By the end of his life, when the darkness was fairly thick over most of Europe, another movement is becoming clear. The rude invaders now develop a concern for *Romanitas*. 'An obvious but remarkable feature of the Western Empire's collapse before the barbarians was the anxiety of Romans and barbarians alike to cling to the ancient forms of political life' (Wallace-Hadrill 1967: 31). The influence of Roman law has been discerned in a number of codes, starting with Euric, 464–84, by whom Sidonius was briefly imprisoned, and continuing to Reccaswinth, another Visigoth, who died in 672 and ruled the Spain that Isidore of Seville had lately dwelt in. The Church brought about a conquest over the invaders by teaching them to read and write, to enshrine their way of life within a Roman casket; and in the long run both the pagans and the Arian heretics succumbed.

When we look at another side of this Church, however, it conveys an impression of being preoccupied with itself. Again a date or two must be put in: the siege of Rome by Attila in 452, and the deposition of Romulus Augustulus by Odoacer in 476. These events lie on either side of the Victorian Easter tables of 457. At the Council of Nicaea, the emperor and bishops had been more absorbed by defining mysteries than by fixing the limits for the Paschal moon; thereafter the argument sank to the low level of politics, and went straight on, Huns or no. Pope Leo was courageous enough to face Attila outside the city of Rome, and perhaps also to think that the Papacy is never in the wrong. Despite an appearance of conformity with Alexandrian practice, *luna xvi* was obstinately retained. Reckoning by *Annus Passionis* furnished a truly Christian era, in which all Christians – quite apart from the Celts – could not acquiesce because the choice between a Latin and Greek Easter sometimes lay open. The occasional conflict can be illustrated from Gregory of Tours, *Historia Francorum*, x. 23. In the year 590 Easter was celebrated at Tours on 2 April, the Latin date of Victorius, but by many others in Gaul on 26 March, the Greek. Never at a loss for miracles, Gregory found that springs near Seville had lived up to a reputation by gushing forth on his own Easter Day. Exactly the same course of events had taken place in 577 (*Historia Francorum*, v. 16).[1] The backbiting on these occasions, however few they were, will have helped to bring the system into disrepute.

Moreover, this new era of the Passion represents yet another addition to a list already becoming formidable. In antiquity, the Greeks had reckoned from the First Olympiad, 776 B.C., and the Romans from the foundation of their capital, *anno ab urbe condita*, in 753 B.C.[2] However doubtful these numbers appear today, at least there was a fair measure of agreement among the classical writers. Into this world of philosophy and learning the Bible made its entry, together with its readers who wanted to find the most fundamental era of all – the date of the Creation. If the Old Testament had been, like the Koran, the product of a single mind, then the reigns of kings and the

---

[1] But whereas at Tours in this year Easter was on the Victorian 18 April, the Spanish celebration is said to have taken place on 21 March, everywhere an uncanonical date; so clearly there is a mistake (Jones 1934: 412, n. 3). The Dionysiac day was 25 April. For an earlier story of miraculous fonts see Jones (1943: 56).

[2] This figure for A.U.C. was given by Varro, and prevailed over others slightly different.

lives of patriarchs would have added up to a single number. Believing every word of what they read, the early Christians did not recognise that they had to deal with a complicated mixture of narratives, put together by a variety of hands, and were puzzled by the anomalies and contradictions. We have seen already (above, p. 47) that Gregory of Tours could work out his own value of the *Annus Mundi*, in the teeth of Eusebius, Jerome and the Victorian estimate. Another hazard had not been fully appreciated until Jerome made a translation of the Old Testament direct from Hebrew into Latin, to form the Vulgate text; then it was found that the all-important numbers were out of harmony with the Greek Septuagint – not that all the discrepancies were removed. The Old Testament 'certainly contains very precise chronological schemes, but these are distinct from, and often inconsistent with, the narratives embedded in them' (Cook 1928: 156–7).

One of the few people to take an interest in this problem was Bede, so that for his chronicles he made a calculation of *Annus Mundi* which was founded on the Vulgate.[3] He arrived at 3952 B.C. by Jerome's text, but despite his authority, in this and other fields, the calculation did not prevail. For so long as the Creation was thought to have taken place in an ascertainable year, the search for *Annus Mundi* went forward, each generation producing a crop of its own solutions. In the eighteenth century, Des Vignolles (1738) was able to collect well over a hundred estimates, nearer two hundred, ranging from 6984 to 3483 B.C., and effort was still being directed to the problem when its foundations were knocked away by Darwin and the geologists.

Aware of physical destruction and social decay, the chronicler or historian of the early Middle Ages was therefore faced with two more difficulties: choice of an era, and the transfer to it of material from other eras. When a man like Gregory of Tours is faulted on chronology, his Church must carry a share of the blame. A chronicler was able to avoid the selection of an era by simply continuing the work of one of his predecessors; but the problem of transfer, even

---

[3] 'He thus adopts to a certain extent a principle of modern historical research, in preferring primary sources to derived ones...in any case the critical sense of Bede is striking' (Levison 1935: 116–7).

in the seventh century, was not at all easy to solve. Thus 'the Annals of Xanten, which record annals for France, *annis* 640–700, are not correct in a single date and are sometimes off by as much as ten years' (Jones 1947: 11). Here the compiler was trying to reconcile the figures from sources which did not share the same era, and his failure is not hard to understand. The 'revival of historiography' in the eighth century, apart from Bede, is confined to Paschal annals or the form of a chronicle; perhaps it would be truer to say 'revival of a sense of history'. Yet the method of Dionysius, and the Alexandrian principles it was founded on, had first to be accepted at Rome, as the right and proper way of calculating Easter, before the Christian era could effectively be used by chroniclers and historians. In this respect the mind of Pope Leo I, capacious and adaptable in many directions, had proved a block to clear thinking. Given a fair chance, Victorius might have created a satisfactory Easter reckoning nearly a hundred years earlier than Dionysius, leaving the way open to an era on which all could agree.

This dividing of the function of an Easter table, as expressed here – furnishing dates for Easter and furnishing an era – may seem to be artificial but does also seem to correspond with the vague boundary between Paschal annals and a chronicle. The annalist entered his notes in a table, alongside the year, whereas the chronicler started with a sheet of parchment blank but for a list of years – defined by a particular era. If that era had, as it were, been hallowed by association with the right way of calculating Easter – a matter of far greater importance to the medieval Church – the chronicler not only felt secure in his own mind but could more readily take in material from elsewhere, from other people of a similar persuasion. The use of *Annus Domini* for historical purposes during the seventh century is, or appears to be, an insular affair; if there were annals or chronicles kept regularly outside England, before 700 and distinctly dated by this era, they have not survived – so far as we can judge (Grosjean 1960a). But the insular usage depended, at first, on the attitude of Rome to the Dionysiac method of calculating Easter. We should therefore enquire when the Papacy abandoned *luna xvi* and the Victorian system in favour of Dionysius and the Alexandrians.

In this matter the pioneering work of Bruno Krusch in the 1880s

and of Schwarz (1905) was overtaken by R. L. Poole (1918a; reprinted 1934: 28–37, from which page-numbers are here taken).
Krusch had thought that the Dionysiac tables were accepted at
Rome in the time of Gregory the Great (died 604); Poole objected
to this view, and we may think rightly. Instead he made another
proposal: 'it is at the Synod of Whitby in 664 that we first find the
Dionysian calculus formally brought forward by Wilfrid' (1934: 32).
True again, so far as England and formality go, but what was
happening at Rome in the meanwhile? The Synod of Whitby is a
Northumbrian affair: the Archbishop of Canterbury neither
attended nor sent proctors; only one bishop of the Roman connexion
took part, Agilbert, who was not then an English diocesan, having
left the West Saxons four years earlier (*ASC*: year 660). The change
of heart by King Oswiu, in forsaking the Celtic-84, surely sprang
from more than the presence of a Gaulish prelate, and of James the
Deacon, a venerable companion of Paulinus, and the eloquence of
Wilfrid, a newly-ordained priest. 'The appeal to St Peter's authority
allowed the king to close the debate in a way which suggests that
his own decision had been made before it began' (*ASE*: 123). We
should, therefore, try to gauge the climate of Papal opinion. Most
unfortunately, Poole seems to have been unaware of the work of
Mac Carthy (1901), which throws light on the Irish sources without
which even an attempt at solving this problem would be far more
difficult. So a fresh start is needed.[4]

When Victorius compiled his tables, the purpose of them was *pro
ecclesiarum pace apostolici pontificis electioni seruatum* (ed. Mommsen
1892c: 684); if both Latin and Greek dates were offered in a particular year, the Pope was to decide the day of Easter. In the immediate
neighbourhood of Rome, or not too far away, any change of policy
over Easter limits would quickly be known – for we need not assume
that successive Popes were all of one mind. In more remote places
the choice could have been made locally, guided by a knowledge of
what the central authority was likely to select; but from the very
sparse evidence it is difficult – it is impossible – to be sure how far a

---

[4] And is the more necessary because Poole's opinions have found their way into the
valuable collection of abstracts and documents, with commentary, made by
Kenney (1929: 222–3).

diocesan bishop was being influenced by Rome or how far he relied on his own judgement. Thus at Tours in 590 Gregory followed the Latin Easter, whereas many others in Gaul chose the Greek (above, p. 53) – and were confounded by the miraculous Spanish springs. Anybody armed with Victorian tables, whether Pope or not, could elect for an Easter based on either *luna xv* or *luna xvi*, depending on the climate of opinion. This point, which may seem to be trivial, perhaps has a bearing on the Paschal controversy in Ireland and Northumbria, as we shall presently see. It is, however, necessary to clear the ground a little further.

As far as we know, the concept of a 532-year cycle was peculiar to the system of Victorius throughout most of the seventh century. Before 716, a 532-year Dionysiac cycle had been worked out in Northumbria (*HE*, V. 21); exactly how much earlier it was current we cannot say, but on all counts not before 660. References to a 532-year cycle in the first half of the seventh century will therefore help towards identifying Victorian tables, and more surely if *luna xvi* is mentioned as well. Moreover, Victorius never hinted at Nicene sanction for his tables. In the preface of Dionysius, on the other hand, we find: *sequentes per omnia uenerabilium cccx et viii pontificum, qui apud Nicaeam . . . conuenerunt, etiam rei huius absolutam ueramque sententiam, qui quartas decimas luna Paschalis obseruantiae x et xix annorum redeuntem semper se in circulum stabiles immotasque fixerunt* (Krusch 1938: 63). Not to be taken at its face value, this statement expresses what might have been hoped for but did not happen. For our purposes, then, any reference to a Nicene background will serve to identify Dionysiac tables, more especially if the limits *luna xv–xxi* are brought in.

About the year 600, the Irish missionary Columbanus wrote to Gregory the Great complaining about the Victorian tables (ed. Gundlach 1892: 156). Officially adopted in Gaul about sixty years earlier, they gave dates for Easter not always in agreement with the Celtic-84, which Columbanus naturally followed. He informs the Pope that in Ireland the reckoning of Victorius is not only unacceptable but treated with pity or derision – adding a few tart remarks about the behaviour of Frankish bishops. He does not mention Dionysius, but the silence could be construed in more than one way;

he may have been ignorant, or the Dionysiac tables were then being consulted but not relied upon or taken to be 'official'. In another connexion Jones (1947: 38) has remarked on the weakness of medieval arithmetic: the difference between observed and calculated full moon might amount to as much as two or three days. The Papacy had endured the Victorian system, controversial though it was, for a century and a half, and surely no change would be made until an alternative system had been tested in full; in other words, until the 95-year term calculated by Dionysius himself had expired in 626, and the next, 627–721 inclusive, was fairly under way. Disagreement over doctrine can be settled by anathema or other suitable measures; the position of the moon in the heavens is subject to its own caprice.[5] The Victorian tables were published in 457 but not officially adopted at Orleans until 541; and surely the lapse of time, 84 years, implies that the newer type of reckoning had been compared with the older.

We should next consider a letter written by Cummian, probably an abbot in Southern or Middle Ireland, to Segene, abbot of Iona from 623 to 652, and as such a leading figure among the Northern Irish. The dating of events has been discussed by O'Connell (1936: 83), following Mac Carthy in the main:

628–9 Victorian tables begin to be adopted in Ireland; Cummian studies them for a year.
630 Synod at Magh Lene. Dissension. Envoys sent to Rome.
631 The envoys spend Easter in Rome.
632 They return in the third year.
632–6 Letter of Cummian probably written.

Cummian's letter (ed. Migne 1863; Oulton 1957) says that when the 532-year cycle was first adopted he gave himself up to a year of study; then he consulted his elders at Emly, Clonmacnoise, Clonfert-Mulloe and two other monasteries which are probably Birr and Mungret. A synod was held in the plain of Magh Lene (Co. Offaly) and those present agreed that Easter should in future be celebrated with the rest of the universal Church. But trouble arose, and envoys were sent to Rome, where they found that the Roman and Irish

[5] Caprice is nearly the right word; in E. W. Brown's tables predicting the behaviour of the moon there are over a thousand terms.

Easters differed by a whole month, *in quo mense integro disiuncti sumus*. From this statement, combined with a new calculation of the Celtic-84, O'Connell deduces that the Easter of 631 is meant (1936: 82). The envoys returned in the third year, evidently 632, when, or shortly after, Cummian will have written to Iona; probably an upper limit is 635 (Smyth 1972: 39–40). His letter strongly defends Victorius; and the documents quoted in it, though some of them are now known to be fabrications, prove that his knowledge of the Paschal controversy was far from superficial.[6] Mention of the 19-year cycle deriving from the 318 bishops is proof that Dionysiac tables, with their preface and explanatory matter, were known in Ireland by about 630 (ed. Migne 1863: col. 975; Mac Carthy 1892: 390); they may have been known a little before 610 (Grosjean 1946: 223–31). Unaware of what Cummian had written, Bede says that the Southern Irish had learnt to observe the canonical Easter, by direction of the Pope, before the arrival of Aidan in Northumbria, 635 (*HE*, III. 3). This statement may be true in a general sense, as a majority verdict, because Bishop Tuda of Lindisfarne (664) had been consecrated at a place in Southern Ireland where the correct Easter was in force (*HE*, III. 26); but Bede seems to have been mistaken in thinking that conformity had spread quite so soon among all the monastic *paruchiae* of the south, where a Victorian chronology can be traced as late as 655 (Kenney 1929: 276–7).

At about this time, and during a pontificate that lasted from 625 to 638, Honorius I wrote to the Irish Church recommending it to conform in the matter of Easter reckoning (*HE*, II. 19). This letter is couched in general terms; the argument amounts to no more than *quod semper*, *quod ubique* and is presumably quoted by Bede as evidence of Papal interest in the chief dispute, that between the Celtic-84 on one hand, and the cycles of Victorius and Dionysius on the other. At this time also there was a synod in *Campo Albo* (Slieve Margy, Queen's Co.), where a new *ordo paschae* was debated, *qui nuper de Roma uenit*; from the presence of Munnu (Fintan), who died in 636

---

[6] A fact which the agitated exclamations of MacCarthy (1901: cxxxix–cxl) do their best to conceal. It may be true that Cummian was not an expert computist (Jones 1934: 418) but we are concerned here with his value as a witness. On fabrications, and the possibility of Paschal dispute before 610, see the notes by Kenney (1929: 217–8), and also Grosjean (1946).

as abbot of Taghmon (Co. Wexford), an upper limit of date can be inferred both for this synod and for Cummian's letter (O'Connell 1936: 81-3). We do not know what this *ordo* was, or whether the letter of Pope Honorius – which seems to have been addressed to the Irish Church in general – will have been the occasion for the synods at Magh Lene or Slieve Margy. More secure evidence of central policy is to be found in a letter written by the Pope-elect, John IV, and others who were administering a vacancy in the see, between August and December 640. Before considering what they have to say, it will be desirable to notice, from the lists conveniently drawn up by O'Connell (1936: 102-4), that Victorian and Dionysiac calculations yielded an identical day for Easter from 595 to 644; then in 645 Victorius offered a choice of Latin and Greek dates; thereafter both were in agreement again until 665, when Victorius gave alternatives.[7] But during this period there were frequent clashes with the Celtic-84.

As Bede's chapter-heading shows (*HE*, II. 19), John IV and his colleagues were concerned with Easter and with the Pelagian heresy, *pro pascha simul et pro Pelagiana heresi*. They address themselves to five bishops, five priests and an abbot – all or mostly in Northern Ireland (Plummer 1896: II, 112-3) – and Bede first gives a summary of the Papal view on lunar limits, *euidenter astruens, quia dominicum Paschae diem a xv^a luna usque ad xxi^{am}, quod in Nicena synodo probatum est, oportet inquiri*. From these particulars the Dionysiac system is clearly meant. Bede goes on: *necnon pro Pelagiana heresi, quam apud eos reuiuiscere didicerat, cauenda ac repellenda, in eadem illos epistula admonere curauit*. After naming the clergy to whom the Pope-elect was writing, with other formalities, Bede's extract from the letter itself mentions that 'some people in your province are trying to revive, or refashion, a new heresy from the old', *nouam ex ueteri heresim renouare conantes*; and there follow a few words directed against *luna xiv*, a principle on which the Celtic-84 rested. After a break in the text, where Bede says that the proper reckoning of Easter was explained, the remainder of the letter is devoted to the evils of Pelagianism. The preoccupation with heresy is a familiar trait in Bede's character;

---

[7] O'Connell quotes the figures as corrected by Schwarz; they differ from those given by Jones (1934: 411 and 413), but the substance of what will follow is not affected.

judging from the Commentaries, more particularly on the Song of Songs, 'his warnings against Pelagianism . . . are so numerous and fierce that one must suppose that Pelagianism was a living question to him' (Lainstner 1957: 160).

Thus the interest of Bede in what John IV had to say would appear to stem at least as much from hatred of false doctrine as from the Easter problem. Nevertheless, when Poole comes to discuss the matter (1934: 30–41) he inclines to the uncharitable thought that Bede had doctored this letter, had changed a reference from *luna xvi* to *luna xv* because 'it disagreed with what he had laid down' – that is, the Dionysiac limits expounded in *De Temporum Ratione*. Clearly, however, Bede knew that what he himself considered the correct, canonical limits for the Easter moon had not always been observed at Rome. Before 532, when the Dionysiac tables came into operation, the Papacy must have been in error by the mere fact of tolerating *luna xvi*: and when he wrote *De Temporum Ratione* (cc. XLII and LI) Bede quoted with approval the opinions of Bishop Victor of Capua, about 550, who inveighed against Victorius and all his works. By 731 almost everyone had abandoned the discordant cycles, except the Church in Wales, which clung to the Celtic-84 until 768, and in some of the provinces of France, where the influence of Victorius was presumably not at an end. Bede had nothing to conceal; and Poole's misunderstanding of the Irish evidence will hardly excuse his failure to allow for the extent of Bede's knowledge, as displayed in *De Temporum Ratione*.

At Rome, therefore, we may reasonably think of a swing away from the Victorian and in favour of the Dionysiac lunar limits as taking place in the decade 630 to 640. The fact of agreement between the rivals, the absence of alternatives, over a long period of years will have helped to make this change smoother and less painful. From the Irish evidence it seems clear that both systems were beginning to make their way against the Celtic-84; and the later stages of this process in Northumbria, where Celtic teaching was dominant until 664, will be discussed in a moment. Meanwhile, from 597, Augustine's mission in the south of England will probably have required Easter tables, in view of the distance from Rome; and sooner or later both varieties will have been in circulation, as they evidently were in Ireland. Three points, however, should be noted here. First, it would seem that Dionysiac tables were not known, even in Kent, before 654, or known only in a superficial way (below, p. 64). Then, there is a considerable gulf between taking the date of Easter on trust and understanding the principles from which the date has been calculated, just as the mariner can pin his faith to tide-tables without a knowledge of celestial mechanics. If any scheme for predicting the Paschal full moon is to receive whole-hearted assent, it must be worked over and comprehended in detail. Cummian's year of study, with the scanty leisure that monastic duties allowed, was none too long. The third point has already been raised, but could do with repeating: no thorough change of heart was possible until the first 95-year cycle of Dionysius had expired in 626, and been found satisfactory. With these considerations in mind we can turn to the kingdom of Northumbria, where Oswald in 635 had transferred Aidan from Iona to the bishopric at Lindisfarne. For the next generation Easter was reckoned by the Celtic cycle – a generation during which the Irish Church, in the south at least, found itself vexed by disagreement, and the future Bishop Wilfrid, throughout his career a source of turmoil and activity, was growing up.

A life of Wilfrid was composed by his faithful follower, Eddius Stephanus, probably before 720 (ed. Colgrave 1927); a shorter and less partial account is given by Bede (*HE*, v. 19). Born about 634, at the age of fourteen Wilfrid entered the monastery at Lindisfarne, where he spent several years and – being a shrewd young man, says Bede, *adulescens animi sagacis* – became dissatisfied with Celtic custom and observances. During the episcopate of Finan, Aidan's successor from 651 to 661, there seems to have been a serious dispute in Northumbria, an Irishman called Ronan, trained in Gaul and Italy, taking the lead against the Celtic-84. But neither he nor the queen's chaplain, who came from Kent, were able to make headway. Nor could James the Deacon, who had stayed behind when Paulinus fled to the south in 633, and was present at the Synod of Whitby; he followed the true and catholic Easter, *obseruabat . . . uerum et catholicum pascha*, even in the midst of a Celtic surround (*HE*, III. 25). One of Wilfrid's motives for going to Rome thus seems fairly evident, and he gained the ear of Queen Eanflaed who sent him to her cousin the king of Kent. At Canterbury, under Archbishop Honorius, he spent a year or thereabouts (Eddius, c. III). On the next stage of the journey, which took place when Wilfrid was about 20 years old, he was joined by Benedict Biscop, the future founder of Wearmouth and Jarrow.

After arriving at Rome, probably in 654 (Plummer 1896: II, 317), Wilfrid received instruction from Archdeacon Boniface, *cuius magisterio iiii euangeliorum libros ex ordine didicit, computum paschae rationabilem, et alia multa quae in patria nequiuerat* (*HE*, V. 19). It will be observed that Wilfrid learnt the correct *computation* of Easter, a matter far removed from the tame acceptance of reckonings made by somebody else. The sense of *computus paschae* can hardly be in doubt, when considered in the light of Ceolfrith's letter, written 706–716 (*HE*, V. 21): *Hic autem, quem uobis sequendum monstramus, computus paschae decennouenali circulo continetur . . . Cuius computum paschalis Theophilus Alexandriae praesul in centum annorum tempus Theodosio imperatori conposuit. Item successor eius Cyrillus seriem XC et V annorum in quinque decennouenalibus circulis conprehendit; post quem Dionysius Exiguus totidem alios ex ordine pari schemate subnexuit, qui ad nostra usque tempora pertingebant.*[8] Thus it will have been the Dionysiac system, down to detail, that Wilfrid learnt from Boniface, the correct computation in Bede's eyes; certainly it cannot have been the Victorian, which Bede had already attacked in 725, when he wrote *De Temporum Ratione* (cc. XLII and LI).

What, then, was the source of Boniface's information about Dionysiac tables? In discussing their transmission Poole (1934: 32–3) supposed that 'the manuscript' of Dionysius and his continuator Felix was originally at the monastery of Squillace (Vivarium), and somehow became known to Wilfrid, or to Benedict Biscop. Yet this notion of 'the manuscript', as a single entity, runs counter to what we have learnt from Ireland, where Dionysiac tables were known by about 630, a good twenty years before Wilfrid paid his respects to Rome, and perhaps before 610 (Grosjean 1946: 223–31). Moreover, these are not elaborate or massive texts: with preface and explanatory matter, the original tables occupy only nineteen pages in the

[8] See also Ducange, s.v. *pascha*, and *Thesaurus Linguae Latinae*, s.v. *computus*.

quarto edition of Krusch, and the preface of Felix – and his tables, had they been printed – barely seven. In other words, this volume of material could be transcribed in a matter of days or weeks rather than months or years. Although Wilfrid did not return to England until 657–8 (Plummer 1896: II, 317), he might have despatched information at any time after 654.

Bede's statement that Wilfrid had not been able to learn the right computation of Easter in England, among other things, *et alia multa quae in patria nequiuerat*, very strongly suggests that Dionysiac tables were not known, even in Kent, earlier than 654. This conclusion needs to be qualified by the possibility that they were introduced into Wessex by Birinus (Harrison 1973d: 113). He had been consecrated in Italy, beginning his work at Dorchester-on-Thames in 634; and Easter tables, whether Victorian or Dionysiac, or both, are likely to be found at this time in the luggage of a missionary bishop (Kenney 1929: 236). Again, we have noticed that acquaintance with these tables is a very different affair from understanding how they were put together. Yet a lack of Dionysiac tables in England – if there was such a lack – is more easily comprehended in the light of what Victorian tables were able to provide. For the most part, during the first half of the seventh century, the predictions of Victorius and Dionysius gave an identical date for Easter. Between 630 and 640 the Papacy seems to have become committed to *luna xv*, if the Irish evidence is anything to go by; and people like Ronan or James the Deacon, trained in Roman custom, did not need Dionysiac tables in order to follow in the wake of Papal opinion. What they did need, and what they could get by letter or word of mouth, was the view current at Rome on the correct lunar limits – as Victorius had intended, whatever those limits might be.

At least the Dionysiac method does not seem to have been known, in the sense of thoroughly comprehended, before 657–8, when Wilfrid came back possessed of a deeper knowledge than he could get from Kent or Northumbria. On any fair estimate, his energetic nature would hardly allow matters to rest there; in later life he is found preaching to the heathen in Frisia and Sussex, a significant streak in his character. If the Papacy had recommended the Victorian system to the Irish in 632 or thereabouts – and Cummian's letter can hardly be construed in any other sense – so also another Pope was backing Dionysius in 640. The tables, complete with their explanatory matter, could be copied quickly, and the demand was small.[9] Thus the Dionysiac method, having reached something like official status, might have become widely diffused about five years before the Synod of Whitby, with an advocate like Wilfrid to speed the process. At all events, though a discussion of the Synod must be postponed until the next chapter, there is no reason to doubt Poole's suggestion that Northumbria formally adopted Dionysiac tables in 664. Soon afterwards, Wilfrid's patron, Alhfrith the sub-king of Deira, sent him to Gaul for consecration according to the Roman rite, and by 669 he had become the sole bishop north of the Humber, seated at York, and in Roman eyes the true successor of Paulinus. Another product of his energy can now be discerned, though not in an altogether clear light and by way of circumstantial evidence only.

After about 670, and perhaps under the influence of Archbishop Theodore of Canterbury, the conveyance of property and privilege in England began to be regulated by charter.[10] In ancient times the transfer of land had often been symbolised by handing over a piece of turf, in the presence of witnesses; greater security was now to be attained by a written deed of gift, couched in solemn language, and subscribed by kings, bishops and other notables. Theodore himself dated by the Indiction (above, p. 41), which is the prevailing style until early in the eighth century; thereafter, if a charter is dated at all the *Annus Domini* also forms part of the dating clause. The question then arises – when, and by whose agency, was the *Annus Domini* introduced into the legal framework? In trying to answer this question, it must be borne in mind that the interpretation of charters is beset by a variety of awkward circumstances.[11] In the

---

9 The sees that can be reckoned as going concerns in 658 are Canterbury, Dorchester, East Anglia, Lindisfarne, Mercia and Rochester; of important monasteries, such as St Augustine's (Canterbury), Malmesbury, Whitby and Melrose there will have been a dozen or so, with the East Anglian *Icanho*, perhaps Iken in Suffolk, founded 654, which if small was certainly influential.

10 Chaplais (1969) has argued for an earlier date, but here we consider only those surviving texts which are usually thought to contain authentic material.

11 Not all of them can be mentioned now; a brief but careful analysis has been provided by Whitelock (*EHD*: 337–49), forming a prelude to translations of selected

first place, only a few of them have survived as contemporary copies.[12] The majority are represented in the collections known as cartularies, which themselves may be no older than the fourteenth or fifteenth centuries, and in their present form could easily be transcripts of transcripts – as some items can be shown to be. Secondly, it is not very common for a charter to have descended in more than one version, unlike a treatise or a chronicle where comparison between the several existing texts will enable its original form to be more clearly restored. Again, charters tend to be suspect because there has been every temptation to forgery in the past, or at least 'improvement'; apart from touching up the list of signatories, to make a more impressive document, quite commonly a clause has been inserted to secure exemption from interference by the local bishop or from all royal dues except the *trinoda necessitas* – making fortresses, building bridges and supporting the armed forces.[13] Thus a charter in its pristine state, fresh from the pen, is something of a rarity. On the other hand, not a few have been copied with great care, preserving for example archaic forms of personal names which had long passed out of use.

Without doubt the majority of early charters were dated, if at all, by the Indiction alone; and the question then becomes – was the *Annus Domini* ever included as well? Writing of the Christian era, Stenton (1971: 186) could say that 'there is no unequivocal proof of its employment in English documents before the appearance of *De Temporum Ratione*'. Put in another way, any document dated *Anno Domini* before the year 725 may well be forged or interpolated. Yet a different opinion had been expressed by Poole (1934: 34), when he said that 'not a few [early] Anglo-Saxon charters which contain the date from the Incarnation have been condemned as

charters, and notes on their provenance and value as sources for history. The standard discussion of charters in Latin is by Stenton (1955); charters in Old English are edited by Robertson (1956); the annotated bibliography by Sawyer is indispensable (1968). Although dealing primarily with later material, the introduction to *Anglo-Saxon writs* (Harmer 1952) is also of great value.

[12] Sometimes called 'originals'; but there is ample evidence for thinking that more than one copy of a charter was written at more or less the ostensible date of the grant, and the longer description ought to be nearer the facts (Stenton 1955: 10).

[13] For an extended treatment of these military obligations see Brooks (1971). No authentic clause of immunity is known before 699.

spurious or corrupt. There seems, however, to be no reason to suppose that the adoption of this era was originated by the treatise of Bede. It is much more likely that it was derived from the Easter tables.' And reference to Table 2 (above, p. 35) will show that no great effort would be required, when dating a charter, to put in the *Annus Domini* as well as the Indiction, when both were to be found in adjacent columns. Whether such a practice is detectable, before 725 or thereabouts, can perhaps be decided on two counts: peculiarities in the style of the dating clause; or circumstances that distinguish one charter from a series of kindred documents (Harrison 1973a: 553).

We may begin with a document which is printed as No. 51 in the first volume of Birch's *Cartularium Saxonicum* (1885) and here cited as *BCS* 51. Although not a contemporary copy, and not to be regarded as an authentic charter, it derives from the pre-Conquest section of Hemming's cartulary, drawn up at Worcester, which is now known to date from the early part of the eleventh century (Ker 1948: 51–2). It has come under fire on more than one occasion, most recently from Finberg (1961: 86 and 172–7), who points out that it seems to have been inflated by an immunity clause; another objection, the lack of witnesses, applies with less force to a transcript because similar examples are known (*EHD*: 338 and 448–9). In this grant from Oshere king of the Hwicce to a monk called Frithuwald, who is otherwise unknown, the date is given as *Anno recapitulationis Dionysii id est ab incarnatione Christi sexcentessimo octuagessimo indictione sexta reuoluta.* The Indiction is wrong for 680, though *sexta* may have been influenced in copying by *sexcentessimo.* But what attracts attention is the phrase *anno recapitulationis Dionysii id est ab incarnatione Christi.* This reference to Dionysius has almost an air of apology, as if the reckoning were in need of explanation – not surprising at a time when Dionysiac tables were familiar enough in the cloister but the era itself was something of a novelty. And the phrase appears to be unique, with one exception now to be discussed.[14]

BCS 43, from the Bath cartulary of the twelfth century, is a grant

14 Ducange, s.v. *recapitulatio*, knows it only in an extract from this charter printed by Hickes (1703: 79). Not only did Hickes emend the Indiction to *octaua*, but he also proposed that the Year of Grace was beginning to be used at this early stage.

by Osric king of the Hwicce to Abbess Bertana, *anno recapitulationis Dionysii, id est, ab incarnatione domini nostri Ihesu Christi sexcentesimo septuagesimo sexto, indictione quarta mense Nouembris viii° Idus Nouembris,* that is, 6 November 675, but reckoned from the beginning of the Indictional year 676 in September. Those witnessing, apart from Osric and his overlord Aethelred of Mercia, are Archbishop Theodore and Bishops Leutherius (Winchester), Wilfrid (York), Haeddi (later of Winchester), Eorcenwold (London) and Seaxwulf (Lichfield), together with four laymen (Birch prints only three names, but a better edition is by W. Hunt 1893: 6–7). Wilfrid may have been in the south for Eorcenwold's consecration. Among other critical remarks, Finberg (1961: 73) points out that although Bede has nothing to say of such an occurrence, the text of the charter implies a fairly recent relapse into heathenism, probably due to the epidemic of 664, in this part of Mercia. Yet Bede was not a journalist, like Defoe, tracing the events of a plague year; he notices only in passing a similar relapse among the East Saxons (*HE*, III. 30), and a forger would be skilful indeed if he could enter into the minds of people anxious to repair the mischief of a decade earlier. Thus a reference to heathenism could tell in favour of this charter, rather than against it. And the absence of an immunity clause is to be noted.

More serious is another of Finberg's points, that reference should be made in the text to separate monasteries for women, *cenobilia etiam loca sparsim uirorum sparsimque uirginum,* at a time when double houses under an abbess were in general favour throughout England. A rather similar problem arises in connexion with St Frideswide's at Oxford (Stenton 1936; *PASE*: 228–9). Yet the words can be interpreted too literally: priests in any case will have been needed for the administration of the sacraments and in the conduct of secular business. Again, Theodore, who signs this charter, did not approve of double houses though he tolerated the foundations already in being, as appears from the second part of his Penitential, VI. 8 (ed. Haddan and Stubbs 1873: III, 195). There are, moreover, some points of detail which would suggest that a genuine text underlies this document. Leutherius signs as *acsi indignus episcopus,* a phrase well-evidenced at this time (Whitelock, in Harrison 1973a: 554).

The authentic *BCS* 107, to be dated 670–76 (*EHD*: 441–2), shares with this charter the formula *pro remedio animae meae et indulgentia* (*relaxacione* 107) *piaculum meorum*; and also a considerable part of the anathema clause, *Si quis uero*, quod absit, succedentium *episcoporum seu regum contra hanc* nostrae *diffinitionis* (*definitionis* 107) *cartulam propria temeritate* praesumere *temptauerit* . . . If we cannot be sure that *BCS* 43 is in mint condition, these features, and above all the peculiar *anno recapitulationis Dionysii*, . . . are difficult to explain away.

A different type of evidence is found in the Mercian confirmation to *BCS* 42, a grant of land in Thanet which forms part of a series preserved by Thomas Elmham (ed. Hardwick 1858). The unreliable nature of some of the material in this compilation has lent a doubtful colour to the rest; but judged by items in a series stretching so far as the 730s, when transcribing their early charters the Canterbury monks were not given to adding the Year of Grace to documents with no date or dated only by the Indiction. In this series *BCS* 42 is exceptionally dated by the *Annus Domini*.[15] And further, it seems probable that documents concerning Minster-in-Thanet have in the past suffered unduly from criticism (Whitelock, in Harmer 1952: 457); and *BCS* 42 is among the charters which can now be regarded in a more kindly light. Thus *BCS* 42 not only looks reliable in itself but stands out in a series otherwise free from intrusion by the Year of Grace. It is a grant by Swaebheard king of Kent to Abbess Ebba *indictione iiii sub die Kalendarum Martis*, so that the year could be 676 or 691. The confirmation reads *Signum manus Aedilredi regis Merciorum dum infirmauerat terram nostram* . . . with the date *Anno ab incarnatione Christi D.C.LXXVI°*, *Indictione.iiii*ᵃ *.viii die mensis Ianuarii, prima feria* – and 8 January was a Sunday in 691. It is possible that a transcriber took the Indictional number *iiii* of the original grant from the confirmation; or he may by mistake have written *indictione iiii* instead of *iii*ᵃ. In another transcript (ed. Turner and Salter 1915: xxxvi–xxxix) the year *DCXCI* is found, with *viii die mensis Ianuarii prima feria* for the day. We may notice that in both versions the style *viii die mensis Ianuarii* is a specimen of 'concurrent' dating, numbering

---

[15] The others are *BCS* 35, 36, 40, 41, 67, 73, 86, 88, 90, 141, 149 and 150 (Harrison 1973a: 555). Conversely, the Year of Grace without the Indiction would be suspicious, as in *BCS* 78 (*EHD*: 446, no. 59), where it most probably has been added in transcribing.

the days of a month in sequence; it is employed in the acts of the Council of Hertford (*HE*, IV.5) but very rarely elsewhere at this period, except in a Canterbury context (Jones 1947: 171–2).[16] If the style derived from a forger we must allow him an uncanny command of his trade.

We still have on our hands the discrepancy of numerals, *DCLXXVI* and *DCXCI*. A possible explanation lies in the fact that scribes were not above altering names or dates when it suited them; and anybody, faced perhaps with a rather faded or illegible figure, might well turn to Bede's Recapitulation (*HE*, V. 24) or to the Chronicle entry derived from it, and there find under 676 *Aedilred uastauit Cantiam*, whereas under 691 he would find nothing. If he then turned to the full account (*HE*, IV. 12), or if he did not, he can scarcely have asked himself whether a king who plundered Kentish churches and monasteries, and so devastated Rochester that the bishop never returned to his see, would in the same year confirm a grant to Minster-in-Thanet. *Sine respectu pietatis uel diuini timoris* is Bede's judgement on Aethelred at this time; yet by 686 or thereabouts the king had undergone a change of heart, for in this year Theodore addresses him as *fili mi dilectissime, tua miranda sanctitas* (Eddius, c. XLIII) – surely a little overstrained, if no substance lay behind it? Certainly in 704 Aethelred forsook the kingdom for the cowl (*HE*, V.24). The phrase *dum ille infirmauerat terram nostram* may represent only a show of force, as opposed to devastation, and on all counts 691 seems preferable to 676. Hart (1966: 120, n. 2) has argued that the earlier date should be chosen because *cum consilio uenerabilis archiepiscopi Theordori* occurs in the text, which is witnessed by him and by Abbot Hadrian; he died on 19 September 690, but reading *indictione iii*[a] will date the grant to 1 March 690, with confirmation on 8 January 691. (See also Appendix 1).

From these Mercian documents we turn now to consider a charter

---

16 For a collection of concurrent dates see Ewald (1887: 362, n. 4). This style occurs also in *BCS* 111, a grant witnessed by Cenred of Mercia, and preserved in a form purporting to be no later than 716, the last year of his successor Ceolred, who confirms it. The date is *anno ab incarnatione domini nostri DCC.IIII.indictione.ii.tertia decima die mensis Iunii quod est Idus Iunii*. There is nothing suspicious about the clause, which seems to show Cenred reigning by 13 June 704. But the copy we possess may belong to the latter part of the eighth century or early ninth (Sawyer 1968: 87).

of Caedwalla of Wessex, *BCS* 72, preserved in the twelfth-century Winchester cartulary. The most recent discussion (*EHD*: 445) shows that it is taken from an eighth- or early ninth-century exemplar, and the date is *Anno ab incarnatione domini nostri Ihesu Christi. DCLXXXVIII. indictione. I.* Among the witnesses are Wilfrid (of York) who befriended Caedwalla (*HE*, IV. 14), and Eorcenwold (London), Haeddi (Winchester) and Hagona *abbas*. Although there may be hesitation over the year (Harrison 1973a: 556), the style of the date is no ground for suspecting what seems to be an authentic text. Once again Wilfrid, Haeddi and Eorcenwold appear among the signatories of a document dated by the Year of Grace, and they also appear in Essex, in connexion with land granted to the abbey of Barking. Hart (1966: 133) has observed similarities between *BCS* 72 and *BCS* 81, the charter of Oethelraed (Hodilred); the year is uncertain (*EHD*: 446–7) but Eorcenwold, Wilfrid, Haeddi and Hagona *abbas* are witnesses, the last presumably being the abbot of *BCS* 72.[17] The same team is found also in Eorcenwold's charter for Barking, *BCS* 87 (better text in Hart 1966: 122–3). Here it is stated that ten years earlier the bishop had visited Rome, obtaining privileges from Pope Agatho *anno ab incarnatione domini* 677° (the number thus stated in the late copy). Then follows *indictione prima*, which is not true for 677 but correct for 688; moreover, Agatho was not consecrated until 27 June 678, and died in 681. Perhaps 'ten years' is a round number; perhaps, too, this document has been tampered with; it will, however, serve to introduce *BCS* 82, Eorcenwold's gift to Battersea (Hart 1966: 135–6). What emerges from Hart's discussion is that a genuine form of words underlies it, and the style of the date, *idibus iunii mensis. indictione vi. anno ab incarnatione domini sexcentesimo nonagesimo iii,* will not be out of place in this context at this time. Apart from Eorcenwold, among the signatories are Wilfrid, Haeddi and Hagona once more.[18]

---

17 This charter is translated, with notes, in *EHD*: 446–8. It is not dated by the Indiction, or by the Year of Grace, although Wilfrid was present; only the month is given, as in *BSC* 34 (below, p. 72).

18 And Hooc *presbiter*, whom Hart would identify, no more than tentatively, with Wilfrid's chaplain (1966: 130). Yet the Hocca mentioned by Eddius (c. XVIII) is a *praefectus*, 'reeve' or 'bailiff', and should be compared with another called Tydlin (Eddius, c. XXXVIII); both will surely have been laymen.

Thus there would seem to be a good deal of evidence from Kent, Mercia, Wessex and Essex – perhaps with Mercian influence to the front – that the Year of Grace was occasionally used, as well as the Indiction, before the writing of Bede's *De Temporum Ratione* in 725. This evidence is circumstantial because none of the charters is preserved, beyond all doubt, in a contemporary copy; still, a few transcripts occur in authentic form, or with little sign of 'improvement', and others, though distinctly corrupt in part, would appear to contain an element of genuine material. It is very unlikely that cartularies or collections from Worcester, Canterbury, Winchester, Bath and London should all bear marks of the *Annus Domini*, if the use of this style were not beginning to make its way in the latter part of the seventh century; very unlikely, too, that there should have been a group of forgers, or a master of interpolation, saturated in the idiom of the seventh century. We started with the question – when, and by whose agency, was the *Annus Domini* introduced into the legal framework? The answer to the first part of the question appears to be: no later than the Bath charter of 675 which combines the archaic formula *anno recapitulationis Dionysii*,... with the signatories Eorcenwold, Haeddi and Wilfrid who are also encountered at Barking in 693. As to Eorcenwold, he was the founder-abbot of Chertsey, and the charter, *BCS* 34, is dated *circa kalendas Martias* (translation in *EHD*: 440–41, where the approximate years 672–4 are assigned; the remainder of the date may have been lost). Eorcenwold had become a legend for sanctity in Bede's lifetime (*HE*, IV. 6) and as bishop of London from 675 to 693 may have been influential in promoting, or helping to promote, the use of a new era during his episcopate. Little is known of Haeddi, except in his capacity as witness, though it is fair to remember that Dionysiac tables could perhaps have been introduced quite early into Wessex (above, p. 64). But of Wilfrid we know that he worked in Northumbria, Mercia, Sussex and among the West Saxons; and he had been active in Mercia and Kent during the years 666 to 669 (Plummer 1896: II, 317).

That Wilfrid was alive to the value of written evidence is clear from Eddius (c. XVII), who describes the dedication ceremony at Ripon, which took place before 678. On this solemn occasion Wilfrid read aloud a list of the lands presented by King Ecgfrith and his brother Aelfwine 'with the agreement and over the signatures of the bishops and all the chief men'. Ripon, therefore, almost certainly did possess a charter (Stenton 1955: 32). And bearing in mind what evidence there is from the south of England, we can inspect the particulars about the foundation of Wearmouth which have been preserved by the anonymous monk and by Bede, doubtless drawing on a common source (*HAA*: 390; *HAB*: 368). Having been given land by the king, Benedict and his monks began to build *anno dominicae incarnationis* [*ab incarnatione Domini*, Bede] *sexcentesimo septuagesimo quarto, indictione secunda, anno autem quarto imperii Ecgfridi regis*. The date would appear to be September or October 673, and clearly these particulars could have been recovered from the margin of an Easter table, with the regnal year added (Harrison 1972: 79–81). Yet perhaps this record, made in the diocese of York while Wilfrid was bishop, from 669 to 678, represents the dating clause of a charter, as the evidence from elsewhere would make probable. The situation is aggravating: Ripon had a charter, but we do not know the date or style; Wearmouth could furnish both, if only we were sure of a charter background.

To be more than fanciful, a theory ought to throw light on material lying outside its stricter limits. If Wilfrid had brought Dionysiac tables to England by 660 – not only the bare list of years, Indictions, and so forth, and the days of Easter, along the lines set out in Table 2, but also the preface and explanations written by Dionysius himself – and if the Year of Grace was an established though optional feature of conveyancing before the end of the seventh century, two small problems can perhaps be cleared up. The Northumbrian priest Willibrord had been consecrated to Utrecht in 695, and spent the rest of his life as an evangelist in the region of the lower Rhine.[19] His Calendar contains an entry dated A.D. 728, almost certainly in his own hand (ed. Wilson 1918: 13, 42 and pl. xi). If the use of *Annus Domini* is supposed to be hardly traceable before Bede's *Chronica Maiora*, prefixed to the *De Temporum Ratione* of 725, this style makes a rather surprising appearance in 728.

[19] On his career see Levison (1940; 1946: 53–69); on his consecration, Levison (1908) and Harrison (1973b: 69–70).

Only twice does Bede employ the Year of Grace in his chronicle, A.D. 532 and 716 – a slender encouragement for Willibrord, then about seventy years of age, to change his habits. Yet the entry will not seem abnormal if we reflect that he received his early education under Wilfrid at Ripon (Eddius, c. xxvi).

Again, the first official use of the new era on the continent appears to be at the *Concilium Germanicum* which took place *anno ab incarnatione Christi septingentesimo XLII* (ed. Boretius 1883: 84). Levison (1946: 83–4) has shown that in 742, when the Frankish throne was vacant, this Council could be most happily dated by employing the Year of Grace instead of a regnal year – a move to be attributed to Anglo-Saxon influence, possibly brought to bear by Boniface himself. Yet in 746–7 Boniface is found writing to Archbishop Egbert of York, asking for copies of treatises by Bede, 'whom lately, as we have heard, the divine grace endowed with spiritual understanding, and allowed to shine in your province' (ed. Haddan and Stubbs 1873: III, 358–60; translation in *EHD*: 757–8). This sentence does not argue a good acquaintance with *De Temporum Ratione*; but the position is easier to understand if we remember Caedwalla's charter of 688, with the implication that the *Annus Domini* could have been familiar in Wessex when Boniface was a youth.[20]

Bede's statement, in *HE*, V. 19, that Wilfrid learnt to calculate the correct Easter in Rome, something he could not learn in his own country, may be thought to dismiss a complicated situation in too few words. The statement rests, however, on sound authority. Bede had met Wilfrid on at least one occasion, though from the context (*HE*, IV. 17) their talk may have been confined to the everlasting topic of virginity. He was in a position to have derived even more from his abbot, Ceolfrith, who had been ordained at Ripon by Wilfrid, afterwards visiting Kent and East Anglia, and spending more time at Ripon before he joined the house at Wearmouth (*HAA*: 389). After Wilfrid's death, among the verses placed on his tomb are the following lines (*HE*, V. 19):

[20] In 736–9 Boniface wrote to Nothelm of Canterbury asking *in quoto anno ab incarnatione Christi praedicatores primi...ad gentem Anglorum uenissent* (ed. Haddan and Stubbs 1873: III, 336). He cannot therefore have seen Bede's *Historia* (Whitelock 1960: 6).

Paschalis qui etiam sollemnia tempora cursus
Catholici ad iustum correxit dogma canonis,
Quem statuere patres, dubioque errore remoto,
Certa suae genti ostendit moderamina ritus.

These lines may only refer to the Synod of Whitby, though the decision in favour of the Roman reckoning of Easter was made by King Oswiu – a secular decision made against the advice of his bishop, Colman – and not by Wilfrid. More likely, it would seem, Wilfrid is being credited with the promotion in England of the Dionysiac cycle, *cursus paschalis*. As to Bede, he is not diminished in stature if we reflect that through him a style virtually restricted, outside the cloister, to the conveyancing of land became the framework for the history of a nation.

CHAPTER 5

BEDE'S HISTORY

❦

Before writing the book by which his name is best known to posterity, Bede compiled two treatises on the reckoning of time: *De Temporibus* in 703 and *De Temporum Ratione* in 725 (both ed. Jones 1943). As companions to them he also compiled the *Chronica Minora* and *Chronica Maiora* respectively (both ed. Mommsen 1898c). For an estimate of the first chronicle it will be enough to quote Levison, usually calm and cautious in expressing opinions: 'He gives a survey which is rather poor in design and performance; the time of single events is not settled distinctly, the duration of generations and reigns is given only to make out the ages' (1935: 116). This theme of the Six Ages of the World, traditional and conservative, informs the *Chronica Maiora* also; and Jones pointedly observes that what Levison says of the first and shorter chronicle applies equally well to the longer (1947: 22). It is true that the *Chronica Maiora* is the production of a very well-informed man, who in the earlier chronicle had displayed an unusual degree of critical sense, when he came to work out a figure for the *Annus Mundi*, by adopting the *Hebraica ueritas* of Jerome's Vulgate in preference to the Septuagint (above, p. 54, n.3). In the period of the Roman and Byzantine Empire, down to Bede's own lifetime, the *Annus Mundi* is equated, rather confusingly, with the year in which an imperial reign ended; and the other defects of his treatment can be realised by examining a few entries which relate to Anglo-Saxon affairs.

Under the *Annus Mundi* corresponding to A.D. 452 we find *Theodosius minor annis XX et vi*, meaning that Theodosius had reigned twenty-six years until this date – which happens to be wrong by two years. The third consulship of Aetius is assigned to *uicesimo tertio Theodosii principis anno*, the true figure being A.D. 446. Under the year corresponding to A.D. 459 we have the end of a reign once more: *Martianus and Valentinianus annis vii. Gens Anglorum siue Saxonum*

Brittaniam tribus longis nauibus aduehitur (ed. Mommsen 1898c: 313).
Vortigern is mentioned a little earlier, but Hengest and Horsa are
not. The arrival of the Angles and Saxons is followed among other
things by the visit of Germanus of Auxerre, in turn followed by
Valentinian's murder of Aetius. Such a degree of confusion in the
chronology will seem less astonishing when we recognise what Bede
had in mind – a picture of the Sixth Age of the World from the
Nativity down to the year 725. For this purpose neither he nor his
readers were in need of a precise chronological sequence. It was
enough to display the pattern of historical events, the rise and fall of
princes and emperors, with the several kinds of detail that an extensive reading could supply. In describing the Sixth Age, for the most
part Bede equated his *Annus Mundi* with imperial reigns – not very
accurately – and then put in various items of information which had
come his way and seemed appropriate to the theme.[1] A few of these
items are separately dated by A.U.C. or the Indiction. Two of them
are dated A.D. 532 and 716; the former refers to the first year of the
Dionysiac cycle, the latter is the year in which the community at
Iona conformed to the Roman calculation of Easter (*HE*, V. 22).
These faint touches of the *Annus Domini* hardly prepare us for what
was to happen in the *Historia Ecclesiastica*, issued six years later.
Always a theologian, Bede would not desert the Bible; and for the
reckoning of time his allegiance was now transferred from the Old
Testament to the New.

There is indeed a remarkable contrast between the jumbled
chronicle and an air of order and simplicity which pervades the
Historia, where the *Annus Mundi* has vanished. In the second chapter
of the first book, *anno ab urbe condita DCXCIII* is promptly trans-
formed into *ante uero incarnationis dominicae tempus anno LX^{mo}*; the
same process takes place in the third and eleventh chapters; and
thereafter, except for the Indiction, the ancient forms of reckoning
are never referred to. Bede evidently decided for a clean break with
the past, though his attitude to the Indiction, still the current style
of the Papal chancery, cannot be discussed for the moment. Instead,
with the haphazard methods of the *Chronica Maiora* in mind, we may

[1] For an exposition see Jones (1947: 22–6).

ask whether Bede's reckoning of time shows any mark of improvement when he came to compose a history. We are not concerned here with his judgment of people or the significance of events. His attitude to the British Church is often thought to be narrow and ungenerous. The heroes of Northumbria, apart from those canonised by popular acclaim, take on a legendary flavour: thus King Edwin 'is portrayed as the intellectual warrior, for ever hesitating, thinking up new tests... We cannot tell if the portrait is true; but we learn much of Bede's ideal of a great Christian king' (Brooke 1967: 96). And sometimes, where another source can be consulted, it is not certain whether his information is quite accurate, as when he deals with the conversion of the Picts (Hughes 1972: 225). No writer can be expected to avoid such faults; yet because Bede is an isolated historian it becomes the more necessary to discover how far his chronology can be trusted. During the last fifty years the *Historia* has undergone several critical examinations, with a confusing outcome, and it is the purpose of this chapter to inspect them.

Broadly speaking, and without trying to be exhaustive, a judgement of Bede's accuracy could become clouded by the operation of four factors:

1. his ignorance, at some points, of a date which would have helped to clarify the sequence of events

2. mistakes in the material he drew upon – occasionally to be remedied from other sources

3. mistakes of his own, such as errors in transcription or the arithmetic, and faulty deductions

4. mistakes not of his making, when it is assumed that considerations which apply to modern history should be applicable to pre-Conquest England.

As to the text, the most recent edition is by Colgrave and Mynors (1969), but that by Plummer (1896) will very seldom need questioning. Bede has also been fortunate in his copyists, and the good fortune is well deserved. He himself, in *HE*, I. 27, has supplied a lengthy transcript of the so-called *Libellus Responsionum*, Pope Gregory's reply to some questions put to him by Augustine. As it happens, a number of other versions are available for comparison; and after a detailed scrutiny of the Bedan transcript – which as it stands is full of errors –

Meyvaert has concluded that Bede 'transmitted his text to us "warts and all" ' (1971: 32). Faced with a document which he must surely have known, or suspected, was corrupt, he did not try to improve upon it; so we may start with a presumption that he strove for accuracy in at least one essential of historical writing.[2]

What seems to be an obvious mistake was long ago pointed out by Plummer (1896: II, 85). In *HE*, II. 5 Bede says that Ethelbert of Kent died in 616, the twenty-first year after Augustine was sent to England, *qui est annus xxi, ex quo Augustinus...missus est*. Elsewhere (*HE*, I. 23; V. 24) he dates the start of the mission to 596, with arrival in 597. So far the calculation is correct; but in the next paragraph we are told that Ethelbert died on 24 February *post XX et unum annos acceptae fidei*. The last phrase, 'receiving the faith', surely means baptism; and the behaviour of Ethelbert, who at first met Augustine in the open air, to avoid magical art, is as surely the behaviour of a pagan (*HE*, I. 25).[3] Since there is no variant reading in the manuscripts, most likely the error is Bede's own. The simplest emendation would be *XV* (*et unum*) for *XX*. Allowing 'sixteen' to be a round number, Ethelbert's baptism may provisionally be assigned to Christmas 599 or to Easter (10 April) or Whitsun (29 May) in the year 600. A letter of July 598 from Gregory to the Patriarch of Alexandria states that Augustine, at the previous Christmas, had baptised more than ten thousand English people, 'as we are informed' (ed. Haddan and Stubbs 1873: III, 12). The failure to mention Ethelbert (or *rex*) is curious and possibly significant, for Gregory can scarcely have been unaware of the solid benefits that accrued from the conversion of a king and the chief men about him (Chaney 1970: 158–67). Ethelbert's hesitation is not without a parallel; Paulinus was consecrated to York in July 625, but Edwin, despite a Christian wife, did not accept baptism until April 627.[4]

---

[2] When transcribing several of Gregory's letters, 'Bede chose fidelity rather than consistency' (Meyvaert 1970: 166).

[3] Ethelbert's son Eadbald at first *fidem Christi recipere noluerat*, but later *suscepit fidem Christi et baptizatus* [*fuit*]...(*HE*, II. 5 and 6).

[4] On the problems of chronology see Markus (1963), Meyvaert (1964) and Hunter Blair (1970). Richardson and Sayles (1966: 162–5) reject the evidence for Ethelbert's baptism; but they do not explain why, if he remained heathen, the day of his death *die xxiiii mensis Februarii* came to be preserved in a Christian context of reckoning, or preserved at all.

79

Another discrepancy, also known to Plummer, has had further attention drawn to it by Levison (1946: 266, n. 4). In *HE*, V. 24 the death of Wulfhere is recorded under 675, whereas under 704 his brother Aethelred enters religion *postquam XXXI annos Merciorum genti praefuit*. A variant reading is *XXX* (Plummer 1896: I, 355, n. 16). On the other hand Bede states that *Wulfheri... defunctus, Aedilredo fratri reliquit imperium*. This phrase may or may not be a stylistic variation, instead of *Aedilredus regnare coepit*. In any case we should not neglect the possibility that Aethelred had ruled with his brother, as joint-king or sub-king, for a while before the latter's death. In Mercia itself, some twenty years earlier, Peada the son of Penda was *princeps* of the Middle Angles in his father's lifetime (*HE*, III. 21); Bede also notices a joint reign in Kent (*HE*, V. 8). And although the date of the Council of Hatfield can be disputed (below, p. 83), if it took place on 17 September 679, in Aethelred's sixth year (*HE*, IV. 15), he could have been reigning alongside his brother in 674, and reckoned his own regnal years therefrom. Before proclaiming an error in Bede's arithmetic these considerations need further study.

And another discrepancy, of a rather different kind, has been noticed by Kirby (1963: 517). A charter of Hlothere king of Kent, *BCS 36*, is dated *anno regni nostri primo, indictione tertia, sub die kalendarum Aprilis*, which is 1 April 675; another charter, *BCS 44*, bears the date *anno quarto regni nostri, indictione vi*, so should be assigned to the year following 1 September 677. Both are known only from transcripts, but the first is thought to be authentic (Stenton 1955: 34–5) and the second, though incomplete, is in substance probably authentic (Whitelock, in Harmer 1952: 457). Bede, however, states that Egbert of Kent died in July 673, *succedente in regnum fratre Hlothere, quod ipse annos xi et menses vii tenuit* (*HE*, IV. 5); and elsewhere he states that Hlothere died on 6 February 685 (*HE*, IV. 24). This particular matter must be kept waiting for a few moments. Kirby thinks that 'while, however, Egbert of Kent died in July 673, charter evidence is consistent and leaves little doubt that Hlothere did not succeed until, at the earliest, 674'. Thus there will have been a gap, or interregnum, from July 673 at least until 2 April 674; or, if the mantle of kingship fell on anybody other than Hlothere we do not know his name. Meanwhile, Poole (1934: 45–6) had discussed the regnal years of Oswiu of Northumbria, whose predecessor Oswald was killed in battle at Maserfeld on 5 August in a year denoted by Bede as 642; but the battle of the river *Winwaed* was fought on 15 November in Oswiu's thirteenth year, in 655 according to Bede. Poole therefore held that 'in the confusion following the defeat at Maserfeld some time elapsed before Oswiu was able to secure the throne' – another interregnum. Although differing from Poole over many points, Kirby (1963: 516) agrees with him on this one: 'That Oswiu's year did not begin before 15 November is indicated by the fact that 15 November 655 was considered to be in his thirteenth year.' Thus the concept of an interregnum has been put forward for two separate kingdoms.

Leaving these particular cases, to which we shall return, the problem of accuracy can be explored within the reign of King Ecgfrith of Northumbria, where numerous dates are given. According to Bede, Oswiu died on 15 February 670 (*HE*, IV. 5), and was succeeded by Ecgfrith who was killed on 20 May 685 in his fifteenth year (*HE*, IV. 24). From this clash of dates Plummer concluded that Oswiu's death and Ecgfrith's accession ought to be placed in 671 (1896: II, 211); and it is by Plummer's remarks that the later work has been stimulated. Kirby (1963) accepted the year 671, from which it follows that many of Bede's earlier dates are a year behindhand, so his text requires emendation in a score of places. Poole, preferring the year 670, also did not shrink from emendation, though the approach was along different lines. His wide experience in medieval chronology can best be shown by the following quotation (1918b: 46–7):

If we suppose a traveller to set out from Venice on March 1, 1245, the first day of the Venetian year, he would find himself in 1244 when he reached Florence; and if after a short stay he went to Pisa, the year 1246 would already have begun there. Continuing his journey westward, he would find himself again in 1245 when he entered Provence, and on arriving in France before Easter (April 16) he would be once more in 1244.

Poole, then, wherever he might find himself at this period, would never be puzzled by the question 'which year is it that I am in now?'

A chronicler in earlier centuries could have been bewildered by the choice of eras;[5] when the era was more or less settled, in what can be called post-Conquest times, confusion arose because kingdom, republic, principality and city-state adopted their own choice of where precisely the year began, as if to disoblige their neighbours. From this extensive knowledge of later medieval habits Poole may have been led to propose a similar solution for the problem which Plummer had raised.

The argument, or the gist of it, can be set out as follows (Poole 1934: 38–53). In the seventh century the *Annus Domini* was a recent import into England; it had not been intended to provide an era for historical purposes but to serve as a reference in Easter tables. Therefore it was taken as running on the same lines as the Indiction; and since the Indiction began on 1 September, four months before what we call the current year, the Year of Grace was reckoned from this day.[6] But the kernel of Poole's argument is formed by an interpretation of the comet which Bede records in 678, *mense Augusto*. Poole had no difficulty in showing that it appeared to European eyes about mid-August 676 and was visible for some three months; unwilling to believe that Bede was wrong, he drew attention to evidence that the year should be 677. He found that this figure occurs in the Recapitulation (*HE*, v. 24) in one of the oldest manuscripts.[7] Reckoning the Year of Grace 677 from the Indiction, that is, from 1 September 676, Poole held that it included almost the whole of the time during which the comet was visible. This interpretation was challenged by Levison, in a long discussion of Poole's theory (1946: 265–79). He pointed out that in the Recapitulation of other manuscripts the figure 678 is preserved; moreover in the main text of the work, *HE*, IV. 12, Bede writes DCLXXVIII, and Plummer gives no variant reading from any of the best manuscripts – neither do Colgrave and Mynors (1969: 370). So the balance of textual evidence would favour 678.

---

[5] Förster (1925) has collected several estimates of *Annus Mundi* from Anglo-Saxon sources alone.

[6] We may recollect, however, that each 19-year cycle of Dionysius (Table 2, above, p. 35) starts on 1 January.

[7] The Moore manuscript (ed. Hunter Blair 1959: f. 127r), where an extra minim has been added to make 678.

And there is another objection to Poole's reasoning.[8] Bede and his contemporaries well knew that the duration of comets can vary; seven to eighty days are the limits given by Bede himself, and no ominous significance was read into the length of time as such (*De Natura Rerum*, ed. Migne 1862: col. 244). What startled them, because comets told of baleful events in the future, was the sudden brilliant appearance of a hairy star in the sky, *apparuit mense Augusto stella quae dicitur cometa*, a sentence that comes next before the downfall of Bishop Wilfrid. A comet appearing in the middle of August was a portent then, but no longer in September or October. Bede in any case made a mistake over the year, perhaps let down by his source or by his own calculation;[9] what matters to the chronologer is that he thought Ecgfrith's eighth year included the month of August.

We now consider a matter to which reference has already been made (above, p. 41). A council was held at Hatfield *sub die xv kalendas Octobres, Indictione viii°*, to which Bede attaches the year 680 in the Recapitulation (*HE*, v. 24). In so doing he followed his own rule, derived from Dionysius, which is expressed in *De Temporum Ratione*, c. XLIX, as follows: to the *Annus Domini* add three and divide by fifteen, the remainder being the Indiction (above, p. 40). Thus the *Annus Domini* is identified with the greater part of the Indictional year running from 1 September to 31 August, not the whole of it; if Bede had written 679 he would have broken the rule. Poole correctly dated this council to 17 September 679 (1934: 44), but for another reason: overlooking the rule which furnished a simple solution he instead thought that Bede began the Year of Grace on 1 September. The complications arising from this proposal are better taken as a separate issue, when further progress has been made in examining Bede's dates. Meanwhile we notice that the council took place in the seventh year of Hlothere's reign, *anno vii°*. If Bede is right in saying that Egbert of Kent had died in July 673

---

[8] What follows in the next few pages is largely drawn from Harrison (1972 and 1973b).

[9] Levison (1946: 268–9) has tried to explain how Bede could have calculated the year; Jones, however, says 'if Bede's mistake must be explained, it is only reasonable to assume that the notice skipped two years in the copying' (1947: 183–4) – whether by Bede or by someone else.

(*HE*, IV. 5) and if Hlothere succeeded immediately, or soon after-wards, the regnal year is correct. But if, following Kirby (1963: 517), the charter evidence is to be preferred and Hlothere began to reign in 674, then the figure should be *vi⁰*. To judge by the number of emendations which have been put forward during the last half-century or so, there is nothing sacrosanct about the *Historia*; and unless Bede worked from a contemporary copy of the acts of the council, his text as it now stands is a transcript of a transcript (see Appendix 1).

Another council took place at Hertford, *xx⁰ iiii⁰ mensis Septembris, indictione prima*, to which Bede adds the year A.D. 673. Again Poole interpreted the date, on his own theory, as 24 September 672; the same result is achieved by applying Bede's rule. And this year, he says, was Ecgfrith's third (*HE*, IV. 5). Kirby (1963: 520) states that 'the 673 date... must have come from somewhere', holding that Bede confused the year of the council with that of the death of King Egbert of Kent, 673. Yet in this context 24 September in the first Indiction could only be the equivalent of A.D. 673, as Bede states; and that year is correct whether the Indictional year began on 1 or 24 September 672.[10] In the same chapter we are told that Oswiu died on 15 February 670; putting together this information with what is found in the acts of the Hatfield council – that it occurred in Ecgfrith's tenth year (*HE*, IV. 15) – there is a case for thinking that Ecgfrith came to the throne between 1 and 17 September 670. The limits can be arrived at in another way. From the particulars about Wear-mouth (above, p. 73), we can safely follow Poole (1934: 46) in fixing the period when the buildings were begun at some time after 1 September 673, in Ecgfrith's fourth year; the upper limit seems to be about 12 January 674 (Harrison 1972: 80). The comet wrongly ascribed to August 678 was in Ecgfrith's eighth year (*HE*, IV. 12) and he himself was killed on 20 May 685, in his fifteenth year (*HE*, IV. 24). To complete the picture, at Jarrow the dedication stone is

---

[10] Kirby, in agreeing with 672 for the year of the council (or synod) also says: 'if it was a native Northumbrian tradition that Hertford was held in the third year of Ecgfrith, Ecgfrith must have succeeded in 670. It is unlikely that this was a native tradition since the synod was not a Northumbrian event...' (1963: 520). Yet Bishop Wilfrid of York was represented at the council by proxies, *per proprios legatarios adfuit*, who if not 'natives' themselves must have reported promptly to Northumbria.

inscribed *viiii kl. Mai anno xv Ecfridi reg.*, and 23 April was a Sunday in 685, the most probable day of the week (Plummer 1896: II, 361). These figures and events are set out in Table 5.

TABLE 5

Regnal years of Ecgfrith from between 1 and 17 September 670	Events
(3) 672–73	Council of Hertford, 24 September 672
(4) 673–74	Wearmouth building after 1 September 673
(8) 677–78	Comet sighted about mid-August 678
(10) 679–80	Council of Hatfield 17 September 679
(15) 684–85	Jarrow dedication 23 April, Ecgfrith killed 20 May, 685

Hitherto in this analysis the notion of a gap or interregnum between reigns has been arrived at only by inference. Positive knowledge of such an episode is to be found in Eddius (c. LIX), where he relates how when King Aldfrith died the throne was in dispute between his son Osred, a child about eight years old (*HE*, v. 18), and an interloper called Eadwulf, who reigned for two months until driven out. Bede does not mention Eadwulf, and Eddius tells the tale in such a way as to magnify the power and influence of Wilfrid; still, the occasion must have been familiar to the contemporary audience for which Eddius was writing, about a decade later. At this point, while agreeing with Poole over the concept of an interregnum, we may glance at a few difficulties of his chronology. If, when composing the *Historia*, Bede changed the structure of the *Annus Domini*, or Year of Grace, by starting it on 1 September instead of 1 January, he acted strangely – and without warning. The ecclesiastical calendar of anniversaries was, and still is, anchored to the Julian framework; and by dividing it, Bede would in effect invite his largely monastic audience to think of Jesus being conceived in one Year of Grace and born in the next. A thought of this description is hardly likely to have entered Bede's orthodox mind, even for the sake of historical convenience.[11] By neglect of the rule for relating *Annus Domini* to the Indiction, the theory creates as many problems as it solves.

In detail, Poole requires us to believe that when Bede ascribed King Edwin's death to 12 October 633 the year he meant was in fact 632, by modern reckoning. Yet on 11 June 634 Pope Honorius wrote to Canterbury making various arrangements about the consecration of successors to that see and to York, and with this letter the *pallium* was sent to both bishops (*HE*, II. 18). Clearly the Pope did not know that Edwin was slain and Paulinus had fled to Kent. If Edwin died in October 633 the ignorance of the Pope is understandable, since, in the confusion following the battle of Hatfield, the news might well not have reached Rome in eight months, allowing for the hazard of winter travel; if his death took place in October 632, it seems very unlikely that the news should have been delayed twenty months (Harrison 1973b: 58). Again Bede goes to some trouble over explaining why Oswald was deemed to reign nine years following on Edwin's death (*HE*, III. 1 and 9), and he gives the year of Oswald's death as 642 (*HE*, V. 24). The day, 5 August, falls within the 'neutral' part of the year, unaffected by the Indiction, and cannot be reconciled with Poole's chronology; he ignored it (1934: 45), but the necessary emendation, to 5 August 641, now seems to have met with approval (Powicke and Fryde 1961: 11). Again, the episcopate of Paulinus is given as *X et VIIII annos, menses duos, dies xxi*, his consecration taking place on Sunday 21 July 625 and death on 10 October 644 (*HE*, II. 9; III. 14). But by any October date in 644 Bede was meaning 643. Poole argued therefore on two grounds: first, that *xxi* must be wrong for the days, for that number would bring the consecration back to Saturday 20 July 625;

---

[11] In the later Middle Ages a reckoning from the Annunciation, 25 March, is often found; here the Year of Grace is defined anew, in accordance with a stricter theology which dates the Incarnation to 25 March. But the proposals of Dionysius have fared better. For a discussion of Annunciation dating in the Anglo-Saxon Chronicle, from about the year 1000, see Whitelock (in Earle and Plummer 1899, reprint of 1952: II, cxliia-c).

and secondly, that there is no more violence in subtracting one from the years than adding one to the days (1934: 45). The second proposition is true; but Levison has pointed to the circumstance that in the Middle Ages the day beginning a period and the day ending it are often both counted as full days (1946: 275, n. 2), by analogy with the reckoning of days in the Roman calendar; and another example is adduced by Grosjean (1960a: 260), also in an English episcopal reckoning. The emendation of $(X\ et)\ VIIII\ annos$ to VIII, respectable enough in itself, could only be justified by a theory free from difficulty in other ways.

From detail we pass to the more general objection that Plummer and Poole were guided by a maxim not far removed from 'No demise of the Crown'; namely, they assumed that a king counted his regnal years from the death of his predecessor, or within a few days of it. The rulers of England have indeed reckoned in this way since the Conquest, except for an interregnum of two months when James the Second fled the country; in pre-Conquest times the assumption will often be true enough, but we may not suppose it always applying to seventh-century Northumbria, or Kent. If Poole had treated the reign of Ecgfrith as he treated that of Oswiu, reckoning the accession backwards from various events dated by regnal years, his chronology would have taken a different form. By discarding the assumption which Plummer and Poole unconsciously made, the particulars in Table 6 are arrived at. Thus to the elements which could combine into kingship at that period – heredity, election, designation and force – we should add the element of time: when did a prince become a king?

Examination of this table may suggest that the compilers of regnal lists could have recorded the length of reigns from accession to accession. Hence Oswiu's 28 years run from November 642 to September 670, roughly and in round number; from his accession to death would account only for 27 years and a few months. Luckily such a list, with years of reign, has survived and been carefully analysed by Hunter Blair (1950). It was compiled, he shows, in 737, and thus might partly derive from Bede; many of its figures, which are identical with the regnal years in Table 6, could have been calculated or taken directly from the *Historia*. Yet the names of kings

TABLE 6

Kings of Northumbria, 616–729

Accession	Regnal years from accession	Death
Edwin after 12 April 616	17	12 October 633
Oswald on 12 October 633	9	5 August 642
Oswiu after 15 November 642	28	15 February 670
Ecgfrith between 1 and 17 September 670	15	20 May 685
Aldfrith after 14 December 685	20	14 December 705
Osred after 14 December 705 or mid-February 706	11	716
Cenred 716	2	718
Osric after 23 April 718[a]	11	9 May 729
Ceolwulf on or after 9 May 729[b]	—	—

[a] Osric's seventh year included 23 April 725 (HE, v.23).

[b] Ceolwulf had been designated to the kingdom by Osric (HE, V.23) so perhaps the accession was immediate. He was reigning by 15 August, because in his sixth year Frithuwold was consecrated to Whithorn on that day in 734 (Grosjean 1960a: 261).

and lengths of their reigns are carried back to Ida, 547, with other details of independent origin. The list furnishes an example of what may have been in front of Bede when he wrote, serving as a broad frame of reference, though we cannot say whether it owes anything to him or not. These lists were drawn up with care; the *infaustus annus* following the death of Edwin, when Northumbria reverted to heathenism, was counted into Oswald's reign by all who reckoned the dates of kings, *cunctis...regum tempora computantibus* (HE, III. 1).

From the secure date 9 May 729 for the death of Osric – in the 'neutral' part of the year, unaffected by the Indiction – it is found that 44 years almost exactly had elapsed since the death of Ecgfrith, 20 May 685. His obit would almost certainly be recorded at Wearmouth and at Jarrow, to both of which he was a benefactor; at the latter he marked out the site of the high altar (*HAA*: 391–2), and in after days it was known as 'Ecgfrith's monastery' (*ASC*: year

794).[12] Edwin's baptism, at Easter in his eleventh year (*HE*, II. 14), represents the kind of information that could be transmitted by word of mouth, too notable an event to be forgotten; the same might apply to the date of Oswiu's victory at the river *Winwaed*, in the form 'two weeks before St Michael's tide in his thirteenth year'. As to Oswald, his fame as a saint and martyr had spread *trans oceanum* to Ireland and Germany in Bede's lifetime (*HE*, III. 13). The day of his death will often have been entered into calendars, such as Willibrord's; and earlier still, at the monastery of Selsey in Sussex, there is evidence of it being entered *in annale*, that is, a list of obits of the type discussed by Grosjean (1961) *in quibus defunctorum est adnotata depositio*... where at the death of a child one of the brethren *inuenit eadem ipsa die Osualdum regem fuisse peremtum* (*HE*, IV. 14).[13] By the combination of regnal years with obits and other events Bede had an important source at his disposal, quite apart from what Paschal annals could contribute.

Yet in some directions his knowledge seems to have been incomplete or made up of conflicting elements. Evidently he was a little unsure of the length of Aldfrith's reign – nineteen years (*HE*, V. 1) or less than twenty (*HE*, V. 18), the king's death being assigned to 705 (*HE*, V. 24). It is unlikely that he succeeded soon after his predecessor died, since to all appearances he was then in exile (Plummer 1896: II, 263), and his path to the throne may not have been smooth, for although he restored a shattered kingdom it was within narrower boundaries, *intra fines angustiores* (*HE*, IV. 24). Furthermore, there is evidence that Aldfrith died on 14 December 705 – a date apparently not known to Bede. This day and month are preserved by the 'northern recension' of the Anglo-Saxon Chronicle, now represented by the D and E versions, whose archetype was

[12] Ecgfrith does not rank as a saint, and his invasion of Ireland is strongly condemned by Bede (*HE*, IV. 24). Yet he appears, with Edwin, among the early additions to Willibrord's calendar, whereas Oswald's name was entered from the first (ed. Wilson 1918). Ecgfrith is also found in a list of obits dating from the first half of the eighth century (Grosjean 1961), but the Osric also commemorated, on 9 May, is surely Ceolwulf's predecessor and not the apostate king of Deira (*HE*, III. 1). These obits may be drawn from the *Historia*.

[13] *Depositio*, burial, often took place on the day of death, unless circumstances prevented it. Thus Ceolfrith was buried the next day, at a place distant *tria ferme milia passuum* (*HAA*: 402).

probably compiled at York in the latter part of the tenth century (Whitelock, Introduction to *ASC*: xiv–xv). And the record does not stand alone in the Chronicle, but forms one of seven items, stretching from 685 to 721, in a series which has been discussed by Hunter Blair (1948). The series furnishes place-names not mentioned by Bede in his account of events connected with them; for instance, King Aldfrith died 'at Driffield'. And combined with the wording of two items which has a contemporary flavour, the evidence would justify Hunter Blair's conclusion that the source is to be found in 'an annalistic chronicle, perhaps in the form of entries in Easter tables' (1948: 112).[14]

Accepting 14 December 705 for Aldfrith's death, and Eadwulf's intrusion for two months, Osred presumably began to reign about the middle of February 706. According to Bede, the Synod of Nidd, where Wilfrid became reconciled with his fellow-clergy, followed soon after Osred came to the throne, *mox* (*HE*, V. 19); according to Eddius (c. LX) the Synod took place in Osred's first year. Wilfrid's death took place four years later (*HE*, V. 19). He died on a Thursday, *quintam feriam* (Eddius, c. LXV), and all the early calendars fix the obit to 24 April (Levison 1946: 278–9). Hence the date would appear to be 24 April 710, agreeing with the length of his episcopate, forty-six years (Eddius, c. LXVI), his consecration being assigned to 664 (*HE*, V. 24). But although the date of Aldfrith's death is in the Anglo-Saxon Chronicle, Poole treated the figures on his view that the Year of Grace begins in September, and hence the true date should be 14 December 704 (1934: 80–81). The day of Wilfrid's death, 24 April 709, now becomes a Wednesday. Poole saw the difficulty and tried to meet it by proposing that Wilfrid had died on a Wednesday night (that is, before midnight). Eddius relates that an abbot – probably Tatberct of Ripon – was accustomed *celebrare . . . omni hebdomada quintam feriam, in qua obiit, quasi dominicam in epulis*

---

[14] It may not be a coincidence that the years 684 to 721, inclusive, represent the last two 19-year cycles calculated by Felix. Although Easter tables had a poor chance of survival, we may adopt Professor Whitelock's informal suggestion that these items could have been preserved in an annotated copy of the *Historia*. Thus the place, Driffield, and the precise day *xix k. Ianr.*, 14 December, were on this theory taken from an Easter table and added next the year 705 in *HE*, V. 18 or V. 24, and so came to the Chronicler.

uenerare, as if a Sunday (c. LXV). It is true that if Wilfrid had died late on a Wednesday night the abbot would indeed celebrate for him on a Thursday, since the ecclesiastical day began at about 19–20 hours (7–8 p.m.) on the previous night. But if all the days throughout the year include part of the previous night, the argument falls to the ground; and we may not in any case assume that Wilfrid died late at night in order to show Bede never making a mistake.

It would appear that Bede did not know the precise date, day and year, of Aldfrith's death, of Osred's accession, of the Synod of Nidd, or of Wilfrid's death. As a rough guide he could turn to the regnal list, and reckoning back from Osric's death on 9 May 729 a total of forty-four years would take him almost precisely to 20 May 685, when Ecgfrith was killed. Then Aldfrith's 'not quite twenty years', *anno regni sui XX° necdum inpleto* (*HE*, v. 18) would bring the calculation to the early part of 705, with Osred's accession and the Synod of Nidd following soon after. Wilfrid's four years of life from the synod now indicates 709 as the year of his death, in Osred's fourth year (*HE*, v. 19) – the month and day being left in the air. Furthermore, an inscription on Wilfrid's tomb, recorded in the same chapter, has these lines:

> *Quindecies ternos postquam egit episcopus annos*
> *Transiit, et gaudens caelestia regna petiuit.*

Three times fifteen is a suspiciously round number, more attuned perhaps to metre than to accuracy. Eddius, on the other hand, prosaically writes *per quadraginta sex annos episcopatus sui* (c. LXVI), and although the phrase could be stretched to mean the forty-sixth year of his episcopate, it could mean what it says. Bede was hardly in a position to ignore the epitaph; but whoever wrote it may have reflected, as a sturdy forerunner of Samuel Johnson, that in lapidary inscriptions a man is not upon oath. Even so, Bede treats the matter in an oblique fashion: he states that Cenred of Mercia went to Rome in the year of Wilfrid's death, and identifies the year with 709, *postquam v annos regnauit* (*HE*, v. 24). If the Twickenham charter is to be believed, as probably it is (above, p. 70, n. 16), Cenred was on the throne by 13 June 704.[15]

---

[15] According to *HE*, v. 20, Abbot Hadrian died in his forty-first year after leaving Rome on 27 May 688 (*HE*, IV. 1). Thus he will have died before May 709, ascribed

Yet the statements of Eddius cannot be overlooked (Levison 1946: 278). For many years he had been Wilfrid's companion, travelling to Rome with him in 703–4, and he wrote at least for the edification of the houses at Ripon, Hexham and Oundle, whose monks now revered their founder as a saint. Without taking his estimate of Wilfrid's character at face value we should allow him a residue of hard fact. Thus it would appear that even for Northumbria – let alone for Kent – Bede occasionally lacked some of the finer detail which is needed to provide a scheme of dates altogether free from uncertainty. In this respect the tabulation of regnal years by round numbers was not without disadvantage. Over a long period, a century or so, the positive and negative errors may be expected to come into balance; Edwin's baptism on Easter Day in his eleventh year and Osric's death on 9 May 729 are warrants for the head and tail of the figures in Table 6. On a shorter term, if Osred had ruled only ten years and just over six months the figure 'eleven' might well interfere with an estimate of when his reign began, not to mention whether the two-month interregnum was or was not included in his tenure. Much is known about the legal and 'sacral' aspects of Germanic kingship.[16] Far less is known of the events which could and sometimes did follow when personal power was extinguished by the death of a king, and the hungry athelings began to prowl. Bede's fidelity to the title of his book, in allowing the claims of ecclesiastical over political history, is justified by an orderly narrative to which few countries in the early Middle Ages can offer a rival, but from his indifference to worldly affairs we are usually, except in Oswald's case, left to make deductions about the timing of kingship.[17]

Finally, the circumstances surrounding the Synod of Whitby should be mentioned. Oswiu's queen, brought up in Kent, cele-

to Osred's fifth year. Apparently Bede may have thought that Osred had succeeded before 27 May 705, as the regnal list by itself, with no other guide, would indicate.

[16] See for instance Whitelock (1952a), Brooke (1967), Binchy (1970), Chaney (1970) and Wallace-Hadrill (1971).

[17] In *HE*, IV. 24 it is stated that after the death of Hlothere's successor Edric the kingdom of Kent was ravaged for a while by *reges dubii uel externi*. In Wessex at this time Caedwalla 'began to contend for the kingdom' (ASC: year 685). For claimants and internal strife see also *EHD*: 26–7.

brated the Roman Easter which sometimes differed by a week from her husband's Celtic observance (*HE*, III. 25). From the table prepared by O'Connell (1936: 104) it can be seen how often this clash was occurring, and further, that in 665 the Celtic and Dionysiac Easters were identical. Thus a synod in 664 would prepare for harmony a year later, although other motives may well have directed Oswiu's final decision. There are, however, some difficulties over the episcopate of Archbishop Deusdedit, who died on 14 July 664. After the death of his predecessor Honorius, 30 September 653, there was a vacancy in the see for a year and six months, until Deusdedit was elected – clearly in March 655 – and he was archbishop for *annos viiii menses iiii et duos dies* (*HE*, III. 20). In one of the oldest texts *vii* has been altered to *iiii*, and Grosjean has argued for the last figure (1960a: 237–8). Previously Levison (1946: 276) had accepted Bede's statement that the consecration took place on 26 March 655, the Thursday next before Easter, but Grosjean convincingly maintains that this day was fully occupied by ceremonies of a different kind, and calculating back from the death of Deusdedit he arrives at 12 March 655. This day was a Thursday, occurring in Lent, but also the Feast of Gregory the Great, to whom an altar was dedicated at the monastery in Canterbury later known as St Augustine's (*HE*, II. 3), and whose memory was venerated by all Anglo-Saxons. It appears that this date should be accepted as by far the likeliest solution to the problem.

The year 664 also witnessed an eclipse of the sun followed by a visitation of bubonic plague (*HE*, III, 27).[18] What seems to be the first record of the eclipse in England is contained in Bede's *Chronica Maiora* (ed. Mommsen 1898c: 313), in the words *eclipsis solis facta est Ind. vii, v.nonas Maias*, 3 May 664, the substance being repeated in *HE*, III. 27, with the addition *hora circiter X*^{a} *diei*, and the *Annus Domini* in place of the Indiction. The true day is 1 May, as noticed in the Annals of Ulster (ed. Hennessey 1887: 119). From calculations made at the Royal Observatory, Brussels, totality occurred in Northern Ireland at about 15 hours 26 minutes, and at Ripon or

---

[18] That is, 664 was a 'plague year', which does not preclude minor outbreaks a few years beforehand, or afterwards. The epidemiology of bubonic plague is far from simple, and the remarks of Grosjean (1960a: 234–5) should be qualified by those of C. Morris (1971: 206–9 and 214).

Jarrow about 25 minutes later (Grosjean 1960a: 239, n. 1). There can be little doubt that the entry was first made in the margin of a Dionysiac table (Jones 1947: 37–8), though we cannot be sure precisely where it was made. Good seeing in Ulster is not incompatible with heavy cloud in Northumbria, or a thunderstorm, in which case the dramatic quality of a total eclipse would be spoilt, and a general darkening of the sky for a few minutes might go unremarked. Strictly, the condition for an eclipse to occur is the phase of conjunction, when the moon is exactly between earth and sun, casting its shadow on the earth's surface; and conjunction takes place on the last day of a lunation, before the new moon. Possibly, however, in the Middle Ages it was thought that eclipses coincided with the new moon (Jones 1947: 37–8). In 664 the lunation ended on 2 May, with new moon the next day, according to Dionysius (Grosjean 1960a: 240, n. 1). The English annalist may not have seen the eclipse for himself, since the belt of totality did not cover the whole country; and he might prefer the day of the new moon indicated by the Dionysiac table, 3 May, even if he had been assured that the event took place on the Kalends of May.

From this analysis of Bede's mistakes and misapprehensions, and remembering the factors which could influence the judgement of his accuracy (above, p. 78), it will be seen that a certain amount of error derived from matters outside his control, such as the day of the eclipse in 664, and the date of Willibrord's consecration (Harrison 1973b: 69). Then there are slips of the pen, exemplified by the episcopate of Deusdedit, and perhaps the date of Ethelbert's baptism and the number of Hlothere's regnal year at the Council of Hatfield. This second factor represents what we should be astonished not to find in the days before printing and proof-correcting. Even within the territory of Northumbria Bede's information, or lack of it at a crucial point, may have led him astray over the death of Aldfrith and consequently that of Wilfrid. Yet there remains a hard core of dates whose accuracy has been in question because, first, it has been assumed that the reign of a king began on, or very close to, the day of a previous king's death, allowing of no sizeable interregnum; and second, the relation between *Annus Domini* and Indiction, as expounded in *De Temporum Ratione*, has been neglected. This treatise is surely not the product of Bede's unassisted imagination, rather, it reflects the Anglo-Saxon attitude both to time-reckoning and the calculation of Easter, current in England about a dozen years before Bede was born, and stretching back (c. xv) to heathen days, to the *antiqui Anglorum populi*. Interpretation of the *Historia* seems to require not only the usual apparatus of criticism but also the help afforded by the treatise on Time (Hunter Blair 1970: 198).

Improving on the *Chronica Maiora*, Bede's attempt in the *Historia* to equate events with imperial years is more successful than his editor was able to allow (Plummer 1896: II, 66). The emperor Phocas began to reign on 23 November 602 (Bury 1898: V, 64; not 2 November 601, as Plummer thought). The battle of *Degsastan*, 603, is assigned to his first year (*HE*, I. 34), the death of Pope Gregory to his second (*HE*, II. 1), and a council at Rome *Indictione xiii^a, tertio die Kalendarum Martiarum*, 27 February 610, to his eighth (*HE*, II. 4). Before enlarging on the career of Gregory, however, at the beginning of *HE*, II. 1 Bede referred his death to 605, as the result of a separate calculation (Jones 1947: 161–2). Returning to the mainstream of dates, the mission of Augustine was despatched in 596 (*HE*, V. 24), correctly assigned to the fourteenth year of Maurice (*HE*, I. 23), who came to the throne on 13 August 582; the imperial year is taken from Pope Gregory's letter to Augustine transcribed in the same chapter.[19] Bede could now work back from the eclipse of 664, with the aid of a Kentish regnal list which is summarised in *HE*, V. 24: Eorcenberht died in the eclipse year, Eadbald in 640 and Ethelbert in 616, which he calculated to be the twenty-first year after Augustine and the missioners had left for Britain (*HE*, II. 5). From the Papal letters to begin with and an eclipse at the end, Bede's chronology for the first half of the seventh century seems to rest on good foundations; and the eclipse also furnished a link with Northumbrian chronology, occurring in Oswiu's twenty-second year (*HE*, III. 26 and 27). The battle of *Degsastan* is tied to the first year of Phocas, and the eleventh of Aethelfrith, consonant with the

---

[19] As Jones observes (1947: 162) there is a systematic error in the *post consulatum* years in this and other letters. Here the figure *xiii* seems to have influenced the number of the Indiction in some texts of the *Historia*, where it appears as *xiii*. But in *HE*, I. 24 another of Gregory's letters, dated to the same day and imperial year, bears the correct Indiction *xiiii*.

accession of Edwin after 16 April 616 (Table 6), since the Northumbrian regnal list gives Aethelfrith twenty-four years (Hunter Blair 1950: 246–7). Taken with the contents of Tables 5 and 6, the main sequence of dates from 596 to 729 appears to be reliable and free from systematic error.

When Poole (1934: 38) attempted to show that Bede 'did not make mistakes', applying to this author criteria he would have applied to no other, he could not help but fail in an impossible task. Reviewing the position at a later date (1947: 40–41), Jones could form a melancholy opinion of Bede's methods and capabilities; for instance, the remark that 'in his statements lie buried as many New Years as were employed in the many sources from which he drew' – with others of a like nature.[20] Such remarks cannot be swept aside. Yet by further exploration a different state of affairs is revealed. The primitive Anglo-Saxon calendar, with its reckoning from Midwinter, coincides nearly enough with the Julian year, and enabled Bede to fix some of his early dates in terms of heathen regnal years, such as the battle of *Degsastan* in 603 (*HE*, I. 34). In their turn, the regnal years of Christian kings provided the chief framework around which the narrative could be built. A secondary framework also existed, in the form of episcopal lists; among the East Angles, however, although Bede knew the length of time for which two bishops had occupied the see (*HE*, III. 20), he did not have enough information to supply dates *Anno Domini*, and cautiously refrained.[21] To all appearances the later material at his disposal had been recorded by the Julian calendar, which even the system of Indictions presupposes; and to judge from *De Temporum Ratione*, the Indiction gave him no trouble. If New Years other than 1 January lie buried they await discovery.

As to Paschal annals, it is admittedly hard to decide whether a particular item of information came from this type of source or some other. Internal evidence would suggest that the eclipse of 664 was

20 '...a type of care and knowledge in authorship which Bede could not easily have possessed...Bede was so little habituated to precision in computistical matters... This kind of inconsistency...indicates how little his mind operated in the fashion of modern diplomatists,...'

21 Bede's mind worked very often in the fashion of a 'modern diplomatist'; the *Historia* is littered with expressions like *interea, mox, plus minus, eo tempore, circiter*, which may fairly be said to outnumber the positive dates.

first recorded in the margin of an Easter table; the chances are that the details isolated and studied by Hunter Blair (1948), or most of them, were also preserved in this way. Jones (1947: 35) advances the view that Paulinus and James the Deacon kept annals in Northumbria; but when the work of James is described (*HE*, II. 20) it would have been uncharacteristic of Bede to omit the mention of annals, had they been known to him, either at that point or in his Preface. Existence must not be equated with availability: if the precise date and place of King Aldfrith's death were recorded by a contemporary annalist, those facts seem to have escaped Bede's enquiry; and in some degree it will therefore be allowed that more entries were made in Easter tables than we are aware of. Yet before postulating Dionysiac annals we need to know when the tables themselves arrived in this country. Jones has stated that the consecration of Mellitus and Justus, A.D. 604 according to Bede (*HE*, II. 3), is 'the first clear indication of a Dionysiac annal created in England' (1947: 165); more likely the figure is based on an episcopal list, and the balance of evidence is in favour of Dionysiac tables being brought back by Wilfrid from Rome in 657–8 (above, pp. 63–5).[22]

Again, with no more than probability to go by, it is to Wilfrid that we may ascribe the introduction of the *Annus Domini* into charters. The monk Dionysius had replaced the era of Diocletian, most notorious of persecuting emperors, by a specifically Christian era, and the reasons that appealed to him will have had no less force in the mind of Wilfrid, another monk. When Bede deserted the form of the chronicle in order to write a history, he will have had several motives for deserting the *Annus Mundi*. Three of these possible motives are relevant here. First, the Christian era was associated with the Alexandrian reckoning of Easter which had shown itself to be reliable.[23] Then, this era had already been adopted in legal instruments – throughout the country, if the analysis developed in Chapter 4 is correct. In the third place, an era to which his contemporaries had already subscribed, and given their sanction, was well suited to harmonising the regnal years of rulers in

22 For comments on the lengthy and very useful analysis of time-references made by Jones (1947: 161–99) see Harrison (1973d).
23 The lunar calculations expounded by Dionysius and Bede are still of use today (Newton 1972: 122).

different kingdoms, and, through the Indiction, the Papal letters on which his account of the Conversion partly relied. By this stroke of imagination, by extending the use of *Annus Domini* from the conveyance of land and privileges to the writing of history, in a form so well adapted to the piety and comprehension of the Anglo-Saxon church, Bede helped also to prepare for the downfall of a system now in the last stages of practicability – the cycle of Indictions.

Although Bede's attitude to the Indiction is not made explicit in the *Historia*, it is possible to infer something about his thoughts. Throughout we discover the Indiction only in official documents – with one exception, and that in a Papal context (*HE*, II. 4). The dating clauses of Pope Gregory's letters are left in their pristine form; a letter of Honorius (*HE*, II. 18) is given the explanatory *id est anno dominicae incarnationis DCXXXIIII*. The acts of the Councils of Hertford and Hatfield are transcribed in *HE*, IV. 5 and 15; to the former the equivalent *Annus Domini* is added separately in the same chapter, and to the latter in *HE*, V. 24. There are no signs of more enthusiasm for the Indiction than for *ab urbe condita*. During the childhood of English charters, while Theodore presided at Canterbury from 669 to 690, there can be little doubt that the Indiction enjoyed the status of a prime reckoning, to which the *Annus Domini* was subordinate; and very probably this state of affairs continued until Bede's death in 735.[24] As the eighth century wore on, leaving behind a more extensive series of annals and charters than the seventh can furnish, there seems to have been a development in favour of the Year of Grace; and to this changing climate of opinion the next chapter will be devoted.

---

[24] In his formal letter, 5 November 734, to the bishop (later archbishop) of York, Bede employed the formal style of the Indiction (Plummer 1896: I, 423; translation in *EHD*: 735–45).

CHAPTER 6

ANNALS AND CHARTERS

❦

At this point it will be convenient to discuss an item of information preserved in the *Historia Brittonum* ascribed to Nennius (ed. Mommsen 1898b). Remarks on Nennius are deferred until the next chapter (below, p. 136); he seems to have compiled his work in 829–30, and we are concerned here with a passage – it might almost be described as annalistic – which occurs only in the oldest text, formerly kept at Chartres, but destroyed in the Second World War. The manuscript is dated to the second half of the tenth century, not earlier, and has been carelessly copied: 'ce manuscrit de Chartres est détestable', says Grosjean (1960b). He restores the entry as follows:

Et in tempore Guorthigerni regis Britanie Saxones peruenerunt in Britanniam, ⟨id est⟩ in anno Incarnacionis Christi, sicut ⟨S⟩libine abas Iae in Ripum ciuitate inuenit uel reperit ab Incarnacione Domini anni.D.usque a Kl.ian.in.xii.luna ut aiunt alii i⟨s⟩tis.ccc.annis a quo tenuerunt Saxones Britanniam usque ad annum supradictum.

To this passage, meaningless as it stands, Grosjean has provided a skilful interpretation.

We first notice some traces of a Celtic background: *ciuitas* is a not uncommon Irish translation into Latin of 'monastery'; and the ferial and lunar notation is that of Irish annals. Why should Slebhine, abbot of Iona 752–67, find himself in Ripon? In part, at least, because since the breach over Easter reckoning had been closed, in 716 (*HE* v. 22), with Iona and its dependent monasteries thenceforward reckoning Easter in the Dionysiac manner, it was natural for an abbot to visit what had been one of the daughter churches in Northumbria.[1] Why, then, should Slebhine make a note about the *Aduentus Saxonum*? The *anni D* of the Chartres manuscript is incomprehensible; perhaps the exemplar was damaged at this point, and

---

[1] Ripon was originally under the Celtic dispensation; it had been given by Alhfrith, son of Oswiu, to some who followed the customs of Aidan, but was soon taken over by Wilfrid, about 660 (*HE*, III. 25).

the transcriber could not puzzle it out, or would not try to find the true figure. From Table 2 (above, p. 35), it is seen that epact XII, the age of the moon 'on the Kalends of January', occurs in the thirteenth year of a Dionysiac cycle. Since these particulars repeat themselves throughout the 95-year term, Slebhine could observe that epact XII marked the year 753, part of his first as abbot; and further, subtracting twice 95 years, A.D. 563 is arrived at – the date when Columba founded Iona. 'La coincidence devait le frapper' (Grosjean 1960b: 388).[2] If historians do not like coincidences, nevertheless such things do occur: and the material was there for Slebhine to see whenever he went to Ripon, and to note down. On independent grounds, the life of Columba by Adomnan, the year 563 is most probable (Anderson and Anderson 1961: 66–7).[3]

Subtracting 300 years from 753, we arrive at 453. There is no particular reason to suppose, with Grosjean, that this figure for the *Aduentus Saxonum* is dependent on, or derived from, Bede's *Historia*, where the process is spread over the seven years of Marcian and Valentinian, after 449 (*recte* 450). The form of the date preserved at Ripon is entirely different; it is precise, couched in Dionysiac terms, and not referred to an imperial reign. How this figure may have been reached will be a topic in the next chapter. Meanwhile we can suppose that the calculation, for what it is worth, is derived from material at Canterbury. Wilfrid had paid a visit there, and Ceolfrith too (*HAA*: 389), some years later, about 670 (Plummer 1896: II, 372), and other visitors from Ripon are not to be excluded. If the arguments of Chapter 4 are valid, and the Dionysiac system was becoming known, in Northumbria at least, by about 660, then the calculation could have been made in its present form at any time afterwards. Whether Bede knew of it we cannot tell. Ceolfrith, a link with Ripon, had died in 716, long before Albinus put the notion

---

[2] Taking 550 as the last of a 19-year cycle (Table 2), the thirteenth year after, with epact XII, will be 563.

[3] Bede says that in 565 Columba *uenit de Hibernia...Britanniam, praedicaturus uerbum Dei prouinciis septentrionalium Pictorum* (*HE*, III. 4). But in *HE*, V. 24 he distinctly implies that Iona was founded after this preaching to the nothern Picts, which appears to be a mistake; the figure was got by subtracting 150 years from A.D. 715, when the Iona monks decided to abandon the Celtic-84, (*HE*, III. 4), adopting Roman customs the next year; and Bede might have been prudent to add *circiter* or *plus minus*, as was often his habit.

of writing an ecclesiastical history into Bede's mind. We ought in any case to be suspicious of the neat round number 300.

We turn now to another aspect of annalistic writing in Northumbria: the status of the Indiction as a prime reckoning, not with Bede but among his immediate successors. The leading figures of the school at York, Archbishop Egbert, Archbishop Ethelbert and Alcuin the Deacon, master and pupil or friend and friend, are in a line of succession for seventy years or so after Bede's death; and besides this obvious and established chain of descent there will have been collaterals of whom we can form only a faint idea. Those seventy years were favourable to the growth of annals, the earliest extending from 731 to 766, annexed to several copies of the *Historia Ecclesiastica*, and forming the so-called 'Continuation of Bede'; a few may have been compiled before his death in 735. For the most part they survive only in late manuscripts, and in their present form have been interpolated; thus the entry for 757 is drawn from the common stock of the Anglo-Saxon Chronicle, not earlier than the latter part of the ninth century. In any case they do not by themselves speak decisively about the Indiction.[4] But they, or materials closely allied with them, form part of the Northumbrian Annals, from 732 (*recte* 731) to 802, now embedded in the *Historia Regum* ascribed to Simeon of Durham.[5] At one time it was supposed that Simeon had drawn on the 'northern recension' of the Anglo-Saxon Chronicle, now represented by versions D and E; but William Stubbs, in his introduction to Roger de Hoveden's chronicle (1868: I, xxvi–xxx), demonstrated that the annals preserved by Simeon were the source upon which these versions of the Chronicle, or rather their archetype, had relied. When the word 'Chronicle' is used here without qualification, it refers to the northern recension.

More recently, Hunter Blair (1963) has argued that the manuscript of the *Historia Regum* dates from about 1170, and was written by a monk of Sawley, in the West Riding of Yorkshire just over the border from Lancashire, near Clitheroe – a monk evidently of antiquarian tastes and, to judge by his handling of place-names, a careful

---

4 Text in Plummer 1896: I, 361–3; translation in *EHD*: 259–60, with comments.
5 Text in Arnold 1885: II, 3–283; translation of extracts in *EHD*: 239–51, which selects information not to be found in other sources.

transcriber of what came his way; but the manuscript tradition is complicated (Offler 1970). As a first step, then, we can compare the dates in the Chronicle versions, representing their archetype, and the dates given by the Northumbrian Annals, whose compiler (or compilers) will simply be called Simeon of Durham – here abbreviated to SD.[6] In addition, Hart (1970) has published a preliminary account of annals copied down at Ramsey (here abbreviated to RA), somewhere about the year 1090. This abbey was founded by Oswald, bishop of Worcester and archbishop of York; it is therefore not surprising that some of these annals are based on a D, E version of the Chronicle, the archetype of which had to all appearances been put together at York about a century earlier (Whitelock, Introduction to *ASC*: xiv). Yet in the section from 732 onwards these Ramsay Annals seem also to depend partly on a copy of the Northumbrian Annals; that is, RA has connexions with SD. And as with SD there are likewise events drawn directly or indirectly from Bede's Recapitulation (*HE*, v. 24), and the Continuation already mentioned.[7] Unfortunately the compiler of RA was not always careful in transcribing dates; in places a revising hand has put *inanis* alongside a few of them (Hart 1970: 39). The compiler is also far more interested in kings than in bishops; on the other hand, SD preserves details of episcopal consecration which are of great value in fixing a precise sequence of dates – subject to qualifications now to be discussed.

Earlier we have seen that a king need not succeed immediately

[6] This convention, though inaccurate, is now established. It appears that, apart from two lengthy interpolations, the Annals were edited and brought to their present form about the year 900 (Hunter Blair 1963: 117–8). But in their original form they could have been compiled not much later than 800. It should be added that a thorough study would take in Henry of Huntingdon and the Chronicle of Melrose, but Stubbs's edition of Hoveden here represents the secondary sources.

[7] Hart (1970: 35–7) thinks that the Recapitulation is based on 'a series of Latin annals entered against Easter tables', in this opinion closely though not exactly following Jones (1947: 32). Yet it is not clear why an unwieldy Easter table should be resorted to, when a single sheet of parchment would suffice. Jones's remark, that 'scratch paper in our sense of the word did not exist', may well apply to the smaller monasteries. But the *Codex Amiatinus* alone required more than 500 calfskins (Bruce-Mitford 1969); and since only the best were selected, there will have been a supply of 'seconds'. The views of Levison carry weight: the Recapitulation he considers to be 'a kind of skeleton or guide'...'remnants of preparatory work' (1935: 136).

after, or very soon after, the death of his predecessor, though often his passage to the throne will have been smooth. A bishop is differently situated: vacancy in the see, long or short, takes nobody by surprise. Other problems make their appearance towards the end of an episcopate. For various reasons a new bishop might be consecrated while the old was still alive. As an example, Laurentius was consecrated by Augustine to succeed at Canterbury (*HE*, II. 4); and it is not enough to plead that Augustine was compelled to take this step, for Laurentius could have sought episcopal orders in Gaul, as in 692 Berhtwold was to do (*HE*, V. 8) and Wilfrid had done earlier still. Moreover, this act was uncanonical, since Pope Hilarius in 465 had forbidden the consecration of a successor by the reigning prelate (Plummer 1896: II, 82). But for reasons of health, or an inclination towards the settled life of a community, a diocesan might be in want of help during the latter days of his work; and in spite of the admonition by Hilarius, bishops may have had good reason to secure a man of their own choice. In Bede, often frustrated by lack of information, the details of episcopal succession are not always clear.[8] Yet about 673, when Bisi of East Anglia fell sick, two bishops were consecrated to replace him (*HE*, IV. 5), and Bosel, bishop of the Hwicce, in poor health, stood down in favour of Oftfor, about 691–2 (*HE*, IV. 21). John of Beverley, retiring to his monastery at *In Derauuda*, consecrated Wilfrid II to York (*HE*, V. 6). Again (*ASC*: year 744) Daniel resigned Winchester to Hunfrith. Under the year 780, SD records that Archbishop Ethelbert of York died, having in his lifetime consecrated Eanbald to the see; and in the same year Cynewulf of Lindisfarne resigned in favour of Higbald, dying three years later (ed. Arnold 1885: II, 47). On the continent, before 739, Willibrord had consecrated a type of suffragan, known as *chorepiscopus* or country bishop – once again in defiance of Canon Law, which forbade more than one bishop in a diocese (Levison 1946: 65–8). In some cases a Papal relaxation of the law may have been procured.

England during the seventh century was the scene of constant missionary effort and enterprise, the process continuing with the

---

[8] On Bede's native sources, and the limitations of his knowledge, see Kirby (1966). It will be allowed, however, that missionary bishops or infant monasteries did not always have the time or the means to indulge in the luxury of annals. On Northumbrian limitations generally, see Bonner (1973: 88–90)

foundation of a bishopric at Whithorn, about 730, in the person of Pecthelm (HE, v. 23). These conditions may in part account for the evidence of irregularity, going back to the time of Augustine himself, and it is not possible to lay down inflexible rules about the occurrence of a consecration during the predecessor's lifetime, or, as will be seen, the particular day. In the Western Church, a Sunday or sometimes a major feast was nearly always preferred; yet this variety of choice was occasionally flouted (Grosjean 1960a: 260–64). When examining the material in SD, RA, the Anglo-Saxon Chronicle, and other sources, these complications will become more evident.

Although a preliminary study of SD, as compared with the Chronicle, has tended to show that the former is generally more reliable, the text is by no means free from mistakes or uncertainty (Harrison 1967, on which most of the following remarks are based). The first annal in SD, for 732, should be dated to 731 (EHD: 239; Hunter Blair 1963: 94). Under 734 the timing of a lunar eclipse is approximately correct, and only a simple emendation is required to restore the true day, 24 January (Hunter Blair 1963: 94–5); then the death of Archbishop Tatwine is assigned to 30 July, and the consecration of Frithuberht to Hexham follows on 8 September, a Wednesday. But this anomaly is explained by the festal character of the day, the Nativity of the Virgin Mary (Grosjean 1960a: 261). Again, at a later time, the Chronicle under 762 (recte 763) refers to the consecration of Frithuwold to Whithorn on 15 August, a Sunday in 734, in the sixth year of King Ceolwulf – an entry not preserved by SD.[9] Since Ceolwulf's predecessor died on 9 May 729 (HE, v. 23) the year of consecration would appear to be correct, unless there was a long interregnum, neither implied by Bede nor supported by considerations to be discussed presently. It will be observed there is no break in the year 734 between the death of Tatwine and the consecration of Frithuberht, apart from other days; thus the Greek Indiction of 1 September appears to be ruled out. Under 740 SD records the death of Earnwine die x kal.Ian.feria vii,

---

[9] It has been suggested (Earle and Plummer 1899: II, lxix) that the Chronicler had access to a version of the Northumbrian Annals which was rather fuller than the version available to SD. This theme has been developed (Harrison 1960), and though some of the conclusions should now be modified the main drift is not affected. The details of Frithuwold's consecration are not in Roger de Hoveden.

Saturday, 23 December. As Hunter Blair points out (1963: 95), 23 December 740 falls on a Friday, and he goes on to suggest that in place of *feria vii* we could read *feria iiii* – in itself plausible enough – and thus, if the year changed in September, the true date would become Wednesday 23 December 739. Without invoking an Indictional year it is possible to read *ix kal.Ian.feria vii*, a figure supported by Roger de Hoveden (ed. Stubbs 1868: 1, 6). This writer, about the year 1200, unquestionably had access to a copy of the Northumbrian Annals, or of material derived from them at second hand (*EHD*: 118).

After eclipses correctly dated in 741 and 752, the latter year corroborated by RA, a significant discrepancy has been found by Hunter Blair (1963: 95). Under 756 an eclipse of the moon is recorded by SD on *viii kl.Decembris*, 24 November; but the reference must be to the eclipse of 23 November 755, the account being of more than ordinary interest because it seems to describe an occultation of the star 114 Taurus (Newton 1972: 589–92). Hunter Blair then goes on to say: 'If the writer reckoned the day to begin at sunset of the previous evening, he was correct in dating the eclipse to 24 November, and if, moreover, he reckoned his year to begin in September, he was equally correct in calling the year 756.' This opinion is hard to resist (Harrison 1967: 197). If the writer of the annals, the original compiler, had not seen the eclipse for himself, the information may well have come to him from somebody who still thought in terms of Indictional reckoning; it is not, however, derived from the Continuation of Bede. The fact of the eclipse occurring later in the annal than an event dated 1 August may only mean that the information was added later, and does not rule out 755. Although evidence will slowly emerge that the bulk of the annals in SD seem to be based on a change of year at Christmas (Midwinter), the faint survival of another system is not altogether surprising. In this connexion it may be noted that a Northumbrian letter of 773 is dated by Indiction alone (*EHD*: 766–7), though from being addressed to Charles the Great an addition of the *Annus Domini* might not have been called for. Earlier, in 734, when formally writing to Egbert of York, even Bede himself was constrained to use the formal style of the Indiction (*EHD*: 735–45).

At this point we should observe that in 754 begins a dislocation of years in the Anglo-Saxon Chronicle, 'by which' says Whitelock, 'all extant versions are dated two – or even further on three – years too early up to the annal for 845' (*EHD*: 30, n.5); moreover, from 759 'the parts of these annals peculiar to the northern recension come from a source without the chronological dislocation of the Chronicle, and are therefore usually two years earlier than the events in the parts of the annal common to all versions' (*ASC*: 32, n. 4). The qualification expressed by 'usually' begins perhaps to apply in the year before. Under 758, SD notices that Eadberht of Northumbria resigned the crown to his son Oswulf, an event dated by the Chronicle to 757. The former says that Oswulf in the course of one year held, lost and forfeited the kingdom, being killed on 27 July, which should therefore be in 759 – agreeing with the Chronicle, whereas the Continuation of Bede gives 758 (this last figure probably being wrong, according to *EHD*: 260, n. 2). The accession of Aethelwold Moll, on 5 August 759, after an interval of just under a fortnight, is supported by RA, Roger de Hoveden (ed. Stubbs 1868: I, 7) and by SD's further notice that in his third year a battle was fought on 6 August, ending *post triduum* on a Sunday; and unless the battle began late in the day and ended early on a morning, perhaps at some stage *iv* days has been misread as *iii*. And 9 August was a Sunday in 761, the year being in agreement with the Chronicle. In 763, however, several troubles are encountered. Three versions of the Chronicle, A, D, E and the bilingual F which depends to a varying extent on A and E, place a hard winter in 761; the dislocation by two years, mentioned earlier, will justify a correction to 763; and the fact that version C gives 762 may result from a blank annal at 761, not in other versions, so that the entry has been put against a wrong number. SD, however, talks of 'an immense snowfall, hardened into ice', with much else of a like nature, from the beginning of winter almost to the middle of spring, and dates 764. He then says, rather vaguely, 'in these times' Frithuwold of Whithorn died and Pehtwine was appointed bishop in his place. There is no annal for 763 in SD, but his reference to the weather should preferably be dated 763–4. Neither the Continuation of Bede nor RA give any help.

We have seen that under 762 (more correctly, it may appear, 763) the northern recension of the Chronicle records the death of Frithu-wold of Whithorn, he having been consecrated on 15 August 734, in Coeolwulf's sixth year, then adding that he had been bishop for twenty-nine years, pointing to 763 for his death, the day being given as 7 May. His successor Pehtwine was consecrated on 17 July, a Sunday in 763. Thus it would not appear that Ceolwulf succeeded after a long interregnum, if any; and the latter part of SD's annal for 764, as it now stands, could well be dated a year too late. In the next year SD records the consecration of Jaenberht to Canterbury, the common stock of the Chronicle (A and C) adding that this event took place on the fortieth day after Christmas Day; the year is given as 762, by mere error for 763 (recte 765). Here we should not over-look the bugbear of inclusive counting; but Plummer was surely right in concluding that 2 February 765 is meant, which although a Saturday in this year was also the Feast of the Purification (Earle & Plummer 1899: II, 49–50). Then in the next year, 766, when the Continuation of Bede comes to an end, it and the northern recen-sion of the Chronicle and SD are in agreement over the deaths of Archbishop Egbert of York and Bishop Frithuberht of Hexham; the Chronicler and SD give 19 November for the former, and SD alone gives 23 December for the latter. At this point Christmas dating seems to be becoming clear, for in 767 the successors to York and Hexham, Ethelbert and Alhmund, were consecrated on viii kal. Mai., which is 24 April and a Friday, according to SD. The Chronicle gives 766, rather than which 767 might appear in better accord with Alcuin's statement that Ethelbert died on 8 November in the fourteenth year from his consecration, 780 according to SD (Earle & Plummer 1899: II, 52); Grosjean also seems to incline in this direc-tion (1960a: 262). Yet perhaps the month has been corrupted by a transcriber: reading viii kal. Mar., 22 February is arrived at, which was Sexagesima in 767. Thus an episcopate from 22 February 767 to 8 November 780 would be in harmony with Alcuin's figure, though in fact Ethelbert had effectively handed over his duties some two years earlier (Earle & Plummer 1899: II, 52). Possibly, however, we should read vii kal. Mai., 25 April, St Mark's day.

It is now necessary to lay the ground for an examination of SD's annals from 768 to 790. A century ago, almost exactly, R. Pauli drew attention to a series of entries which refer to continental affairs (summary in Hunter Blair 1963 : 92–4). They include the death of Pippin (768) and of Carloman (771); Charles the Great's first campaign against the Saxons (772), his capture of Pavia (774) and second Saxon campaign (775). As Hunter Blair observes, the entries 'are certainly to be regarded as primary sources of information, not merely as derivatives of continental annals'; moreover they serve to check the accuracy of SD at this stage. Under 774 the Chronicle and SD, confirmed by RA, record the succession of Ethelred to the Northumbrian throne, followed by Charles's second campaign of 775, in SD only. Then in 776 the Chronicle states that Pehtwine of Whithorn died on 19 September, having been bishop for fourteen years; the consecration of his successor Ethelbert is referred to 15 June 777. There is no annal of 776 in SD, who places the death of Pehtwine in 777, after being in charge of Whithorn for fourteen years, and merely adds that Ethelbert succeeded him. Yet we have seen that 763 is the most likely year for Pehtwine's consecration. The Chronicler ought to have arrived at this figure by adding the twenty-nine years of Frithuberht's episcopate to the year of consecreation, 734. Instead he dates the annal to 762 (*ASC*: 32); then, adding another fourteen years, Pehtwine's death is entered under 776.[10]

If 777 is the correct year, as in SD, then Pehtwine died on 19 September, and his successor at Whithorn, Ethelbert, was consecreated on 15 June, a Sunday. Yet if the irregularities already mentioned are borne in mind (above, p. 103), this departure from the usual chain of events is not astonishing. Archbishop Ethelbert of York, we may presume, will have officiated; or, if there was in truth a technical breach of Canon Law, condoned it. He himself was to retire in 778, in favour of Eanbald (Earle & Plummer 1899: II, 52). Moreover, he can scarcely have been ignorant of the precedents in Bede's *Historia*, still less of the fact that Wilfrid II of York had resigned in favour of Egbert, his immediate predecessor. Although

---

10 Roger de Hoveden, perhaps following a copy of the Northumbrian Annals, assigns Pehtwine's death clearly to 777, but adds *xx° iv° anno episcopatus sui* (ed. Stubbs 1868: I, 23). Apart from the mistake about length of time, here as elsewhere also it is sometimes hard to decide whether anyone died after *z* years or in the *z*th year.

this particular situation is a trifle obscure, we can now begin to construct Table 7 (modified from Harrison 1967: 194–5). Here between 774 and 790, there appears to be a more or less systematic error in the Chronicle entries, which is further complicated by the information provided under the year 778. According to SD, in Ethelred's fourth year *tres duces, Ealdwulf uidelicet, Cynewulf et Ecga...necati sunt...iii kal.Octobris*, 29 September.[11] In favour of Hart's contention (1970: 37) that RA drew directly on a copy of the Northumbrian Annals, the Ramsey entry for 774 has *anno iiii regni eius* (Ethelred) *tres duces occisi sunt*. The Chronicle, however, has another tale to tell: Ealdwulf son of Bosa was killed at Coniscliffe, Cynewulf and Ecga at *Helathirnum*, on 22 March. Then Hoveden (ed. Stubbs 1868: I, 24) here seems to be following the style of the Chronicle account, in separating the death of Ealdwulf from the other ealdormen, and preserving the place-names. Perhaps, therefore, the archetypal entry ran somewhat as follows: 778, Ealdwulf son of Bosa was killed at Coniscliffe on 29 September; 779, Cynewulf and Ecga were killed at *Helathirnum* on 22 March. At least a transcriber of SD appears to have simplified the circumstantial detail now furnished by the Chronicle, or was working from a shorter copy of the Northumbrian Annals.[12]

Comment on the remaining entries also begins in 778, under which the Chronicle places the accession of King Aelfwold; it is supported by Simeon's own work, the *Historia Dunelmensis Ecclesiae*, where the resignation of Bishop Cynewulf of Lindisfarne, 780, is said to have taken place in Aelfwold's third year (ed. Arnold 1882: I, 50). Yet the Chronicle, on internal evidence, is far from accurate, and Simeon's *Historia*, partly based on the Northumbrian Annals, does not always carry conviction.[13] When referring the accession of Aelfwold to 778, the Chronicle seems to depend on a reign of four

[11] The Chronicle translates *duces* by 'high reeves;' Whitelock prefers the normal meaning 'ealdormen' (*EHD*: 244, n. 6).

[12] Compare the remark of Whitelock (*ASC*: 34, n. 1) that 'Simeon, who does not distinguish between two events, gives the date as 29 September.'

[13] Thus at the beginning of II. 4 (ed. Arnold 1882: I, 49), Aethelwold Moll comes to the throne in 760 (SD, 759) and is made to reign six years, whereas there can be little doubt that he lost the kingdom to Alhred in 765 (SD). Then Simeon says that in Alhred's ninth year, which should be 773, Ethelred succeeded, though both the Chronicle and SD agree over 774, which is also Hoveden's year.

TABLE 7

The uncorrected dates of the Chronicle and SD are given in round brackets ( )

	Historia Regum (SD)	*Chronicle* (D, E)
774	Accession of K. Ethelred. Capture of Pavia	Accession of K. Ethelred
775	Second Saxon campaign of Charles the Great	[No annal]
776	[No annal]	—
777	Consecration of Bp. Ethelbert [no day given] Death of Bp. Pehtwine, 19 Sept.	Consecration of Bp. Ethelbert, 15 June. Death of Bp. Pehtwine, 19 Sept. (776)
778	Death of Ealdorman Ealdwulf and two others, 29 Sept. [No place given]a	Death of Ealdorman Ealdwulf at Coniscliffe, 29 Sept.a
779	Accession of K. Aelfwold	Death of two ealdormen at *Helathirnum*, 22 March (778). Accession of K. Aelfwold (778)
780	Abp. Ethelbert dies, 8 Nov. [day from Alcuin]	Abp. Ethelbert dies (779)
781	Apb. Eanbald receives the *pallium* (780). Tilberht consecrated, 2 Oct.	Apb. Eanbald receives the *pallium* (780). Tilberht consecrated, 2 Oct. (780)
782	[No annal]	—
783	Werburh diesb	Werburh dies (782)b
784	[No annal]	[No annal independent of the common stock]
785	[No annal]	—
786	Abbot Botwine dies. Legatine Synodc	Abbot Botwine dies (785). Legatine Synod (785)c
787	Synod at *Pincanheale*, 2 Sept.d	Synod at *Pincanheale*, 2 Sept. (788)d
788	Death of K. Aelfwold, 23 Sept.	Death of K. Aelfwold, 23 Sept. (789)
789	[No annal]	—
790	K. Osred expelled	K. Osred expelled

a Supposing two distinct events which are not separated by SD, who places the death of three ealdorman on 29 September, whereas the Chronicle makes them all die on 22 March.

b Widow of K. Ceolred of Mercia, later abbess (SD).

c Professor Whitelock suggests that because the Chronicle (D, E) tacks on the Legatine Synod to the record of the Chelsea Synod in the common stock (A, B and C), wrongly dated 785 (*recte* 787), and confuses them, the previous annals became dislocated.

d Neither the place nor the purpose of this synod are known.

years by his predecessor Ethelred, from 774, whereas SD from the
same year gives *uix quinque annos*. Then from 778 the Chronicle
calculates that Aelfwold reigned ten years – the length of time in
agreement with SD – but assigns his death to 23 September 789.
We revert with more confidence, then, to SD, who states that Aelfwold's third year included 2 October 781; hence he should have
succeeded after 2 October 778. His death on 23 September 788,
supposing 'ten years' to be a round number, might suggest that
these regnal years were counted from early in 779; we have seen
that two high reeves, or ealdormen, may have been killed as late as
22 March 779, and SD places responsibility for all the deaths on
Ethelred, who then, says the Chronicle, was driven out by Aelfwold.
The interval from March 779 to September 788 is as consonant with
'ten years' as the Chronicle's interval March 779, as corrected, to
September 789; and the Chronicle's uncorrected 778 can hardly be
sustained. It should be added that RA puts the accession of Aelfwold
in 779, together with Hoveden.

Under 779, version E of the Chronicle places the death of Bearn
on 24 December, version D on 25 December; thus if the year
changed at Christmas the latter figure would indicate 780, in agreement with SD. The death of Archbishop Ethelbert of York also
seems to be correctly fixed by SD to 780 (Earle & Plummer 1899:
II, 52). But neither source would appear to be accurate over Eanbald's reception of the *pallium*, dated by both to 780; Alcuin, who
had been sent to Rome to fetch it, on his return met Charles the
Great at Parma in the spring of 781 (Levison 1946: 243), the year
also in Roger de Hoveden (ed. Stubbs 1868: I, 24). In the same year
there is a puzzling entry in SD, stating that Alhmund of Hexham
died on 7 September and Tilberht was consecrated in his room on
vi non.Octobris, 2 October; Hoveden agrees with the year; but the
Chronicle, supporting the day, gives 780 for the year. And 2 October
was not a Sunday in 780 (Monday) or 781 (Tuesday), and is not a
major festival. Grosjean offers no solution (1960a: 262). In Willibrord's Calendar, however, the original hand marks 3 October, *v
non.Oct.*, as the commemoration of two priests, both named Hewald,
who were killed while serving with the mission to Germany (ed.
Wilson 1918). They were and still are venerated at Cologne, and

Bede devotes almost a whole chapter to them (*HE*, v. 10). Possibly
the eve of their festival, or the day itself if emended, was thought to
be suitable for a consecration; Northumbrians were justifiably proud
of Willibrord and his companions. Lame or improbable though this
attempt at explanation may be, any other must explain a ceremony
which appears deliberately to have dodged a Sunday and the Feast
of St Michael on 29 September.

The Legatine Synod is assigned to 786 by SD (text in Haddan and
Stubbs 1873: III, 447–62; translation in *EHD*: 770–74). It is dated
A.D. 786, the tenth Indiction, with no month or day. Thus the year
might be ambiguous, because according to Bede's rule, discussed
earlier, the greater part of 786 belongs to the ninth Indiction; but
we shall see, later in this chapter, that the Indiction was on the way
to losing the primacy it had once enjoyed, or perhaps had already
lost it. More significant, however, is the Chronicle's dating to 785,
for no part whatever of that year fell into the tenth Indiction. But in
790 the Chronicle and SD agree over the expulsion of Osred, thus
completing the particulars in Table 7. In the same year, too, all
sources agree over the return to power of Ethelred, including RA;
the latter by mistake says *Osred dolo occiditur*, though under 792 it
correctly states that Osred was captured and killed – on 14 September, in the Chronicle and SD. As to the remaining entries, the Chronicle is most probably right in assigning the consecration of Badwulf
to 791, as against 790, since 17 July was a Sunday in that year
(*EHD*: 246, n. 7; Grosjean 1960a: 263); both it and SD are in general
agreement over the death of Osred, 14 September, and the marriage
of Ethelred, 29 September, in 792, which would exclude the Bedan
Indiction as a starting point for the year. Although SD records the
death of Pope Hadrian, on 26 December, under the year 794 (*recte*
25 December 795), and the Chronicle is also in a state of confusion,
the problems have been discussed already (Harrison 1967: 197) and
need not be expanded here.

Following Hunter Blair (1963: 93 and 95–6) we may note the
confirmation of SD's dates for Charles the Great's victory over the
Avars in 795, and his visit to Rome in 800, besides the lunar eclipse
of 796, correct to the day and hour. A small emendation (earlier
proposed in *EHD*: 249, n. 2) will fix the election of Eanbald II to the

see of York on Sunday 14 August 796. In the next year, the Chronicle and SD combine into an informative sequence of events: Eanbald II of York received the *pallium* on 8 September (Nativity of the Virgin Mary), Ethelbert of Hexham died on 16 October, and *post excursum paucarum dierum, hoc est iii.kal.Novembris,* Heardred was consecrated in his place. This day, 30 October, was a Monday in 797, but a Sunday in 798 (*ASC*: 38, n. 1); yet judging by the prompt attention to vacant sees in Northumbria at this period, and the words 'after a few days', it is most likely that Hexham will not have been without a bishop for just over a year. An emendation to *iv.kal.Novembris* is therefore reasonable. Eanbald I of York, dying on 10 August 796, had a successor only four days later. Grosjean (1960a: 263) would propose 30 October 796, a Sunday, but perhaps does not make allowance enough for the overall accuracy of SD.

The remaining annals are of little account when the drift of this tedious but unavoidable enquiry comes back into view: among Bede's successors, was the beginning of a year governed by an Indiction on 1 or 24 September? The lunar eclipse of 23 November 755, recorded by SD under 756, would point to an Indictional source; beyond this particular item the available evidence, though not abundant, is in favour of Christmas (or 1 January). The years of value, with days, are: 734 (31 January, 30 July, 8 September); 765 (2 February, 30 October);[14] 781 (7 September, 2 October); 792 (14 September, 29 September); 797 (8 September, 16 October). This meagre collection excludes the figures in Table 7, which a future editor of SD might disagree with, and takes no account of paired years, where the break between them is difficult to explain unless the reckoning did change at Christmas, and more certainly did not change on 24 September. Thus 8 September 734 is followed by the death of Bede in 735 – most probably towards the end of May (Plummer 1896: 1, lxxi–lxxiii); 765 (30 October) and 766 (death of Archbishop Egbert, as in the previous footnote); 786 (Legatine

---

14 The exact day, 2 February, for Jaenberht's consecration was known, because in the common stock (A, B and C) on which the northern recension is founded; and 30 October for Aethelwold's loss of the Northumbrian kingdom seems secure enough; Alhred's succession in 765 is confirmed by the Chronicle; then both sources, together with the Continuation of Bede, agree over 766 for the death of Archbishop Egbert of York.

Synod) and 787 (2 September); 796 (28 March, precise day of a lunar eclipse, with others to 10 August) and 797 (8 September and 16 October); 800 (24 December) and 801 (15 January). Without any pretence that SD can always be relied on, or that his system of reckoning is completely uniform, as we now have it, the trend seems to be clear. And the final words derive from Alcuin, most famous of Bede's spiritual heirs: in opposition to those at the court of Charles the Great who argued in favour of the Indiction, Alcuin preferred to begin the year *cum nato Christo et crescente luce* (ed. Dümmler 1892: 231; Levison 1946: 277). Here is the Roman *sol inuictus* again.

Although, until the eighth century, information about Mercia is relatively sparse, when compared with several other kingdoms, in that century and more especially the next it happens that Mercian charters are abundant. We shall find, moreover, that some of the most useful, for the purpose in hand, are preserved in contemporary copies. When studying the use of an Indiction in this type of document, as related to the *Annus Domini* in a dating clause, evidently the charters issued on days lying between 1 or 24 September and Christmas Day or 1 January will throw the strongest light on the problems which arise. Two such documents will be considered now, partly because they help to define what the term 'contemporary copy' can in practice mean. *BCS* 378 and 379 were both issued in the year 824, *Indictione ii*, at a council held in the second year of Beornwulf of Mercia at *Clofeshoh*.[15] The former is witnessed by several bishops and then, before the laymen, by Beonna *electus*; the latter similarly but by Beonna *episcopus* (of Hereford). Moreover the latter alone is dated 30 October and employs rather different phrases and expressions. Leaving aside, for consideration in due course, the fact that 30 October 824 should be in the third Indiction, there remains the query - were there two councils at *Clofeshoh* in 824, separated by the interval between Beonna's election and consecration, or only one? The matter seems to have been settled by Brooks.[16] In his view, 'there is no significance in the fact that *BCS* 378 and 379 are in

---

[15] A place not yet identified, in spite of many efforts.
[16] In Harrison (1973b: 60, n. 3), from which paper most of the following section is derived.

different formulas. *BCS* 378 is in favour of Canterbury, and drafted by the Canterbury scriptorium, *BCS* 379 in favour of Worcester and drafted by that scriptorium.' Allowing that the news of Beonna's consecration will have reached Worcester first, none the less these two documents, originating at the same Council, may well have been written down weeks or possibly months apart. A further point is that among the witnesses of *BCS* 379 we find a man Nothelm, *praeco a domino Eugenio papa* (Thorogood 1933: 358); *praeco*, herald, can here be taken to mean 'representative', and since Eugenius was elected on 24 May 824 the year is not in doubt.

The principle of working backwards, from the more secure dates to the less secure, will be applied here to the Mercian evidence. Beornwulf's predecessor Ceolwulf I was 'consecrated' – whatever that may mean – according to *BCS* 370 (contemporary copy) on 17 September 822, the fifteenth Indiction. If calculated from the Greek Indiction of 1 September the true year should be 821; yet 17 September in 822 was an Ember Day, suitable for ordinations, though not in 821; and this fact alone will raise doubt over the Indictional reckoning. Better information comes from the next earlier reign, of Cenwulf (Coenwulf), which has the advantage that documents are frequently dated by regnal years, in addition to other styles; and it seems fairly clear, from other sources, that he came to the throne between 14 and 17 December 796. This narrow limit is advantageous, for example, when considering a series of documents also emanating from a council at *Clofeshoh* in the year 803, the eleventh Indiction. They are *BCS* 308, 309, 310 and 312, and are of special importance for three reasons. First, *BCS* 310 and 312 are contemporary copies; and second, an assembly which included the archbishop of Canterbury, several other bishops and a few prominent abbots (including Beonna *presbiter abbas* who is presumably the future bishop of Hereford) will have represented 'official' thinking and practice. The third point of importance lies in the detail: *BCS* 308 is dated to 6 October, *BCS* 309 to 12 October, in Cenwulf's seventh year, *feria v* – and 12 October was a Thursday in 803; *BCS* 310 and 312 also bear the date 12 October. From these charters alone (and more evidence can be found in Harrison 1973b) the conclusion seems to be that, by the early part of the ninth century, the Indiction was being copied mechanically from the column next to the *Annus Domini* in a Dionysiac table (above, p. 35). Otherwise expressed, the Indictional number is one too few, if the year began on 1 or 24 September, because any day in October 803 falls strictly within the twelfth Indiction. The testimony of two reliable transcripts and of two contemporary copies, all giving the eleventh Indiction, is difficult to shake.

Charters from the reign of Offa, though sometimes embellished with phrase like *Indictione viiii, decenoui xi.luna viii*, are not normally helpful to this particular line of enquiry. But *BCS* 236, from the Worcester cartulary, is probably genuine and is dated 780, third Indiction, *passio sancti Mauricii*, 22 September. It has been argued by Chaplais (1968) that this document shows use of the Bedan Indiction of 24 September; yet the observation would be true only if we were assured that the scribe did not merely copy the Indiction from a Dionysiac table, as already suggested. Taking leave of Mercia, and moving into the next century, the genuine *BCS* 419, from Kent, reads 838, *Indictione.i.iii feria.die.uero.xiii.kl.Decembr.* and 19 November was a Tuesday in 838.[17] Again, the contemporary copy *BCS* 449 has 845 *Indictione viii, die ii feria, xvi kl.Decembr.* and 16 November was a Monday in 845. These Indictions, keeping in mind the time of year, are also one too few.

Yet the conclusions can only be tentative, in this sense: of the several kingdoms which are involved, none had a 'chancery' in any recognisable form, and in practice there may have been more variation of style than we are prepared to admit. Unless contemporary copies are available, which is none too often, there can be difficulty in deciding whether correction, omission or addition of a dating clause could have taken place. But the councils at *Clofeshoh* in 803 and 824 were preceded by a different type of record, the Northumbrian Annals (SD), where in spite of doubt or hesitation, and in spite of the lunar eclipse in November 755, there remains a positive balance of evidence in favour of a yearly reckoning from Christmas or 1

---

[17] The statement in Harrison (1973b: 65) that this charter came from Wessex is, unfortunately, wrong. There is another mistake on the same page: *BCS* 451, of 26 December, tenth Indiction, should be dated 846 in modern reckoning, not 848 as stated. If the year changed at Christmas, as most probably it did, the year is 847 by ninth-century reckoning.

January. In some cases these days may have been regarded as more or less equivalent since the Octave of Christmas was a season of feast and rejoicing; and the chronologer should perhaps make allowance, as usual, for variation in practice at different times and in different places. The chief point, the only point of importance, is that soon after the eighth century had begun the Indiction ceased to be the prime reckoning for purposes of administration or as a guide to the chronicler and historian.

In the light of these considerations we proceed next to the collection of documents which form the Anglo-Saxon Chronicle. Their relationship has been explained and reviewed by Whitelock (Introduction to *ASC*); here for the moment we shall be taking account only of a series of annals belonging to the latter half of the ninth century. The current view of the chronology in these annals is derived from Beaven (1917), who thought that from the year 851, at latest, the reckoning was calculated from 'autumn'. There can be little or no doubt that his opinion is correct, though we should not be too readily persuaded to look for a more precise solution. The text of the Chronicle furnishes a very meagre supply of detail: after Easter (853); in the harvest season (877); after Twelfth night, at Easter, the seventh week after Easter (878); an eclipse, but not even the month given (879); before Christmas (885); a comet, after Easter at the Rogation days or before (891); the death of King Alfred, six days before All Saints' day (900). The last item apart, woolly writing of this character does not suggest an urge to restore the Indiction in either of its forms; the word *tacencircol* never occurs. It is very rare in Old English, being found only in two Sherborne charters.[18]

The autumn reckoning is no doubt connected with the circumstance that the Danish armies sought their winter quarters at this season, or a little later. In other words, the chronicle writers were thinking in terms of a campaigning year rather than a calendar year, more especially in the annals from 892 to 896 (Whitelock, in Earle

---

[18] After the reign of Alfred, the problems of dating are not quite at an end; for a detailed discussion see Whitelock in the 1952 reprint of Earle and Plummer (1899). In some sections, for instance, the year began on 25 March, Lady Day. It should be noticed that a source used by Aethelweard, correctly giving 26 October 899 for Alfred's death, did not use an Indictional year (ed. Campbell 1962: xlii).

and Plummer 1899, reprint of 1952: cxli). Nevertheless it is such a peculiar and individual style as to raise the question of where this section of the Chronicle can have been put together. In the opinion of Stenton (1925; *PASE*: 106–15) it was compiled for a person of quality in the south-western shires. Couched in diocesan terms, Sherborne would be implied rather than Winchester. Perhaps it is only of incidental interest that two bishops of Sherborne were fighters: Ealhstan (824 to 867) took the field against the Danes in 845, and his successor Heahmund was killed in battle at *Meretun* in 871. The views of Stenton have been challenged by Davis (1971) in a series of arguments which are not easy to summarise; but in the present context it is only suitable to observe that Carolingian influences did not extend to the technique of annalistic writing. Thus the contemporary Annals of St Bertin (ed. Grat *et al.* 1964), which run from 835 to 882, are far more precise in chronological detail; moreover, their style of dating is conventional and in no way peculiar, although the Northmen were also a pest on that side of the Channel. At all events, the revival of an Indiction as the beginning of the year would appear to be very unlikely in the latter half of the ninth century, to judge from the internal evidence of the Chronicle itself, let alone the evidence of charters.

Briefly, then, it would seem probable that in the seventh century, covering the early part of Bede's life, the Greek Indiction of 1 September reigned supreme. It was the style employed by the Papal chancery, and the earliest English charter to have survived in contemporary manuscript, *BCS* 45, Hlothere's grant of 679, is dated by Indiction alone. Moreover in Chapter 4 we recognised that when the style of *Annus Domini* appears, in the later years of the seventh century, it is found only in transcripts – though cartulary copies can be reliable. But after about 735 (as in *BCS* 154, 162 and 178) the *Annus Domini* and the Indiction almost invariably occur together; indeed, *BCS* 296, dated only by the latter style, is known to be spurious (Levison 1946: 249, n. 3). How far the writings of Bede were responsible for the downfall of the Indiction in England, or whether he only mirrors the opinion of his time, is a matter yet to be examined; but even a casual reader of the *Historia* can seldom have been in doubt over the author's purpose. As to the other Indiction of 24 September, associated particularly with Bede's name, it does not seem ever to have been in use, though a study of the later annals in the Chronicle might yield a trace of it. But it is the earlier annals, the earliest of all, that we must now explore.

CHAPTER 7

THE ANGLO-SAXON CHRONICLE

❦

Hitherto we have been considering mainly the northern recension of the Chronicle, now represented by versions D and E. Their archetype was a copy similar to those called A, B, C and F, the first being written in one hand up to the year 892. The earliest annals, which are here taken to include everything from 700 back to 449 (*recte* 450), are not quite identical in all these six versions; thus E has a lengthy passage at 443 (*recte* 446) which is not found in the rest of the common stock.[1] Apart from additions made at a much later date in the northern recension, however, there is reasonably good agreement over fact and figures before 700; and all versions reflect the matter contained in the original up to 892. As well as these texts in the vernacular there are two Latin translations of special importance: that due to Aethelweard, about 980 to 990 (ed. & tr. Campbell 1962); and extracts preserved in the Annals of St Neots, a manuscript of the early twelfth century (ed. Stevenson 1904).

In the versions A–F a few particulars which Aethelweard has preserved do not appear at all, yet he is not in the habit of introducing extraneous annals into the translation (*ASE*: 20), and we may conclude that some of the material in his Old English text had been dropped by later transcribers or that this text preserved statements of fact which were not in the archetype of other versions (*PASE*: 121–2). The Annals of St Neots are valuable in another way, because they do not show the dislocation of years between 756 and 845 which is found in all extant copies, and Aethelweard, and thus

---

[1] The manuscript of D has lost a gathering, hence the annals from 286 to the middle of 693 are absent, and E becomes the sole authority for the northern recension in these years, except that the additions in A show these annals were in the predecessor of E. The annal for 443 in E was added to A at Canterbury in the late eleventh century. C. F. C. Hawkes (1956) places altogether too much reliance on this late entry, which is based on Bede and misdated by three years, *xliii* being written for *xlvi*, a common error. F is chiefly a late copy of A, with no great weight for the earliest annals.

represent an even earlier stage in the manuscript tradition (Earle and Plummer 1899: II, cii–civ). There is no particular reason to suppose that they were compiled at this priory near Huntingdon, for the background is East Anglian (Stevenson 1904: 100); and apart from Bede, and continental sources resembling the Annals of St Évroul, *Annales Uticenses*, they seem to contain passages drawn from the northern recension of the Chronicle. The date of Ethelbert of Kent's accession is given at 565, with a reign of fifty-three years, yet his death is recorded at 616 – precisely as in the E version. By Plummer (1896: II, 85) it was suggested that since Bede allots a reign of fifty-six years, with death in 616 (*HE*, II. 5) the E version has mistakenly written *liii* for *lvi* at this point – a plausible emendation – and the faulty arithmetic of E is faithfully followed by the Annals.[2] Again, at 731 there is an entry taken presumably from the northern recension, concerning Ceolwulf of Northumbria, which has been mangled in the process (Stevenson 1904: 107), though it is fair to add that this opinion is not accepted by all scholars. The presence of a chronicle resembling D and E at an East Anglian centre is not remarkable, for the existing version E was at Peterborough by 1121 or thereabouts; and what may be another copy had reached Ramsey somewhere near 1090 (Hart 1970).

The marriage of Ethelbert with the Frankish princess, Bertha, seems to have taken place before his accession in 560. Gregory of Tours was acquainted with her mother Ingoberg, as well as with two half-sisters who were unsatisfactory nuns at Poitiers and Tours. He knew next to nothing about Kent, or Britain as a whole, but did know a very great deal about the Merovingian rulers in the latter half of the sixth century; and he says that Bertha was married to the son of a certain king of Kent, *quam in Chancia regis cuiusdum [filius] matrimonio copulauit* (*Historia Francorum*, IX. 26; *ASE*: 105). Hence the marriage took place before 560, though likely enough not by more than a year or two; and Bede, whose information is here *a traditione*, mentions that Ethelbert received the girl from her parents, *a parentibus* (*HE*, I. 25), which means before 568, before her father

---

[2] If Ethelbert's reign seems unusually long, so long as to have led a few scholars to doubt the veracity of Bede's sources, it will be remembered that the Merovingian Lothar is credited with reigning fifty years, in a savage climate of royal assassination and battlefields (*Historia Francorum*, IV. 14).

Charibert was dead. (Perhaps the 588 of *ASE:* 105 is a misprint). More information about Bertha derives from another contemporary source. Writing to her in 601, Gregory the Great expresses concern at the slow rate of conversion; whether *tota gens* means all the Angles, as the Pope habitually referred to them, or only the inhabitants of Kent, is not quite clear.[3] He continues: 'For since you, illustrious lady, are, as I said, furnished with the right faith, and are also instructed in letters', *et recta fide gloria uestra munita, et literis docta est,* 'this ought not to have been a slow and difficult task for you' (ed. Haddan and Stubbs 1873: III, 17–18; tr. Mason 1897: 58–9). Bertha, then, was literate; and she came of a literate family. Her father Charibert, King of Paris from 561 to 567, is praised for his command of Latin by Venantius Fortunatus (*Carm.* VI, 2, ed. Leo 1881: 131–4) in these terms,

> *cum sis progenitus clara de gente Sygamber*
> *floret in eloquio lingua latina tuo.*
> *qualis es in propria docto sermone loquela*
> *qui nos Romanos uincis in eloquio?*

(lines 97–100). The sentiments of formal panegyric often reach down to the level of humbug, but even a Fortunatus would jib at ascribing Roman eloquence to a man with no Latinity at all; and Charibert's half-brother Chilperic wrote halting verse in the style of Sedulius (*Historia Francorum,* VI. 33).

Though not a friend to the Church, it is unlikely that Charibert would send an uneducated bishop to accompany his educated daughter to England, in the capacity of chaplain. A gold 'medalet' bearing Liudhard's name and rank was almost certainly struck in this country, not abroad (Grierson 1952). If Liudhard is a shadow in other respects, his literacy can hardly be in doubt – and surely he will have had a deacon or two? The presence in Kent, from about 560 onwards, of people able to read and write has largely been ignored by historians.[4] It will not be pretended for one moment that

---

[3] Kent remained partly heathen until the reign of Eorcenberht, 640–64, who destroyed the idols (*HE,* III. 8); and Wihtred's laws, 695, have injunctions against heathenism (*EHD:* 363).

[4] Though not by Wallace-Hadrill (1971: 26) who observes that 'no doubt Bertha corresponded with her relatives (Gregory says she was learned in letters), and Bishop Liudhard, too, with former colleagues'. Tolstoy (1964: 295–6) takes

annalistic writing, whether by entries into an Easter table or in the form of a chronicle, did take place at this stage. Yet a few items may have been noted down. 'In no family was hereditary descent more strictly observed and buttressed than in the Merovingian . . . If he took little else from his formidable connexions, Aethelbert would surely have learned how to make the most of his blood' (Wallace-Hadrill 1971: 45). Thus the record of his pedigree, as given by Bede (*HE*, II. 5) might belong to the sixth century rather than the seventh. It is not known when, or for how long, this king achieved the over-lordship, *imperium*, of southern England. A man aspiring to this position could have caused such names of British kings as Conmail, Condidan, and Farinmail to be written down, since their deaths at Dyrham (*ASC*: year 577) removed a significant obstacle to expansion; the spelling of these names is in an early form, and to a Celtic scholar they 'have the look of contemporary records' (Jackson 1953: 464 and 677), though in Old English they need not be older than the ninth century. Again, Vortigern appears in Bede's *Chronica Maiora* spelt Uertigernus, which, as Kirby has observed, is very early indeed (1968: 48). He also says: 'It is of great importance that behind our earliest literary materials for the conquest of Kent lie not only Kentish oral tradition but ancient written records deriving probably from the late sixth or the early seventh century.' Hitherto the picture has been drawn somewhat out of balance: the Britons bask in the light of learning – and unquestionably Gildas was an accomplished man – while Kent is covered by inspissated gloom. In this matter we have to deal with possibilities rather than probabilities, yet the possibilities, however, faint, are nonetheless real.

It will be more pertinent to ask – how did Bertha and her chaplain manage to ascertain the date of Easter? Liudhard might have received notification, year after year, by a messenger from his former metropolitan, presumably the bishop of Sens. Yet he was truly working *in partibus infidelium*, and it is far more probable that he possessed a copy of the Victorian Easter tables, official in Gaul since 541. From a Victorian table the approximate date of the *Aduentus*

literacy back to 449 (*recte* 450), but there is no direct evidence before 560. Literate Frankish merchants would hardly be in a position to take part in recording national affairs.

Saxonum, as it appears in the style given by Bede (*HE*, V. 24), could have been worked out. Three postulates are needed, which taken singly or collectively are not unreasonable.

1. Anybody furnished with an Easter table would know which calendar year he was in, and we saw in Chapter 3 that the Victorian tables up to 457 contained a list of consuls which were useful in defining past dates (above, p. 33).

2. The calculator would know which regnal year he was in. A Northumbrian list of kings, with their lengths of reign, has been preserved (Hunter Blair 1950), and from Chapter 1 it is evident that the lunar–solar year is of the same length as the Julian. Bede assigns to Ethelbert fifty-six years, and the Chronicle twenty-four years, 488–512, to Oisc (Aesc in its later form).[5] Unfortunately neither Bede nor the Chronicler, from their differing points of view, had any interest in Octa and Eormenric.

3. An elementary knowledge of Roman history, ascertained from such chroniclers as Prosper – only enough to distinguish the names of emperors in a consular list. From the work of Renatus Frigeridus it was possible for Gregory of Tours, for instance, to recognise Valentinian and Aetius in their separate roles (*Historia Francorum*, II. 7).

During the summer of 616 a child could have remembered some such words as these: 'King Ethelbert reigned fifty-six years, and before him Eormenric *x* years, and Octa *y* years and Oisc twenty-four years, and that was (about?) thirty-five years before he came across the sea with his father Hengest.' This type of calculation would be possible at a later period than 616, or could have been reckoned from an earlier year of Ethelbert's reign. From a particular year, checked by the date of Easter, the length of reigns could be added up, and in sum appears to have given a figure within the following limits in a Victorian table (ed. Mommsen 1892c: 722; Krusch 1938: 47–8), the consular list being, with A.D. dates,

---

[5] It is sometimes objected that Oisc could not have died as late as 512 if he were involved in the *Aduentus Saxonum*, fighting as early as 455, or a few years before. Yet he may only have been a stripling at the time, though capable of being present in the field. King Alfred, it is well known, was a warrior at nineteen; the Northumbrian Aelfwine fell at the battle of the Trent when about eighteen (*HE*, IV. 19); and Guthlac was under arms, a gang-leader, at fifteen (Colgrave 1956: 3, 80 and 82).

450 *Valentiniano vii et Abieno*
451 *Marciano et Adelfio*
452 *Herculano et Asporatio*
453 *Opilione et Vincomalo*
454 *Aetio et Studio*
455 *Valentiniano viii et Anthemio*

Apart from Aetius, whose consulate of 454 was soon brought to an end by his murder, the patricians are obscure figures. Marcian, though emperor in 450, before which he is not named, and consul in 451, does not appear again, nor does Valentinian, in turn murdered in the first year of his eighth consulate. The exact limits for the *Aduentus Saxonum*, if found in this way, would therefore seem to be 450 to 455.[6]

The advantage of referring a date back to imperial or consular years lies in its being independent of an era, such as the *Annus Mundi* – though capable of being translated into Julian terms – the disadvantage that the date is vague rather than precise. By the standards of the sixth century this disadvantage was of no great moment. Whenever possible, Gregory of Tours would fix an event to the *x*th imperial or consular year, giving however no exact date on his own scale of *Annus Mundi*; when the sources failed in this degree of precision he was content with the indefinite, as 'in the reign of Constans lived James of Nisibis . . . Maximus also, bishop of Trèves . . .' (*Historia Francorum*, I. 29). The barbarians had absorbed *Romanitas*; Bertha's great-grandfather Clovis received the dignity of a proconsul from the emperor Anasatasius, and was vested in a purple tunic (*Historia Francorum*, II. 38). Their descendants were satisfied if anything in the national history could be placed, however indistinctly, within the framework of an empire which had not been able to govern them. There is, moreover, no reason to think that the calculation was made by Bede himself; in the *Chronica Maiora* (above, p. 76) he refers the *Aduentus* to the joint reign of Marcian and Valentinian as if it were a matter of common knowledge, which with great probability it was – and from a Kentish background (Myres 1951: 231). The Ripon estimate (above, p. 99) should be

[6] It will be evident also that even if there were no Victorian tables in England a traveller in Gaul could have made the calculation there.

approached with much greater caution. The year 453 could have been ascertained by adding regnal years together, and then working backwards from a fixed *Annus Domini*; yet in the form preserved by Nennius a round number inevitably attracts suspicion, besides involving coincidence. Only in its favour as an independent calculation is the Dionysiac type of reckoning, with no tinge of Roman history.

Familiar as he was with sermons and the literature of exhortation, Bede may well have doubted whether Gildas was aiming to provide a strictly historical narrative. By preserving the letter to Aetius (above, p. 23) Gildas had furnished what Bede could have thought was a lower limit for the *Aduentus Saxonum*. Yet bearing in mind the proposal of Stevens (1941: 362), that the 'barbarians' of this letter are Saxons, not Picts and Scots, it must be recognised that Bede knew better than any modern scholar what barbarians were; his great-grandparents, or grandparents perhaps, fell into that category. Had an estimate of the *Aduentus* given a bracket of years at some time earlier than 446 Bede would have taken it in his stride. As things turned out, the year 446, or soon after, accorded well with the dates 449 (450) to 456 (457).[7] Furthermore, Bede had a double interest in the tale which Gildas unfolds: the letter to Aetius, as providing an approximate date; and the sins of the Britons, for which they were punished by a foreign invasion. Bede's dislike of them was founded not only on their method of reckoning Easter, but also on their neglecting to convert and baptise the Anglo-Saxons. The Church had clear views on the value of baptism; Augustine of Hippo had not been alone in teaching that the un-baptised were consigned to the flames of Hell, real not metaphorical flames which burn for ever and ever. The vision of Drycthelm is in keeping (*HE*, V. 12), the vision of Fursa even more explicit (*HE*, III. 19); another glimpse of the next world revealed the souls of very many young children in torment because Bishop Daniel of Win-

---

[7] Bede's figure of 449 is not easy to explain, except as an arithmetical slip. He certainly knew the chronicles of Prosper and Marcellinus Comes (Plummer 1896: II, 25–26), and the existing texts give the equivalent of 450 for the accession of Marcian (ed. Mommsen 1892a and 1893b). Though Marcellinus reckoned by an Indictional year, Marcian came to the throne on 25 August, so the error should not have arisen in that way.

chester had neglected to baptise them (Plummer 1896: II, 308; Jones 1947: 211, n. 88). Any pious Anglo-Saxon, supposing his kinsmen condemned by this ugly doctrine, can be excused a failure in charity towards people who, sharing the same views, had neglected a signal duty. It would not be safe to underline Bede's indebtedness to Gildas in historical matters while overlooking the moral issues, as they were then understood.

For the remaining annals, which are not referred to the imperial scale, it will be suitable to begin the search for methods of dating by an examination of the internal evidence. A duplication of West Saxon entries from 495 to 527 has long been known (*PASE*: 121), and the essential detail is set out in Table 8, modified from Harrison (1971), where it is found that the paired events are separated by an interval of nineteen years, the length of a lunar cycle. Under 501, the landing of Port (is this a nickname?) and his sons at Portsmouth seems to be unconnected with Cerdic's operations. In the left hand column, at 519, Aethelweard's annal for 500 has been incorporated. We have seen that on occasion the text from which he translated preserves items, to all appearances authentic, which are not found in any other version of the Chronicle; and in some respects it is closer to the original (Introduction to *ASC*: xviii). How, then, did this duplication arise? The Dionysiac tables used in England from about 660 onwards comprised a 95-year term, in five separate cycles of nineteen years, each cycle being written down as a unit, as in Table 2 (above, p. 35). When forming a chronicle it was not necessary, or even desirable, to work out a complete Easter table. The simplest approach, when dealing with dates as far away as 450 or earlier, would be to extrapolate backwards, arranging the *Anni Domini* in separate units of nineteen years to avoid confusion – a hope, in the event, not to be realised altogether. It will be observed that since a 19-year cycle runs from 494 to 512, and the next from 513 to 531 (both inclusive), the paired dates 495 = 514, 500 = 519 and 508 = 527 fall as a block into one cycle or the other. This arrangement is surely beyond coincidence. What has happened, it would seem, is that a version of virtually the same story, told in different words, has been transferred to the wrong Dionysiac cycle.

The annal for 530, though forming part of the Cerdic saga, has no

TABLE 8. *Successive decennovenal cycles run from 494 to 512 and from 513 to 531*

501   Port and his sons landed at *Portesmutha* (Portsmouth) with two ships

514 (from 495) Cerdic and Cynric came to Britain with five ships and landed at *Cerdicesora* and fought the Britons the same day	514 The West Saxons came into Britain with three ships at *Cerdicesora*; and Stuf and Wihtgar fought the Britons and put them to flight
519 (from 500, Aethelweard) In the sixth year after their arrival they conquered Wessex	519 Cerdic and Cynric succeeded to the kingdom and fought the Britons at *Cerdicesford* (Charford)
527 (from 508) Cerdic and Cynric killed the British king Natanleod and 5000 men; and the land up to *Cerdicesford* (Charford) was called *Natanleag* (Netley) after him	527 Cerdic and Cynric fought the Britons at *Cerdicesleag*

530   Cerdic and Cynric captured the Isle of Wight

534   Cerdic died, Cynric ruled for 27 years, and they gave the Isle of Wight to Stuf and Wihtgar

pair at 511. Thus the capture of the Isle of Wight, and the part played by Stuf and Wihtgar, in the annal for 514, may not have been in the tradition represented by the left-hand column in Table 8; and in any case the adjustment here proposed makes Cerdic's life fall within more probable limits. Of more importance is the uniting of a measure of intervals in the discordant items – discordant, as they originally stood, not in sense but in time. There are two ways in which this measure of intervals, 501 to 514, 514 to 519, 519 to 527, and 527 to 530 could have been derived from oral tradition. In the first place, an event can be referred to the regnal year of a particular king; thus Bede records that the battle of *Degsastan* occurred in Aethelfrith's eleventh year (*HE*, I. 34; below, p. 132). Given a list of regnal years continuing into the Christian period, when Dionysiac tables were circulating, for example the reign of Cenwalh, 641–72, and working backwards, the Year of Grace corresponding with the event is found. Naturally the dangers of such a form of reckoning need to be emphasised.[8] Yet a certain amount of care seems to have been taken over the regnal years themselves. Although the information dates from no earlier than the reign of Oswald, who died in 642, there existed a group of people whose business it was to keep the regnal list; with their agreement, *cunctis placuit regum tempora computantibus*, the *infaustus annus* of his predecessors was counted into his own reign (*HE*, III. I). Oswald started life as a pagan, to be converted when in exile at Iona, but no harm would be done by his following a pagan custom of preserving regnal years. These years seem to have been rounded off: for instance, ten years and five months would count as ten, and ten years and seven months as eleven. It has already been pointed out (above p. 92) that in the short term an error of a year could readily arise, but over a long stretch the errors from this cause alone would tend to cancel out, as in Table 6.

In the second place a narrative form could be adopted, as exemplified by the far later chronicle of Aethelweard (Tolstoy 1964: 280). Here the dates are relative to one another, thus: 'after a lapse of three years [from Aelle], Cerdic and his son Cynric joined battle with the Britons; in the sixth year from their arrival they encircled Wessex; in the seventh year after his [Port's] arrival Cerdic with his son Cynric slew Natanleod; when the sixth year was completed, . . .' (tr. Campbell 1962: 11–12). There are dangers in this form of computation, too; not all writers are careful to distinguish between '*x* years' and 'the *x*th year', cardinal and ordinal; versifiers could fall into the same trap. Yet the mistake which lies exposed in Table 8, so far from detracting from the value of the dates, will serve to increase confidence in them, for at least in both sets the same

---

[8] As by Kirby (1968: 45–6). But in the examples he puts forward the length of a generation is not strictly comparable with the length of a reign. At the same time, however, the importance he attaches to regnal lists, as opposed to Easter table entries, is instructive.

measure of intervals between events had been preserved. How a mistake could have arisen is far more difficult to understand, perhaps impossible. In a previous discussion (Harrison 1971) it was assumed, for the sake of simplicity, that the luni–solar calendar operated on a Metonic cycle of nineteen years, in which case the placing of a block of events into the wrong Dionysiac unit would be more comprehensible. Even though the majority of people may have used an 8-year cycle in their day-to-day affairs, a more sophisticated group in charge of regnal time-keeping may have used the full Metonic cycle; the same principle underlies them, 'octaëteris' being a portmanteau word for the first eight years of the longer cycle. But if, after archaeological study, there is positive evidence of an 8-year cycle, the problem will be harder to solve. In any case the duplication could have been brought about, in a manner still obscure, by the union of two forms of reckoning: an absolute chronology based on a regnal list, and the relative chronology cast in narrative form.

From Wessex we may now glance back to Kent. Here it is possible that the reign of Oisc (Aesc), 488–512, formed a pivot on which other dates were made to hinge; just as an event can be fixed to 'the xth year of King Y' so to 'the xth year before King Y.' The Kentish royalty called themselves Oiscingas (*HE*, II.5) and Stenton describes Hengest as 'a chieftain of very noble descent...' who 'fights battles which open the way to an occupation by men of his race in the next generation' (*ASE*: 17). In 488 the kingdom existed as a territorial fact, by reason of this occupation, and perhaps only then was Oisc invested with an aura of sacral kingship which his father did not enjoy; he stood for good luck and security. However that may be, a matter beyond chronology, at this point a few words on the structure of the annals must be interjected. Stevens (1941: 369) has complained of the Chronicle that 'parallel stories of Kentish, Sussex and Wessex settlements have been artificially laid end to end in a continuous narrative...' Although not literally true, the misunderstanding should not be passed over. A West Saxon chronicler was outlining the history of Germanic expansion westwards in Britain; the Northumbrian annal at 547 is clearly an addition from Bede (*HE*, v. 24). At this remove of time we are in the dark about the chronicler's choice of material, though he laid emphasis on his own royal house. In part, at least, he may have chosen for record the episodes, of greater or lesser importance, to which he could attach a date – or thought he could. The story begins in Kent, where by 488 the kingdom had attained to stability. Meanwhile, 477, Aelle invaded Sussex and during his lifetime became the overlord of the southern peoples. The year of his death is not known. Then in 514 – if Table 8 is accepted – another seizure of land took place under Cerdic; the culmination of West Saxon power came with the overlordship of Ceawlin, who died in 593. It is due to Bede that the *imperium* of Aelle and Ceawlin is known (*HE*, II. 5). Since a westward drive naturally took the invaders further from their homelands, with longer sea-passages, there is nothing 'artificial' in the stories, which would on geographical grounds have seemed unnatural if they were in any way parallel. As to the artificiality of the dates, and the supposition of grouping by fours and eights, now deeply embedded in the literature, reference should be made to Appendix 2.

Nobody, however, will affirm in a court of law that each and every one of these dates is correct. Errors in copying apart, the human memory is not infallible. Yet neither the individual nor the collective memories of an almost entirely illiterate people should be played down too far. At this present time it is less easy than in a not very distant past to suppose that because men cannot read or write they are defective in other ways; the 'savages' of the last century have proved, on better acquaintance, to possess talents which nobody had troubled to look for. Something, moreover, can be inferred about this matter. Although there is no evidence for official 'lawspeakers' (Whitelock 1952a: 135), the ninety clauses of Ethelbert's code (part translated in *EHD*: 357–9) must be largely founded on the memory of ancient custom and penalties, and by no means all the current law was written down. Ability to remember both facts and figures was therefore required. In the north of England, the first converts were made in 626 (*HE*, II. 9), and when a child of parents who were almost certainly themselves born heathen is found to have a good memory, the fact is surely to be ascribed to heredity rather than baptism.[9] Notches on wooden tally-sticks, or on more durable

---

[9] Thus Wilfrid, born in or about 634, had the psalter by heart (Eddius, c. II) and so did Ceolfrith, born about 642 (*HAA*: 401).

materials, can serve as an *aide mémoire*; and alliterative verse is also
a help. Even though Welsh or Irish poetry is free from indications of
time, and in general 'chronology is a concept foreign to oral literature' (Hughes 1972: 145), there are traces of what may be called
'domestic' saga – the songs sung in the petty kingdoms to praise and
magnify their lords and the ancestral heroes. Descended from the
Mercian royal house, a bandit now becoming reformed in his ways,
Guthlac 'contemplated the wretched deaths and the shameful ends
of the ancient kings of his race in the course of the past ages' (tr.
Colgrave 1956: 83). More to the point, Bede knew that the battle of
Degsastan took place in Aethelfrith's eleventh year, which with the
aid of a Northumbrian king-list enabled him to fix the date to A.D.
603 (*HE*, I. 34); and the circumstantial detail of the battle of Chester,
in the same king's reign, may well derive from a similar type of oral
tradition (*HE*, II. 2). These are only two out of several examples
hinting at lost material (Wright 1939: 32–3).[10]

We have seen that the Annals of St Neots, because they do not
suffer from the dislocation of numbering common to all other
versions, are representative of an earlier manuscript tradition.
Before the middle of the ninth century, and going back to the death
of Ine, 726, the entries become more and more meagre in themselves
and thinly scattered, apart from a long passage at 757. Although
Wheeler (1921) argued from the frequent occurrence of royal
genealogies between 648 and 726, with very few thereafter, that a
change of authorship had occurred in the latter year, and that the
previous annals from 648 are contemporary, his line of approach
does not seem to be well founded (Sisam 1953: 336–7). But a little
while later, a different twist to the argument was given by Stenton
(1926; *PASE*, 119–22). Writing of the year 648 he remarks that

in itself the annal for this year does not look like the beginning of a chronicle.

---

[10] A statement in the Chronicle (*ASC*: year 626 doubtfully) that Penda was fifty
when he became king, and reigned thirty years, is the subject of some informal
comments by Professor Whitelock: 'These round figures are used in *Beowulf*.
Grendel seized thirty thanes, Beowulf had the strength of thirty men and came
from Frisia with thirty suits of armour; Hrothgar reigned fifty years before
Grendel's attack; Beowulf reigned fifty years and the dragon was fifty feet long.
Penda was the sort of man about whom poems would be sung.' Such remarks are
helpful in guarding against round numbers, or the thought that every 'domestic'
saga contained reliable indications of time.

It is surely inconceivable that a clerk who wished to compose such a record would open with the unprefaced words 'In this year Cenwalh gave to Cuthred his kinsman three thousands of land by Ashdown – Cuthred was the son of Cwichelm [etc.].' Cuthred was not the founder of a dynasty; he died in 661 without recorded issue. Even if the chronicler began to write in 648 it is surely not unreasonable to assume that he would have recorded retrospectively the conversion of his people and their rulers, to which no fewer than six annals, for which no ulterior source has been found, are actually devoted in the preceding section of the extant chronicle. The character of annalistic writing does not change in 648...Is it not far more probable that this seventh-century chronicler began his work at a much earlier point, that we owe to him the preservation of the West Saxon traditions of Cerdic, Cynric and Ceawlin?

If the concept of a proto-chronicle (or early set of annals) is to be sustained, the various types of evidence for it must be set out. In his introduction to the Annals of St Neots, Stevenson drew attention to the fact that the copy of the Chronicle on which it was based had kept the archaic spelling Oisc, which appears as Aesc in other versions, and is not known from any other source than Bede (*HE*, II. 5). Sisam held that this spelling was taken from Bede (1953: 338, n. 3); but in the very same annal, for 455, the *Uurtigernus* of Bede is spelt *Guirthegirnus*, so the argument has little force. The form Wihtgaraburg or Wihtgarabyrig is an archaic genitive, at 530 and 544 in various Chronicle versions (Stevenson 1904: 172–3); the spellings of Farinmail, Condidan and Conmail, 577, have already been noticed, if in fact they were as early as Celtic scholars have supposed. Evidence of another kind is provided by Stenton (1926: 163–4; *PASE*: 119). 'The remarkable precision', he says, 'of the annal for 661 which records that Cenwalh fought at Posentes byrig *at Easter* suggests contemporary writing. If possible, it is certainly improbable that any annalist of a later generation would have set down that there was a great destruction of birds in 671.' The improbability becomes greater by considering the next sentence, in Aethelweard's version only: 'so that on sea and land a very foul stench was noticeable from the (carrion of) small birds and larger ones' (tr. Campbell 1962: 20–21). Such vivid writing is more likely to derive from a man who could not forget the smell than from an annalist of later days. Moreover, it is recorded that Cuthred, who died in 661 without leaving any descendants of note, was the godson of Birinus at his baptism in 639 – again a detail which few would remember for long. Signs of a contemporary hand will encourage the thought that if the compiler had been guessing about earlier dates and events he was in a position to have guessed a great deal more; but there is no padding or embroidery, no attempt to link the earliest entries together or breathe life into a fossil record.[11]

After referring to the frequent difficulty of identifying some of the place-names, Stenton concluded that this proto-chronicle, or set of annals, might have been composed 'at or shortly after the middle of the seventh century' (1926: 166; *PASE*: 120–21). His opinion can now be supported by the various reasons put forward in Chapter 4 for thinking that in the decade 660–70 the Dionysiac tables had begun to circulate in England, together with a thorough knowledge of the principles on which they were founded. Still earlier, by about 640, they seem to have been approved at Rome. And in the decades after 670 there is evidence that the *Annus Domini* was finding its way into legal instruments, as a subsidiary element in the dating clause. It is very unlikely that a chronicle reckoning by the Year of Grace could have been compiled earlier than 660, unless Birinus had brought Dionysiac tables to Wessex, and much more probable that the materials for the section from 450 to about 660 were collected soon after the latter date, to be continued by various hands until the manuscript, or a copy of it, with or without occasional gaps, became the foundation of all extant versions. Where it was compiled is perhaps a matter of guesswork, though a case could be made out for Malmesbury, founded by the Irish scholar Maildubh about 640.[12] Wessex was relatively remote from East Anglia, but reference to affairs in that kingdom – 654, King Anna slain, and Botwulf built the minister at *Icanho* (perhaps Iken in Suffolk); 673, foundation of Ely

---

11 Under 664 the day of the eclipse, 3 May, clearly derives from Bede; thus the whole annal, though there may well originally have been an entry here, must be disregarded in this context.

12 An objection is that Pecthelm, monk and deacon under Aldhelm, was known to Bede (*HE*, v. 18); and presently we shall see that Bede was ignorant of the Chronicle. But their talk may only have been of visionary matters (*HE*, v. 13), and an interesting feature of the story is that it seems to involve a literate layman in the reign of Cenred (died 709). And Bede may not have known Pecthelm for long, that is, earlier than the writing of *HE*, III. 7.

– is most readily explained by circumstances in the life of Cenwalh, who reigned from 641 to 672, and was succeeded for a year by his widow Seaxburh. While a heathen still, he had married a daughter of Penda; but on putting her away was attacked by the Mercians in 645 and took refuge for a time at the East Anglian court. Here, under the influence of King Anna, his mind turned to Christianity and he was baptised in 646. According to Eddius (c. VII) he was a strong supporter of Roman usages, in which he encouraged his friend Alhfrith, son of Oswiu (*ASE*: 67–8 and 122); Alhfrith in turn was a friend of Wilfrid, to whom he gave Ripon, about 660. It is not far-fetched to imagine Dionysiac tables in Wessex by 670, even if Birinus had not resorted to them. But Professor Whitelock makes another suggestion about East Anglia: a late compiler, or inter-polator, could have used a version of Bede's Recapitulation (*HE*, V. 24) to which marginal additions had been made at an East Anglian house, or perhaps Peterborough; and there is no sign of interest in East Anglia except in this section where *HE*, V. 24 is a main source (though the exact date of the 664 eclipse is found in *HE*, III. 27).

As Plummer observed of Bede, 'it is plain that he could obtain no reliable details as to the conversion of the West Saxons' (1896: II, 141). Information at the beginning of *HE*, III. 7 is dated only by reference to the reign of Cynegils and the presence of Oswald at the font when the king was baptised, and no precise figures are given for events in the succeeding reign of Cenwalh either. Bede's inform-ant was Daniel bishop of Winchester (Preface to *HE*); if a proto-chronicle did exist, or an early set of annals compiled from about 670 onwards, and Daniel was unaware of it, perhaps an application to Sherborne would have met with better success. It is from Ald-helm, bishop of Sherborne, that further light is shed on Bede's ignorance of West Saxon affairs. According to *HE*, IV. 12, on Cen-walh's death several *subreguli* took over the government for about ten years, whereas the Chronicle says that his widow Seaxburh reigned a year and was succeeded first by Aescwine and then by Centwine. Here the Chronicle version should be preferred, for Aldhelm describes Centwine as a strong king who ruled for many years (Wheeler 1921: 165; *ASE*: 68). Thus when Bede was writing, in 731, we can envisage a source of information beyond his ken, which is not unusual, though he may have heard of a disputed succession. It is virtually certain that he did not know Adomnan's Life of Columba (Plummer 1896: II, 131), though extracts from *De Locis Sanctis* appear in *HE*, v. 15–17, and, more strangely still, did not know the Life of Gregory the Great by an anonymous monk of Whitby, written before 714 (Colgrave 1968: 56–9).

If a start was being made, perhaps about 840–50, but far more likely in Alfred's reign, on the archetypal version of the Chronicle as we now have it, in its various copies, and behind that archetype there was a proto-chronicle, or a set of annals covering the earlier years, though not necessarily in a continuous fashion, then we should enquire how far a more ancient text, or series of texts, could be related to other material.

1. The regnal table, or king-list with lengths of reign, prefixed to the A version of the Chronicle was considered by Sisam to be 'an older independent document of some official standing, which the compiler of the Chronicle adopted without critical scrutiny' (1953: 333).[13] The questions remain – how much older and how far independent?

2. The *Historia Brittonum* usually connected with the name of Nennius (ed. Mommsen 1898b; tr. Wade-Evans 1938; in part tr. *EHD*: 236–8). From a recent analysis the date of compilation is found to be 829–30 (Dumville 1974). The later sections of this work, 56 and 58–61, contain northern material which has a genuine flavour and to some extent could have been written down in the seventh century (Jackson 1963). But in earlier sections we encounter a romancing style, with conversations between Hengest and the fair Rowena, and much else of similar value. If there was a proto-chronicle, of the type and age suggested, the oral transmission of a part of this southern detail could be accounted for. In the opinion of Kirby, 'this Kentish material reached Nennius through Powys' although it 'lacks a chronological framework and, apart from a mention of Thanet, geographical detail' (1968: 54–5). As to attempts at fixing a date for the *Aduentus Saxonum*, they again seem to be derived; a discussion is provided by Tolstoy (1964: 276–98). More recently, Dumville has concluded that the year 428 has no historical

13 Translation, with comments, in *ASC*: 3–4; see also Kirby (1965).

validity (1974: 445), but until his new edition of the *Historia Brittonum* has been published any further remarks on the text would be unsatisfactory. Meanwhile, in the present state of knowledge, it does not appear necessary to postulate a 'Kentish chronicle' (J. Morris 1965; 1973), presumably thought to be independent of the Anglo-Saxon Chronicle or of the elements which went into its final composition.

In spite of the doubts and hesitation which will be found in the preceding pages, it is possible to give a tentative outline of developments in chronology from the earliest times to the death of Alfred. The attitude of Anglo-Saxons to the reckoning of time was practical throughout and firm. If the pagan system is primitive in one sense it is not in another. A luni-solar calendar can be adapted to fixing a particular day in the year, as Midwinter, but is far less suitable than the Julian when a series of festivals or commemorations must occur on specific days. Ill-adapted for use by the Church, except in determining the particular day of Easter in any one year, a luni-solar cycle is an effective guide to agricultural life, with the days of a lunar month giving as much precision as can reasonably be required for assemblies of a hostile or peaceful character: except in emergency, says Tacitus, the Germans meet at new moon or full moon. In this sense the Anglo-Saxon calendar was far from primitive. Unlike many others of the same type, all over the world, it seems to have operated under firm and definite rules; and with its double months related to the solstices, and a third intercalary month in embolismic years, during the summer, is the product of a relatively sophisticated people. Practical, then, among barbarians, it could not survive for for long in an age when Christianity and letters were virtually inseparable.

Perhaps England was lucky in that the conversion of the south was beginning to take place only shortly before the Paschal controversy had started to die down on the continent, more especially at Rome; the Britons alone, with a far older type of computation to defend, would stand against innovation for a long while. As a result of the Synod of Whitby, in 664, everyone under the jurisdiction of Canterbury obeyed the same method of calculating Easter. From that moment the Anglo-Saxons, always practical, became still more firm. They were in a strong position: neither the Victorian system nor the Celtic-84 were deeply dug in, and the manifest advantages of the Alexandrian computation, as Dionysius had explained it, will have made an appeal to others besides Wilfrid. He, returning from Rome about 658, trained in the centre of western Christendom, was to achieve a personal success at Whitby, soon followed by his consecration. Dallying too long in Gaul, he did not attain to the see of York until 669; in this year Theodore arrived at Canterbury, and with him, perhaps, the concept of a solemn charter (but see Chaplais 1969). Although other enthusiasts will have taken their part, the evidence would suggest that Wilfrid was a prime mover in establishling the *Annus Domini* as a feature of dating clauses, though at the start optional, and subsidiary to the Indiction. Wilfrid's roving life after 678, the year of his first expulsion from York, must surely have aided in the spread of this element in the legal framework until the close of the seventh century.

At Wilfrid's death, when his personal influence was already in decline, and during the first thirty years of the eighth century, the Dionysiac tables had reached a position never again to be challenged. In 715 the monks of Iona decided to abandon the Celtic-84, and next year celebrated Easter according to the Roman custom. A little while before, it is clear from Ceolfrith's letter to King Naiton that the concept of a Great Paschal cycle of 532 years, originally due to Victorius, was being applied to the Dionysiac system. Rather more that ten years later, in 725, Bede composed *De Temporum Ratione*, which enjoyed a European fame throughout the Middle Ages. Thus England, and England alone, had acquired an era at once stable and Christian.[14] The reckoning *Anno Domini* was indissolubly linked with the only computation of Easter which had proved to be accurate; and this latter fact, of immense consequence to the Church at large, helped to ensure the spread of the Christian era in the valley of the Rhine, and northwards, by the hands of Willibrord and Boniface. Among continental monasteries, from the latter half of the eighth

---

[14] The Spanish era, from 38 B.C., continued in isolation until 1339 in Aragon, 1383 in Castile and 1420 in Portugal, though not officially abolished until 1558 (Poole 1934: 3–4 and 26–7). It began, however, from an arbitrary date which had no significance for the Church.

century, annalists or chroniclers usually adopted this era, and by the ninth its roots were established almost everywhere.[15]

If, as is likely, Bede was born in 673, then by a coincidence of years what may be the dating clause from the foundation charter of Wearmouth is styled A.D. 674, second Indiction, that is, the autumn of 673; later it would be transcribed by him and by the anonymous author of the Life of Ceolfrith. Although Bede's attitude to historical matters in the *Chronica Maiora* of 725 is conventional enough, apart from his revision of the *Annus Mundi*, and far from satisfactory in the execution, within six years he had become the most significant historian of the early Middle Ages. In his hands the Christian era was lifted from a narrow legal background into a larger usefulness where it has remained ever since. Apart from the wealth of information he supplies, the writing of history, in the proper sense, was thereafter placed on a more secure foundation than almost anyone had known since classical antiquity. Fortunate in the circumstances of his early life, Bede was now able to reduce any kind of date to a uniform system – Indictional years, imperial or consular years, and the regnal years of several kingdoms. Whatever the limits of outlook, shared by most others of his day and age, he is unusually careful and clear-headed in the handling of chronology; his mistakes are a trifle, a brick or two out of place in the solid architecture. A tribute from Jones (1947: 43) is both accurate and concise: 'Bede would not invent a date.'

At the same time he set his face firmly against the Indiction, ambiguous as a system of dating, and clearly becoming obsolete. In determining to be rid of it, Bede nonetheless respected the material of Papal or conciliar origin, but as a rule when transcribing an Indictional figure he separately added the equivalent Year of Grace. To what extent he led, or conformed with, current opinion is perhaps of no moment; what matters is that in England, to all appearances, Bede killed the Indiction. His spiritual descendants were no less firm. During the eighth century a series of Northumbrian Annals shows only a faint trace of Indictional reckoning, with

---

[15] According to Poole (1934: 178–9), the adoption at Rome of dating by the Year of Grace, under John XIII, took place about 970, through the influence of Otto the Great; but the regular use of this style is not older than the pontificate of Leo IX, 1048–54.

many more entries in favour of a change of year at Christmas; towards the end of the century Alcuin is found lending his support. A number of Mercian charters, more especially documents issued by two councils at *Clofeshoh,* serve to complete the picture: after Bede the Indiction is retained as no more than a formality.

Meanwhile, though from circumstantial evidence only, it appears that some of the material which now forms part of the Anglo-Saxon Chronicle may have had its origin in the decade 660 to 670, or soon after. The earliest manuscript is not older than 891; yet there are features, such as archaic grammatical form, spelling of personal names, and the frequency of obscure place-names, which suggest a far earlier textual base, apart from touches looking as if they proceeded from a contemporary hand. It is only possible, rather than probable, that material of subsequent value was written down in the sixth century, before the arrival of Augustine. But the assignment of Hengest and Horsa's landing to the joint reign of Marcian and Valentinian appears to stand on a different footing from the remainder of the annals. Commonly ascribed to Bede, perhaps because it is first recorded in the *Chronica Maiora,* this type of reckoning could well derive from any period within the century preceding 660; it is as appropriate to the age of Gregory of Tours, or Bertha and Liudhard, as the Ripon estimate is to the years after 660. That some kind of entry once stood roughly at 449 is shown by the mention of Ebbsfleet (*Ypwinesfleot*), which occurs in no other source. Possibly, then, the proto-chronicle, or earliest native annals, began here, for we do not know when the still earlier entries were made, and the origin of some of them, apart from Bede, is doubtful.[16] As to the remaining annals, before 600, the combination of a luni-solar calendar with regnal lists affords a base for the reckoning, and the Wessex entries from 495 to 527 by their duplication seem to reveal a measure of internal consistency. In the absence of a sufficient documentary background, all that can be safely said amounts to this: the earliest dates in the Chronicle may have suffered from errors in transcription, but in substance they need not be founded on guesswork, and there is a little evidence that some of the figures are not. Thus the genesis

---

[16] The entry under 418 is puzzling; for different types of explanation see Charlesworth (1949: 35–6) and W. H. Davies (in Kirby 1968: 42, n. 7).

of the Chronicle, so far from being obscure, could be more rational and straightforward than critics have been able to allow.

For the Anglo-Saxon chroniclers, no matter when they lived and worked, as for Bede, the sign-posts of history had originated within various systems of reckoning: pagan and luni-solar, imperial or consular and Julian, with or without the Indiction, and the eras of Victorius and Dionysius.[17] The study of time-reckonings is only one form of historical criticism, to be tempered by others, and all told amounting to the rigours of common sense. It may be hoped that none of the suggestions which have been put forward are extravagant or absurd; though perhaps too much weight has been given to what is simple and probable, with too little regard for the tangles which future explorers may discover. In a phrase, therefore, this essay must be regarded as a 'first approximation', and no more.

---

[17] The 'autumn' dating of annals in the Chronicle from about 850 until just after the reign of Alfred is idiosyncratic enough to suggest a group of clerks with a secular outlook; perhaps a continental parallel may be found.

APPENDIX I

SUCCESSION AMONG KENTISH KINGS

With reference to *BCS* 42 (above, p. 69), Professor Whitelock has kindly allowed this quotation from an unpublished lecture, delivered some years ago, to be printed here with supplementary notes; to which a few additions are distinguished by square brackets.

Whatever its date, this is an important text for what it tells us about Swaebheard. He calls himself *rex Cantuariorum*, and the charter is dated 1 March in the second year of his reign, the fourth Indiction. The grant is made with the consent of Aethelred of Mercia, and with the counsel and consent of Swaebheard's own father, King Sebbi, whom we know to have been king of Essex. The fourth Indiction could be either 676 or 691. The confirming clause, by Aethelred of Mercia, which is also in the fourth Indiction, gives the Incarnation date 676...The copyist who added it may have been influenced in his choice by reading in Bede or the Anglo-Saxon Chronicle that Aethelred ravaged Kent in that year. The alternative possibility for the Indiction, 691, would fit Swaebheard rather well. March 691 would be in his second year if he had come to the throne before March 690; he attests Oswine's charter of 27 January 690, *BCS* 35, without title [wrongly dated to 675 by Birch]. Yet the charter [*BCS* 42] claims to have been made with the counsel of Archbishop Theodore, and is attested by him. He died on 19 September 690; so, unless his name is assumed to be a later addition to a charter which mentioned no archbishop, (the see was vacant 690–92), it cannot belong to 691. It is therefore dated 676, e.g., by Stenton [*PASE*: 51] and connected with the ravaging of Kent by Aethelred of Mercia in that year. This date has been held to be supported by the occurrence of six of the lay signatories on a charter of Hlothere of 679 (*BCS* 45), but this argument loses force when we find four of them attesting some twenty years later.

The following six occur in *BCS* 45, a contemporary copy: Gumberct, Gebred, Osfrid, Hagona, Bernhard and Gudhard. Four of these names, Gebred, Hagona, Bernhard and Gudhard occur among *BCS* 96, 97 and 98, all of 697. *BCS* 97 has also Aehcha who is (I think) the Ecce of *BCS* 42. Hagona and Beornheard are found in *BCS* 99, of 699. For the years intervening between 676 and 699, or before 676, it will be convenient to make a list.

BCS 36. Charter of Hlothere (preserved in the Trinity Hall MS.), April, first year of reign, third Indiction, i.e., 675; therefore, if the Indiction figure is correctly copied, Hlothere did not succeed until April 674. Bede dates Egbert's death to July 673, in which year he places the Council of Hertford. He says Hlothere reigned eleven years and seven months, so it looks as though he had a detailed regnal list of some kind. The witness list of *BCS* 36 has two of those in *BCS* 42, Ecca and Osfrid. Here we should look at *BCS* 35 (also from the Trinity Hall MS). It is a charter of Oswine, second year of his reign, third Indiction, 27 January; and it is witnessed by Swaebheard. The Indiction would be for either 675 or 690. Birch chose 675, but it is generally taken to belong to 690. This latter date would put both Oswine and Swaebheard into Bede's period of doubtful kings after Eadric [*reges dubii uel externi*, *HE*, IV. 26, and Swaebheard was an East Saxon outsider]. Note that apart from the addition of the signatures of the two kings, the list is identical with that of *BCS* 36, including Ecca and Osfrid. Unfortunately both charters have only this curtailed list, and one cannot help wondering whether the cartulary scribe has copied one from the other. But if this charter is of 690, Ecca can be added to those witnesses of *BCS* 42 who appear as late as 690.

BCS 40. Grant by Oswine, who claims royal descent [*in regno patrum meorum*]; witnesses Swaebheard and Acce (for Ecce). No date. [Also from Trinity Hall MS]

BCS 41. Charter of Suabert. Is this an error for Swaebheard? No date. Witnessed only by two of the signatories of *BCS* 42, Gumberct and Aecci (Ecce). [Trinity Hall MS.]

BCS 44. Hlothere, fourth year of reign, sixth Indiction, i.e. 678. Fragment only, no signatures. [See below].

BCS 45. Hlothere (as above, month of May, seventh Indiction, 679). This charter has the six agreements with the list in *BCS* 42, mentioned already, and five other names, Irminred, Aedilmar, Aeldred, Aldhod, and Velhisc. (Compare 'Welisc presbyter' in Caedwalla's charter, *BCS* 72 of 698. The name is *very* uncommon.)

BCS 73. Oswine, grant of land inherited from his 'parents' [*de terra iuris mei quae mihi ex propinquitate parentum meorum uenit*], and confirmed by Aethelred of Mercia. Dated July, second Indiction, i.e. 674 or 689. Witnessed by Sabertus (is he Suabertus of *BCS* 41, Suabherdus?), Ecca as in *BCS* 42, Osfrid as in *BCS* 42 and 45, Aedilmar (*BCS* 45), Burgred, Eana, Frod (*BCS* 97 and 98), Uaeba (Ueba in *BCS* 99), and Suydred (perhaps Scirierdi of *BCS* 99; it is the Scirheard of *BCS* 91, below). [Trinity Hall MS.]

BCS 86. Grant by Wihtred, 17 July, third year of reign, seventh Indiction, i.e., 694. This shows that Bernhard, who is in *BCS* 42 and 45, was still signing in 694; he is also in *BCS* 99, of 699 (Beornheard). Trinity Hall MS.

BCS 89. Caedwalla's grant. [No date, but he reigned about 686–8.] Note about this that the parts printed by Birch in square brackets are not in the manuscript, and appear to be Kemble's invention. That means that the list beginning with Caedwalla's name probably goes down to 'Signum Cuffan'. [In other words, *Donatione uero Sigheri infra cernuntur* could be interpolated.]

If so, it shows that King Sighere was probably subservient to Caedwalla; and this list includes Gebred and Egeran (for Egesan, with a common misreading of *s* as *r*), both of whom occur in *BSC* 42. Snoccan and Teodan occur as witnesses also in Caedwalla's Farnham charter, *BCS* 72 [translation in EHD: 445]; Aedbert could be 'Eadbertus abbas' on that charter. So we get Egesan of *BCS* 42 as late as about 686–8. I take it, then, that we have three confirmations: one by Swaebheard (with Sebbi of Essex called 'bishop' in error); one by Wihtred, with Beornheard as witness, as in *BCS* 42 (both confirmations have Haecci, who could be the Ecce of *BCS* 42); and one by Aethelred of Mercia, including Teoda *princeps*, presumably the same person as the man Teoda in Caedwalla's list of signatories and in the Farnham charter (*BCS* 72).

BCS 91 is probably spurious. The names may come in part from genuine lists, e.g. Ecca and Scirhead.

BCS 96. Grant by Wihtred, 2 April in the sixth year of his reign. Gefred and Guthard (as in *BCS* 42). [Trinity Hall MS.]

BCS 97. Grant by the same, July, tenth Indiction, i.e., 697. Hagana and Bernhaerd, as in *BCS* 42; and I think Aehcha is the Ecce of *BCS* 42.

BCS 98. Grant by the same, July, with *xiii*^ma instead of *xm*^a for the Indiction [see Birch's note]. It has the same witness list.

BCS 99. Grant by the same, 8 April, eighth year of reign, twelfth Indiction, i.e. 699. It has Ecca, Hagana and Beornheard, as in *BCS* 42. It also has agreements with *BCS* 73, e.g. Ecca, Ueba and Scirierd (if that is the same as Suydred), which supports taking *BCS* 73 as to be dated 689 rather than 674.

If, then, we were to date *BCS* 42 to 676, it would mean that during the reign of Hlothere there was a king belonging to the East Saxon royal family ruling in Kent for over a year, for some time before 1 March 675, without Bede mentioning this. Moreover, this same East Saxon ruler then disappears from all sources until he appears as a witness in Oswine's charter of 689, *BCS* 73. What was he doing in the interim of 13 years?

I would take the fourth Indiction in the date of the grant as a copyist's error, taken from the date of the confirmation. A grant made on 1 March, in the fourth Indiction, cannot have been confirmed on Sunday 8 January, in the same Indiction. The 8 January was a Sunday in 691. Surely, then, it is likely that the confirmation was made on 8 January 691, and the grant on the previous 1 March, the Indiction being altered by adding a minim to make it conform with the confirmation clause by someone who did not notice that a different event was being dated. If we date the charter to 1 March 690, it is right that Theodore should be concerned...As the charter is in Swaebheard's second year, he must have been king when he attests Oswine's charter of 689, without title, and it may be that joint rulers did not always add their titles when attesting the texts of their colleagues.

These observations of Professor Whitelock are complementary to those already made (above, p. 69). We can therefore return to the point raised by Kirby (1963: 517); from the evidence of *BCS* 36 and 44 (see above, in Professor Whitelock's notes) it appears that Hlothere did not begin to reign until April 674 at the earliest. Yet Swaebheard cannot have succeeded on or soon after Egbert's death, July 673 (*HE*, IV. 5), if his second year takes in 1 March 676, the fourth Indiction. But if, following Professor Whitelock's argument, the transcriber added a minim to the Indiction of the original grant, then this grant will be now dated 1 March 675, which could have fallen into Swaebheard's second year, supposing him on the throne not long after July 673. His career at this time may have been so short and inglorious as to deserve no mention from Bede, who seldom took much interest in the details of political life. Still, a ruler once expelled does not often return more than a dozen years later; Wiglaf of Mercia (*ASC*: year 830), for a short while dethroned by the West Saxons, hardly affords a fair parallel. On balance, the evidence seems to favour 1 March 690 for the original grant (above, p. 70). And an interregnum can apparently last for a long time, as in Mercia from about 655–8, when it is not certain that anyone but Oswiu of Northumbria effectively ruled the kingdom (Hunter Blair 1950: 253).

These puzzles in the decade 670–80, which Bede was seemingly unaware of, may be thought to imply that his earlier succession of Kentish kings could be at fault. Yet the instability of the kingdom at this period, and later, during the reign of Caedwalla of Wessex (686–8), surely owes as much to external as to internal influences. 'By 670, when Oswiu died, it is probable that the whole of southern England was under Wulfhere's lordship, for between 670 and his death in 674 [675, according to *HE*, V. 24] he invaded Northumbria at the head of an army drawn from all the southern English peoples. He was defeated by Ecgfrith, Oswiu's son, and the confederation he had formed was dissolved' (*ASE*: 85). The battle took place in 674 (Hunter Blair 1950: 254–5). Thus Wulfhere could have been the effective ruler of Kent for about a year after Egbert's death in July 673, during an interregnum. A northward expansion of Mercian overlordship being checked in 674, Aethelred's treatment of Kent in 676 may reflect a change of direction to the south-east. From *BCS* 34 it appears that Egbert of Kent was recognised as a king in

Surrey at least for a few years before his death (*ASE*: 61), even though the consent of Wulfhere seems to have been required for the later endowment of Chertsey Abbey (*BCS* 54). Ethelbert's overlordship had suffered by competition from Raedwald of East Anglia before 616 (*HE*, II. 5), yet there is no sound evidence of a serious disturbance in the line of Kentish kings before 670. Eadbald was still heathen when he mounted the throne, but his earlier years were not counted as *anni infausti*; his successor Eorcenberht (640–64) was powerful enough to overthrow the idols and enforce the Lenten fast (*HE*, III. 8). In any case the mainstream of Bede's chronology runs back to the battle of *Degsastan* in 603, tied to the first imperial year of Phocas.

APPENDIX 2

NUMEROLOGY

The dates attached to historical events are sometimes found to be arranged in a regular pattern, and there is a temptation to separate the numbers from their context and then to read more into the pattern of isolated numbers than is warranted. On all counts it will be agreed that the element of chance in history is very considerable: the aftermath of a trifling injury or disease can fell a man almost without warning, against all probability. When a king dies, or a battle is fought, the date in terms of years, months or days is for most practical purposes a chance affair, no matter how it may come to be interpreted in later times. Otherwise expressed, the event is brought about by a multitude of variable factors. In spite of these obvious considerations, the study of numbers divorced from their context seldom seems to lose its grip on historical writing; wary of coincidence, the mind nevertheless continues to be fascinated by regularity in a pattern of dates.

This type of thinking is exemplified by Lappenberg (1845: I, 75–8 and 245), whose ideas have enjoyed a lasting currency in one form or another. He observed in the Anglo-Saxon Chronicle a frequent interval of four or eight years between events: as, 457, 465, 473, 485; 491, 495; then six other groups, and finally 607, 611 (details in Earle and Plummer 1899: II, cxii). The regnal years among early kings of Kent also attracted his attention, with four or eight as divisors: Oisc (Aesc) 24 years, Octa and Eormenric together 48 years—though the length of each separate reign is not known—Ethelbert 56 years, Eadbald 24 years and Eorcenberht 24 years likewise. Yet taking all the dates in the Chronicle from 449 (*recte* 450) as far as 611 or 664, Lappenberg did not notice that this sort of game can be played as well with threes, sixes and the occasional nine (Harrison 1971: 529, n. I). Even the pattern of an *octaëteris* can reveal a puzzling regularity (above, p. 5, n. 6), and of far more interest is what astronomers call Bode's Law, though it is only an approximation. The mean distances of the planets from the sun are represented in the following way: take the series 0, 0.3, 0.6, 1.2, 2.4, . . ., and to each number add 0.4, giving 0.4, 0.7, 1.0, 1.6, 2.8, . . ., roughly the proportionate mean distances. The last figure can be taken as a disintegrated planet, in the form of a belt of asteroids; but Uranus does not provide a close fit; and after Bode's death, the discovery of Neptune by Le Verrier and by Adams in 1846, capped by the ninth planet, Pluto, in 1930, put Bode's series out of court. Attempts were made to explain the figures by Newtonian dynamics, but with no success; and in the text-books of today this 'law' is mentioned as a curiosity, perhaps as a warning.

Attempts have also been made to account for Lappenberg's findings. He himself was aware of the *octaëteris*; yet to maintain that the Christian kings of Kent were obliging enough to die in their beds, or do away with themselves, at the behest of a multiple of eight, is surely not a compelling line of argument. None perished in battle, so far as we know; Eorcenberht may have died of the plague in 664. Northumbria, moreover, does not conform to this pattern of regnal years, even in pagan times when an *octaëteris* might underlie the calendar; the full list of kings has been examined by Hunter Blair (1950). The grouping by fours has invited an explanation which is given here in a recent form. Referring to Table 2 (above, p. 35), and marking the letter B at the left, it is seen that 'the margin was divided into isolated spaces by recurrent indications of leap years', and thus 'the curious fact that the entries relating to the English conquest tend to be spaced out at intervals of four or eight years suggests that they were derived from notes inserted retrospectively into chronological tables devised for the finding of Easter' (*ASE*: 15–16). A rubricated letter B could indeed occupy a fair amount of space in the margin – if that is what is being implied. Yet Jones, writing from an extensive knowledge of these tables, has complained that 'the fours and eights, such as they are, do not occur in any fixed relation to the bissextile years, and the marginal *B(issextilis)* is not enough to govern any annalist in analogous existing copies. In fact, had it not been for Lappenberg's ingenuity, I doubt whether the fours and eights would ever have been noticed' (1947: 191).

Again, a chronicler needs only a list of *Anni Domini* and perhaps *Indictiones* for his work, the remaining columns of an Easter Table being of virtually no use to him – at least when handling information from heathen times. Can we be sure that the letter B was in any way necessary to a chronicler, whenever or wherever he lived? For what it is worth, the oldest surviving text of the Anglo-Saxon Chronicle does not mark the bissextile years (Hunter Blair 1956, reprint of 1970: pl. III); far more ancient chroniclers like Prosper and Hydatius also ignore them. In any case, even assuming that Easter tables were involved – and an assumption it is, however reasonable – scribes accustomed to glossing a text did not hesitate to write between the lines and sometimes down the margins, as illustrated by Poole (1926: 5–6) and by Garmonsway (1953: xxiv–xxv). There seems to be no palaeographical ground for thinking that in terms of space the marginal B governed their entries; in the example given by Smalley (1974: 57) the scribes wrote round it.

The leap-year theme has also been developed by Alcock (1973: 43). 'Much stress' he says 'has been laid on the fact that, even before the conversion of Kent in 597, a significant proportion of the annals follow a four-year cycle. It has been suggested that this is because events were entered, long after they had actually occurred, in an Easter table in which the leap years had been specially indicated. There are entries for the years 540, 544, 547, 552, 556, 560, 565, 568, but none for the intervening years. All of these, except for 547 and 565, are of course leap years, and it was certainly common practice to mark off the leap years in an Easter table, so the hypothesis seems sensible. It immediately exposes the artificiality of much of the pre-Christian chronology of the Chronicle.' The entries at 540, 547 and 565 surely ought to be deleted, since they are taken from Bede's Recapitulation (*HE*, v. 24) and could have been added at any time after 731. We are now left with a Lappenberg sequence: 544, 552, 556, 560 and 568, intervals of four and eight, every one a leap year.

Yet it is in the selection of these numbers that the 'artificiality' lies. When all the pagan dates are included, from 455 to 593, no firm conclusion can be drawn. Neither of the years 449 (*recte* 450) is a leap year; these figures from Bede are in any case excluded, and there is also uncertainty over the Northumbrian entry at 588, which is bissextile. Removing extraneous matter as far as possible, there are 27 or 28 entries of which 8 are leap years. Out of 28 random dates, the number of leap years to be expected is 7.23 ± 2.3, the probability of an even larger deviation being about 30 per cent; less accurately expressed, the ratio of bissextile to common years is 1:3.4 or 3.5, whereas the expected ratio, on random distribution, is 1:4. In a controlled experiment, and aware of all the circumstances, a statistician might persuade himself to think the results were significant enough for the experiment to be worth repeating; historians, dealing with events which are complex in origin and out of control when they happened, will perhaps incline to forget the matter.

When examining the statements which have been made about the relation between entries in Easter tables and the marginal B(issextilis), it is not easy to distinguish between two lines of thought, neither of which is clearly stated. Either the rubricated B cluttered up the margin, or, by an unexplained process of thought it attracted an entry. Once again we remember that a chronicler need not have used Easter tables – and would be better off without them, because given more room. Even so, neither palaeography nor statistics appear to support those who look for an 'artificial' arrangement of numbers, divorced from events, in the Anglo-Saxon Chronicle. It is, however, another matter when events seem to be duplicated and the numbers attached to them differ by nineteen (above, p. 127). Here a systematic error can be detected, arising from the transposition of these events into the wrong Dionysiac cycle.

As a final comment, the regnal years of Kentish kings are given in round numbers, which is an approximate measure; the lengths of reign in months or days would provide no neat and attractive pattern, for Ethelbert died on 24 February 616 and Eorcenberht on 14 July 664 (HE, II. 5; IV. 1), and Eadbald on 20 January 640 (Powicke and Fryde 1961: 7).

BIBLIOGRAPHY

❦

ABBREVIATIONS

ASC Translation of the *Anglo-Saxon Chronicle*, see Whitelock, D. with Douglas, D. C. and Tucker, S. I. 1961.

ASE *Anglo-Saxon England*, see Stenton, F. M. 1971. To be distinguished from the annual of the same name.

BCS Birch's *Cartularium Saxonicum*, see Birch, W. de G. 1885.

DTR Bede's *De Temporum Ratione*, see Jones, C. W. 1943.

EHD *English Historical Documents*, I, see Whitelock, D. 1955.

HAA Anonymous *Historia Abbatum*, see Plummer, C. 1896.

HAB Bede's *Historia Abbatum*, see Plummer, C. 1896.

HE Bede's *Historia Ecclesiastica*, see Plummer, C. 1896.

MGH The *Monumenta Germaniae Historica* series (in Bibliography only, under the names of editors).

PASE See Stenton, F. M. 1970.

SD Simeon of Durham, see Arnold, T. 1882–5.

RA Ramsey Annals, see Hart, C. R. 1970.

SPELLING

By the usual convention, familiar personal names are given in modern spelling, the less familiar in an Old English form: thus, Ethelbert king of Kent and Alfred or Egbert of Wessex, but Aethelweard the chronicler and Ecgfrith of Northumbria. Place-names not yet identified will be found in italics, as *Clofeshoh*. Latin variants like Baeda and Beda are retained in the Bibliography, where also foreign place-names are given in the English form, as Hanover not Hannover.

Aethelweard, see Campbell, A. 1962.

Alcock, L. 1973. *Arthur's Britain*. Revised ed. London.

Alcuin, see Dümmler, E. 1895.

Ammianus Marcellinus, see Rolfe, J. E. 1939.

BIBLIOGRAPHY

Anderson, A. O. & Anderson, M. O. 1961. (ed. & tr.) *Adomnan's Life of Columba*. London.

Anderson, M. O. 1973. *Kings and kingship in early Scotland*. Edinburgh.

Arnold, T. 1882 & 1885. (ed.) *Symeonis monachi opera omnia*, 2 vols. Rolls series, London.

Beaven, M. L. R. 1917. The regnal dates of Alfred, Edward the Elder and Athelstan. *English Historical Review*, 32: 517–31.

Beck, C. W. 1970. Amber in archaeology. *Archaeology*, 23: 7–11.

Bede, *De Natura Rerum*, see Migne, J. P. 1862.
  De Temporum Ratione, see Jones, C. W. 1943.
  Historia Abbatum, see Plummer, C. 1896.
  Historia Ecclesiastica, see Colgrave, B. & Mynors, R. A. B. 1969; Plummer, C. 1896.

Bickerman, E. J. 1968. *The chronology of the ancient world*. London.

Biddle, M. 1972. Excavations at Winchester. *Antiquaries Journal*, 52: 94–8.

Binchy, D. A. 1970. *Celtic and Anglo-Saxon kingship*. Oxford.

Birch, W. de G. 1885. (ed.) *Cartularium Saxonicum*, 3 vols. London.

Boniface of Mainz, see Dümmler, E. 1892.

Bonner, G. 1973. Bede and medieval civilization. In *Anglo-Saxon England*, ed. P. Clemoes, 2: 71–90.

Bonser, W. 1963. *The medical background of Anglo-Saxon England*. London.

Boretius, A. 1883. (ed.) *Capitularia Regum Francorum, MGH, Legum*, 2. Hanover.

Borius, R. 1965. (ed.) *Constance de Lyon, vie de Saint Germain d'Auxerre*. Paris.

Bresslau, H. 1923. Die ältere Salzburger Annalistik. *Abdhandlungen der Preussischen Akademie der Wissenschaften, Phil.-Hist. Klasse*, 2.

Brooke, C. (N.L.) 1967. *The Saxon and the Norman kings*. London.

Brooks, N. 1971. The development of military obligations in eighth- and ninth-century England. In *England before the Conquest*, ed. P. Clemoes & K. Hughes: 69–84. Cambridge.

Brown, D. 1974. Problems of continuity. In *British Archaeological Reports*, ed. T. Rowley, 6: 16–19.

Bruce-Mitford, R. L. S. 1969. The art of the Codex Amiatinus. *Journal of the British Archaeological Association*, 32: 1–25.

Bury, J. B. 1898. (ed.) *The decline and fall of the Roman empire*, by E. Gibbon, 7 vols. London.
  1923. *A history of the later Roman empire*, 2 vols. London.

Campbell, A. 1962. (ed. & tr.) *The chronicle of Aethelweard*. London.

Chaney, W. A. 1970. *The cult of kingship in Anglo-Saxon England*. Manchester.

Chaplais, P. 1968. Some early Anglo-Saxon diplomas on single sheets: originals or copies? *Journal of the Society of Archivists*, 3: 315–36.
  1969. Who introduced charters into England? The case for Augustine. *Journal of the Society of Archivists*, 3: 526–42.

Charlesworth, M. P. 1949. *The lost province*. Cardiff.

Cockayne, O. 1864. (tr.) *Leechdoms, wortcunning and starcraft of early England*, 2 vols. Rolls series, London.

Colgrave, B. 1927. (ed. & tr.) *The life of Bishop Wilfrid by Eddius Stephanus.* Cambridge.

1956. (ed. & tr.) *Felix's life of St Guthlac.* Cambridge.

1968. (ed. & tr.) *The earliest life of Gregory the Great.* Lawrence, Kansas.

Colgrave, B. & Mynors, R. A. B. 1969. (ed. & tr.) *Bede's ecclesiastical history of the English people.* Oxford.

Collingwood, R. G. & Myres, J. N. L. 1937. *Roman Britain and the English settlements.* Oxford.

Columbanus, see Gundlach, W. 1892.

Constantius of Lyon, see Borius, R. 1965; Levison, W. 1919.

Cook, S. A. 1928. Chronology: the Old Testament. In *The Cambridge ancient history*, ed. J. B. Bury *et al.* 1: 156–66. Cambridge.

Cummian, see Migne, J. P. 1863; Oulton, J. E. L. 1957.

Cunliffe, B. (W.) 1970. The Saxon culture-sequence at Portchester castle. *Antiquaries Journal*, 50: 67–85.

Dalton, O. M. 1927. (tr.) *The history of the Franks by Gregory of Tours*, 2 vols. Oxford.

Davis, R. H. C. 1971. Alfred the Great: propaganda and truth. *History*, 56: 169–82.

Des Vignolles, A. 1738. *Chronologie de l'histoire sainte*, 2 vols. Berlin.

Dicks, D. R. 1970. *Early Greek astronomy to Aristotle.* London.

Dionysius Exiguus, see Krusch, B. 1938; Migne, J. P. 1865.

Dümmler, E. 1892. (ed.) *S. Bonifatii Epistolae, MGH, Epistolae Merovingici et Karolini Aevi*, 1: 216–431. Berlin.

1895. (ed.) *Alcuini Epistolae, MGH, Epistolae Merovingici et Karolini Aevi*, 2: 18–481. Berlin.

Dumville, D. 1974. Some aspects of the chronology of the Historia Brittonum. *Bulletin of the Board of Celtic Studies*, 25: 439–45.

Earle, J. & Plummer, C. 1892 & 1899. (ed.) *Two of the Saxon chronicles parallel*, 2 vols. Reprint of 1952 with an appendix on chronology by D. Whitelock, II: cxxxix–cxliid. Oxford.

Edwards, H. J. 1917. (ed. & tr.) Caesar, *De Bello Gallico.* London.

Eusebius of Caesarea, see Fotheringham, J. K. 1923; Lake, K. 1926.

Evison, V. I. 1965. *The fifth-century invasion south of the Thames.* London.

Ewald, P. 1887. (ed.) *Gregorii Papae I Registrum Epistolarum, MGH, Epistolae*, 1. Berlin.

Finberg, H. P. R. 1961. *Early charters of the west midlands.* Leicester.

1972. (ed.) *The agrarian history of England and Wales*, 1, pt. 2. Cambridge.

Förster, M. 1925. Die Weltzeitalter bei den Angelsachsen. In *Neusprachliche Studien: festgabe K. Luick*: 183–203. Marburg.

Fotheringham, J. K. 1923 (ed.) *Eusebii Chronici Canones*, Latin version. London.

Frazer, J. G. 1913. *The golden bough*, X. London.

Frere, S. S. 1967. *Britannia*. London.

Gallic Chroniclers, see Mommsen, T. 1892b.

Garmonsway, G. N. 1953. (tr.) *The Anglo-Saxon Chronicle*. London.

Germanus of Auxerre, see Borius, R. 1965; Levison, W. 1919.

Gildas, see Mommsen, T. 1898a; Williams, H. 1901.

Gjerstad, E. 1961. Notes on the early Roman calendar. *Acta Archaeologica (Copenhagen)*, 32: 193–214.

Grat, F., Vielliard, J. & Clémencet, S. 1964. (ed.) *Annales de St Bertin*. Paris.

Gregory of Tours, see Dalton, O. M. 1927; Krusch, B. & Levison, W. 1951.

Grierson, P. 1952. The Canterbury (St Martin's) hoard. *British Numismatic Journal*, 27: 39–51.

Grosjean, P. 1946. Recherches sur les debuts de la controverse Pascale chez les Celtes. *Analecta Bollandiana*, 64: 200–244.

  1957a. Notes d'hagiographie Celtique, 28: La seconde visite de S. Germain d'Auxerre en Grand-Bretagne. *Analecta Bollandiana*, 75; 174–80.

  1957b. Notes d'hagiographie Celtique, 29: Le dernier voyage de S. Germain d'Auxerre. *Analecta Bollandiana*, 75: 180–85.

  1960a. Notes d'hagiographie Celtique, 48: La date du colloque de Whitby. *Analecta Bollandiana*, 78: 233–74.

  1960b. Notes d'hagiographie Celtique, 49: Pour la date de fondation d'Iona et celle de la mort de S. Colum Cille. *Analecta Bollandiana*, 78: 381–90.

  1961. Un fragment d'obituaire anglo-saxon du viiie siècle. *Analecta Bollandiana*, 79: 320–45.

Gundlach, W. 1892. (ed.) *Columbani Epistolae*, MGH, *Epistolae Merovingici et Karoline Aevi*, I: 154–90.

Haddan, A. W. & Stubbs, W. 1873. (ed.) *Councils and ecclesiastical documents relating to Great Britain and Ireland*, III. Oxford.

Halkin, J. 1972. La nouvelle année au 23 septembre. *Analecta Bollandiana*, 90: 56.

Hardwick, C. 1858. (ed.) *Historia monasterii S. Augustini Cantuariensis*. Rolls Series, London.

Harmer, F. E. 1952. *Anglo-Saxon writs*. Manchester.

Harrison, K. 1960. The pre-Conquest churches of York: with an appendix on eighth-century Northumbrian annals. *Yorkshire Archaeological Journal*, 40: 232–49.

  1967. The beginning of the year among Bede's successors. *Yorkshire Archaeological Journal*, 42: 193–7.

  1971. Early Wessex annals in the Anglo-Saxon Chronicle. *English Historical Review*, 86: 527–33.

  1972. The reign of King Ecgfrith of Northumbria. *Yorkshire Archaeological Journal*, 44: 79–84.

  1973a. The *Annus Domini* in some early charters. *Journal of the Society of Archivists*, 4: 551–7.

BIBLIOGRAPHY

1973b. The beginning of the year in England, *c.* 500–900. *Anglo-Saxon England*, ed. P. Clemoes, 2: 51–70.

1973c. The primitive Anglo-Saxon calendar. *Antiquity*, 47: 284–7.

1973d. The Synod of Whitby and the beginning of the Christian era in England. *Yorkshire Archaeological Journal*, 45: 108–14.

Hart, C. R. 1966. *The early charters of eastern England.* Leicester.

1970. The Ramsey computus. *English Historical Review*, 85: 29–44.

Hawkes, C. F. C. 1956. The Jutes of Kent. In *Dark-age Britain*, ed. D. B. Harden: 91–111. London.

Hawkes, S. C. & Dunning, G. C. 1961. Soldiers and settlers in Britain, fourth to fifth century. *Medieval Archaeology*, 5: 1–70.

Heggie, D. C. 1972. Megalithic lunar observatories: an astronomer's view. *Antiquity*, 46: 43–8.

Hennessy, W. M. 1887. (ed.) *The annals of Ulster*, 4 vols. Vol. 4, introduction by B. Mac Carthy (1901). Dublin.

Hickes, G. 1703. *De Antiquae Litteraturae, . . ., Dissertatio.* Oxford.

Historia Francorum, by Gregory of Tours, see Dalton, O. M. 1927; Krusch, B. & Levison, W. 1951.

Hodgkin, R. H. 1952. *A history of the Anglo-Saxons*, 2 vols. Oxford.

Hoffmann, H. 1958. Untersuchungen zur Karolingischen Annalistik. *Bonner Historische Forschungen*, 10. Bonn.

Holweck, F. 1925. *Calendarium Liturgicum Festorum Dei et Dei Matris Mariae.* Philadelphia.

Hoskins, W. G. 1960. *The westward expansion of Wessex.* Leicester.

Hughes, K. 1972. *Early Christian Ireland: introduction to the sources.* Ithaca, N.Y.

Hunt, R. W. 1961. (ed.) St Dunstan's classbook from Glastonbury. *Umbrae Codicum Occidentalium*, 4. Amsterdam.

Hunt, W. 1893. (ed.) Two chartularies of the priory of St Peter, Bath. *Somerset Record Society*, 7.

Hunter Blair, P. 1948. The Northumbrians and their southern frontier. *Archaeologia Aeliana*, 26: 98–126.

1950. The Moore memoranda on Northumbrian history. In *Early cultures of north west Europe*, ed. C. Fox & B. Dickins: 243–59. Cambridge.

1956. *An introduction to Anglo-Saxon England.* Cambridge.

1959. (ed.) The Moore Bede. *Early English manuscripts in facsimile*, 9. Copenhagen.

1963. Some observations on the Historia Regum attributed to Simeon of Durham. In *Celt and Saxon: studies in the early British border*, ed. N. K. Chadwick: 63–118. Cambridge.

1970. The historical writings of Bede. *Settimane di studio del Centro italiano di studi sull'altro medioevo (Spoleto)*, 17: 197–257.

Hutton, M. 1946. (ed. & tr.) Tacitus, *Germania.* London.

Hydatius, see Mommsen, T. 1893a.

Jackson, K. H. 1953. *Language and history in early Britain.* Edinburgh.

1963. On the northern British section in Nennius. In *Celt and Saxon: studies in the early British border*, ed. N. K. Chadwick: 20–62. Cambridge.

Jaffé, P. 1885. (ed.) *Regesta Pontificum Romanorum*. Leipzig.

Jankuhn, H. 1952. The continental home of the English. *Antiquity*, 26: 14–24.

Jarrett, M. G. 1963. The military occupation of Roman Wales. *Bulletin of the Board of Celtic Studies*, 20: 206–20.

Jones, C. W. 1934. The Victorian and Dionysiac paschal tables in the west. *Speculum*, 9: 408–21.

1943. (ed.) *Bedae Opera de Temporibus*. Cambridge, Mass.

1947. *Saints' lives and chronicles in early England*. Ithaca, N.Y.

Kenney, J. F. 1929. *The sources for the early history of Ireland*, 1, *Ecclesiastical*. Columbia, N.Y. Reprinted 1966, with additions by L. Bieler. Dublin.

Ker, N. R. 1948. Hemming's cartulary. In *Studies in medieval history presented to F. M. Powicke*, ed. R. W. Hunt, W. A. Pantin & R. W. Southern: 49–75. Oxford.

Kirby, D. P. 1963. Bede and Northumbrian chronology. *English Historical Review*, 78: 514–27.

1965. Problems of early West Saxon history. *English Historical Review*, 80: 10–29.

1966. Bede's native sources for the Historia Ecclesiastica. *Bulletin of the John Rylands Library*, 48: 341–71.

1968. Vortigern. *Bulletin of the Board of Celtic Studies*, 23: 37–59.

Kirk, J. R. 1956. Anglo-Saxon cremation and inhumation in the upper Thames valley in pagan times. In *Dark-age Britain*, ed. D. B. Harden: 123–31. London.

Krusch, B. 1938. Studien zur christlich-mittelalterlichen Chronologie. *Abdhandlungen der Preussischen Akademie der Wissenschaften, Phil.Hist. Klasse*, 7, No. 8.

Krusch, B. & Levison, W. 1951. (ed.) *Gregorii Turonensis Opera, MGH, Scriptores Rerum Merovingicarum*, 1. Hanover.

Kurze, F. 1889 (ed.) *Thietmari Chronicon, MGH, Scriptores in usum scholarum*. Hanover.

Labat, R. 1963. Mesopotamia. In *Ancient and medieval science*, ed. R. Taton: 65–120. London.

Laistner, M. L. W. 1957. *Thought and letters in western Europe*. London.

Lake, K. 1926. (ed. & tr.) Eusebius, *The Ecclesiastical History*, 2 vols. London.

Lappenberg, J. M. 1845. *A history of England under the Anglo-Saxon kings*, tr. B. Thorpe, 2 vols. London.

Lehmann, P. 1925. Fuldauer Studien. *Sitzungsberichte der Bayerischen Akademie der Wissenschaften, Phil.-Hist. Klasse*, 3.

Leo, F. 1881. (ed.) *Venanti Fortunati Opera Poetica, MGH, Auct. Antiquiss.* 4. Berlin.

Lethbridge, T. C. 1956. The Anglo-Saxon settlement in eastern England. In *Dark-age Britain*, ed. D. B. Harden: 111–22. London.

BIBLIOGRAPHY

Levison, W. 1908. Willibrordiana. *Neues Archiv*, 33: 517–30.

1919. (ed.) *Constantius, Vita S. Germani, MGH, Scriptores Rerum Merovingicarum*, 7:247–83. Berlin.

1935. Bede as historian. In *Bede: his life, times and writing*, ed. A. Hamilton Thompson: 111–51. Oxford.

1940. St Willibrord and his place in history. *Durham University Journal*, 32: 23–41.

1941. St Alban and St Albans. *Antiquity*, 15: 337–59.

1946. *England and the continent in the eighth century*. Oxford.

Lietzmann, H. 1903. *Die drie ältesten Martyrologien*. Bonn.

Lowe, E. A. 1950. *Codices Latini Antiquiores*, 5. Oxford.

1959. *Codices Latini Antiquiores*, 8. Oxford.

Loyn, H. R. 1962. *Anglo-Saxon England and the Norman Conquest*. London.

Mac Carthy, B. 1892. The Codex Palatino-Vaticanus, No. 830. *Royal Irish Academy, Todd lecture series*, 3. Dublin.

1901. Introduction to the Annals of Ulster: see Hennessy, W. M. 1887.

Malinowsky, T. 1971. Über den Bernsteinhandel zwischen den südöstlichen baltischen Ufergebieten und dem Süden Europas in der frühen Eisenzeit. *Praehistorische Zeitschrift*, 46: 102–10.

Mansi, J. 1763. (ed.) *Sacrorum Conciliorum Collectio*, ix. Florence.

Marcellinus Comes, see Mommsen, T. 1893b.

Markus, R. 1963. The chronology of the Gregorian mission to England. *Journal of Ecclesiastical History*, 14: 16–30.

Marshack, A. 1964. Lunar notation on upper palaeolithic remains. *Science (USA)*, 146: 743–5.

Mason, A. J. 1897. (tr.) *The mission of St Augustine to England according to the original documents*. Cambridge.

Meaney, A. L. 1964. *A gazetteer of early Anglo-Saxon burial sites*. London.

Meyvaert, P. 1964. *Jarrow lecture: Bede and Gregory the Great*. Jarrow.

1970. The Registrum of Gregory the Great. *Revue Bénédictine*, 80: 162–6.

1971. Bede's text of the Libellus Responsionum. In *England before the Conquest*, ed. P. Clemoes & K. Hughes: 1–33. Cambridge.

Migne, J. P. 1862. (ed.) *Bedae de Natura Rerum, Patrologia Latina*, 90: cols. 187–278. Paris.

1863. (ed.) *Cummiani Epistola, Patrologia Latina*, 87: cols. 969–78.

1865. (ed.) *Dionysii liber de Paschate, Patrologia Latina*, 67: cols. 483–508.

Miller, M. 1975. Bede's use of Gildas. *English Historical Review*, 90: 241–61.

Mommsen, T. 1891a. (ed.) *Consularia Italica, MGH, Auct. Antiquiss.* 9: 274–339, 744–50. Berlin.

1891b. (ed.) *Liber Paschalis Codicis Cizensis, MGH, Auct. Antiquiss.* 9: 507–10, 740–43. Berlin.

1892a. (ed.) *Prosperi Chronica, MGH, Auct. Antiquiss.* 9: 385–485. Berlin.

1892b. (ed.) *Chronica Gallica, MGH, Auct. Antiquiss.* 9: 631–66. Berlin.

1892c. (ed.) *Victorii Cursus Paschalis*, MGH, *Auct. Antiquiss.* 9: 684–735. Berlin.

1892d. (ed.) *Adnotationes Antiquiores ad Cyclos Dionysianos*, MGH, *Auct. Antiquiss.* 9: 753–6. Berlin.

1893a. (ed.) *Hydatii Chronicon*, MGH, *Auct. Antiquiss.* 11: 13–35. Berlin.

1893b. (ed.) *Marcellini Comitis Chronicon*, MGH, *Auct. Antiquiss.* 11: 60–108. Berlin.

1893c. (ed.) *Victoris Tonnennensis Chronica*, MGH, *Auct. Antiquiss.* 11: 184–206. Berlin.

1894a. (ed.) *Isidori Historia Gothorum, etc.*, MGH, *Auct. Antiquiss.* 11: 267–95. Berlin.

1894b. (ed.) *Isidori Chronica*, MGH, *Auct. Antiquiss.* 11: 424–81. Berlin.

1894c. (ed.) *Marii Aventicensis Chronicon*, MGH, *Auct. Antiquiss.* 11: 232–9. Berlin.

1898a. (ed.) *Gildae de Excidio Britanniae*, MGH, *Auct. Antiquiss.* 13: 25–85. Berlin.

1898b. (ed.) *Nennii Historia Brittonum*, MGH, *Auct. Antiquiss.* 13: 147–219. Berlin.

1898c. (ed.) *Bedae Chronica*, MGH, *Auct. Antiquiss.* 13: 247–327. Berlin.

Morris, C. 1971. The plague in Britain. *Historical Journal*, 14: 205–15.

Morris, J. 1965. Dark age dates. In *Britain and Rome*, ed. M. G. Jarrett & B. Dobson: 144–85. Kendal.

1973. *The age of Arthur*. London.

Myres, J. N. L. 1951. The Adventus Saxonum. In *Aspects of archaeology*, ed. W. F. Grimes: 221–41. London.

1956. Romano-Saxon pottery. In *Dark-age Britain*, ed. D. B. Harden, 16–39. London.

1969. *Anglo-Saxon pottery and the settlement of England*. Oxford.

1970. The Angles, the Saxons and the Jutes. *Proceedings of the British Academy*, 56: 145–74.

Myres, J. N. L. & Green, B. 1973. The Anglo-Saxon cemeteries of Caistor-by-Norwich and Markshall, Norfolk. *Society of Antiquaries, Research Committee Reports*, No. 30. London.

Nennius, see Mommsen, T. 1898b; Wade-Evans, A. W. 1938.

Neugebauer, O. 1957. *The exact sciences in antiquity*. Providence, R. I.

Newton, R. R. 1972. *Medieval chronicles and the rotation of the earth*. Baltimore and London.

Nilsson, (N.) M. P. 1916. Studien zur vorgeschicte des Weinachtsfester. *Archiv für Religionswissenschaft*, 19: 50–150.

1920. *Primitive time-reckonings*. Lund.

O'Connell, D. J. 1936. Easter cycles in the early Irish church. *Journal of the Royal Society of Antiquaries of Ireland*, 66: 67–106.

Addendum, ibid., 67: 311.

Offler, H. S. 1970. Hexham and the Historia Regum. *Transactions of the*

BIBLIOGRAPHY

Architectural and Archaeological Society of Durham and Northumberland, 2: 51–62.

O'Rahilly, T. F. 1946. *Early Irish history and mythology*. Dublin.

Oulton, J. E. L. 1957. The epistle of Cummian. In *Studia Patristica*, ed. K. Aland & F. C. Cross, 1: 128–33. Berlin.

Page, R. I. 1970. *Life in Anglo-Saxon England*. London.

Plummer, C. 1896. (ed.) *Baedae Opera Historica*, 2 vols. Oxford. Includes also the *Historia Abbatum* by an anonymous monk.

Poole, R. L. 1918a. The earliest use of the Easter cycle of Dionysius. *English Historical Review*, 33: 57–62, 210–13.

1918b. *Medieval reckonings of time*. London.

1926. *Chronicles and annals*. Oxford.

1934. *Studies in chronology and history*. Oxford.

Powicke, F. M. & Fryde, E. B. 1961. (ed.) *A handbook of British chronology*. London.

Prosper, see Mommsen, T. 1892a.

Renfrew, C. 1973. *Before civilization*. London.

Richardson, H. G. & Sayles, G. O. 1966. *Law and legislation from Ethelbert to Magna Carta*. Edinburgh.

Robertson, A. J. 1956. (ed.) *Anglo-Saxon charters*. Cambridge.

Roger de Hoveden, see Stubbs, W. 1868.

Rolfe, J. E. 1939. (ed. & tr.) *Ammianus Marcellinus*. London.

Sawyer, P. H. 1962. *The age of the Vikings*. London.

1968. *Anglo-Saxon charters: an annotated list and bibliography*. London.

Schwarz, E. 1905. Christliche und jüdische Ostertafeln. *Abdhandlungen der Köngl. Gesellschaft zu Göttingen, Phil.-Hist. Klasse*, 8, No. 6.

Scudamore, W. E. 1880. Paschal epistles. In *Dictionary of Christian antiquities*, ed. W. Smith & S. Cheetham, 2 vols. London.

Shrewsbury, J. F. D. 1970. *A history of bubonic plague in the British Isles*. Cambridge.

Sisam, K. 1953. Anglo-Saxon royal genealogies. *Proceedings of the British Academy*, 39: 287–346.

Smalley, B. 1974. *Historians in the middle ages*. London.

Smyth, A. P. 1972. The earliest Irish annals. *Proceedings of the Royal Irish Academy*, 72 C: 1–48.

Stenton, F. M. 1925. The south-western element in the Old English Chronicle. In *Essays in medieval history presented to T. F. Tout*, ed. A. G. Little & F. M. Powicke: 15–24. Manchester.

1926. The foundations of English history. *Transactions of the Royal Historical Society*, 4th ser. 9: 159–73.

1936. St Frideswide and her times. *Oxoniensia*, 1: 103–12.

1955. *Latin charters of the Anglo-Saxon period*. Oxford.

1970. *Preparatory to Anglo-Saxon England*: collected papers, ed. D. M. Stenton. Oxford.

1971. *Anglo-Saxon England*, 3rd ed. (1st ed. 1943, 2nd ed. 1947). Oxford.

Stevens, C. E. 1941. Gildas sapiens. *English Historical Review*, 56: 353–73.

1957. Marcus, Gratian, Constantine. *Athenaeum (Pavia)*, 35: 316–47.

Stevenson, W. H. 1904. (ed.) *Asser's life of King Alfred, with the Annals of St Neots*. Reprinted 1959, with a supplement by D. Whitelock. Oxford.

Strong, D. E. 1966. British Museum: *Catalogue of the carved amber, Department of Greek and Roman antiquities*. London.

Stubbs, W. 1868. (ed.) *Chronica Rogeri de Hoveden*, vol. I. Rolls series, London.

Sulimirski, T. 1970. *The Sarmatians*. London.

Swanton, M. J. 1974. Finglesham man. *Antiquity*, 48: 313–15.

Talbot Rice, T. 1957. *The Scythians*. London.

Thietmar of Merseberg, see Kurze, F. 1889.

Thom, A. 1971. *Megalithic lunar observatories*. Oxford.

Thompson, E. A. 1957. A chronological note on St. Germanus of Auxerre. *Analecta Bollandiana*, 75: 135–8.

Thomson, G. 1943. The Greek calendar. *Journal of Hellenic Studies*, 43: 53–65.

Thorogood, A. J. 1933. The Anglo-Saxon Chronicle in the reign of Ecgberht. *English Historical Review*, 48: 353–63.

Tolstoy, N. 1964. Early British history and chronology. *Transactions of the Hon. Society of Cymmrodorion* (no vol. number): 237–312.

Turner, G. J. & Salter, H. E. 1915. (ed.) *The register of St Augustine's abbey, Canterbury*. London.

Van de Vyver, A. 1957. L'evolution du comput Alexandrin et Romain du 3e au 5e siècle. *Revue d'histoire ecclésiastique*, 52: 1–25.

Verlinden, C. 1954. Frankish colonization: a new approach. *Transactions of the Royal Historical Society*, 5th ser. 4: 1–17.

Victorius of Aquitaine, see Mommsen, T. 1892c; Krusch, B. 1938.

Wade-Evans, A. W. 1938. (tr.) *Nennius's history of the Britons and the story of the loss of Britain*. London.

Wallace-Hadrill, J. M. 1960. (ed.) *The fourth book of the chronicle of Fredegar*. London.

1967. *The barbarian west: 400–1000*. London.

1971. *Early Germanic kingship in England and on the continent*. Oxford.

Wheeler, G. H. 1921. The genealogy of the early West Saxon kings. *English Historical Review*, 36: 161–71.

White, D. A. 1961. *Litus Saxonicum*. Madison, Wisconsin.

Whitelock, D. 1952a. *The beginnings of English society*. London.

1952b. On the commencement of the year in the Saxon chronicles. See Earle, J. & Plummer, C. 1899.

1955. (ed. & tr.) *English historical documents*, I, c. 500–1042. London.

1959. See Stevenson, W. H. 1904.

1960. *Jarrow lecture: After Bede*. Jarrow.

BIBLIOGRAPHY

Whitelock, D. with Douglas, D. C. & Tucker, S. I. 1961. (tr.) *The Anglo-Saxon Chronicle: a new translation.* London.

Williams, H. 1901. (tr.) *Gildae De Excidio, Cymmrodorion Record Series,* 3. London.

Wilson, H. A. 1918. (ed.) The calendar of St Willibrord. *Henry Bradshaw Society,* 55.

Wright, C. E. 1939. *The cultivation of saga in Anglo-Saxon England.* Edinburgh.

INDEX

꤮

Abbreviations: abp., archbishop(s) of; bp., bishop(s) of; e., emperor; k., king(s) of; q., queen of; r., river. Place-names not identified are given in *italics*. The names of those witnessing charters, except kings, bishops and abbots, are not included, being all in Appendix 1. Material in footnotes is indexed under page-numbers only.

Abraham, *see* era
accession to the throne, Northumbria, 87–8
Adams, J. C., 148
Adomnan, abbot,
  De Locis Sanctis, 136
  see Columba
Aduentus Saxonum, 18–21, 99–101, 123–6
Advent, 38
Aelfwine, 73, 124
Aelfwold, k. Northumbria, 109–111
Aelle, k. Sussex, 131
Aesc, *see* Oisc, k. Kent
Aescwine, k. Wessex, 135
Aethelfrith, k. Northumbria, 51, 95–6, 129, 132
Aethelred, k. Mercia, 68–70, 142–4
Aethelweard, *see* chroniclers
Aethelwold Moll, k. Northumbria, 106, 113
Aetius, 23–4, 77, 124–6
Agatho, Pope, 71
Agilbert, bp. Dorchester, 56
Aidan, bp. Lindisfarne, 51, 59, 62, 99
Alaric, k. Goths, 24
Alban, martyr, 18, 28
Albinus, abbot, 17, 100
Alcuin, 8–9, 101, 107, 111, 114
Aldfrith, k. Northumbria, 85, 88–91, 94, 97
Aldhelm, bp. Sherborne, 134–5
Alexandria
  mathematics, 31
  Paschal epistles, 31
  bp., *see* Cyril, Dionysius, Theophilus
Alfred, k. Wessex, 13, 117, 124
Alhfrith, sub-k. Deira, 65, 99, 135
Alhmund, bp. Hexham, 107, 111
Alhred, k. Northumbria, 109, 113
All Saints' day, 117
amber, 11

Ambrose, bp. Milan, 43
Ambrosius Aurelianus, 22
Ammianus Marcellinus, 15
Anastasius, e., 125
Angeln, *Angulus*, 20
Anglesey, 25
Anglo-Saxon Chronicle
  beginning of year, 86, 117–18, 141
  dislocation of dates, 106, 109–111, 120
  duplicated events, 127–30, 140, 150
  early entries, 132–5, 140
  numerology, 147–50
  versions, 13, 89–90, 101, 113, 120
Anna, k. East Anglia, 134–5
annals and chronicles, 44, 55
  Burgundian, 48
  Consularia Italica, 46
  Corvey, 45
  Fulda, 45
  Irish, 32–3, 44–5, 49, 93, 99
  'Kentish', 137
  Melrose, 102
  Murbach, 45
  Northumbrian, 101–114, 116
  Paschal, 44, 47–50, 55, 90, 94, 96–7
  Paschale Campanum, 46, 48
  Ramsey, 101–114, 121
  St Bertin, 118
  St Évroul, 121
  St Neots, 120–1, 133
  Salzburg, 45
  Xanten, 55
  see also Anglo-Saxon Chronicle, Bede, Simeon
anno ab urbe condita, see era
Annunciation, feast of, 34, 117
Annus Domini, and Indiction, 40, 67, 82–3, 86, 94
Annus Mundi, 33, 47, 54, 76–7, 82, 97, 125, 139
Annus Passionis, 33, 46, 53

INDEX

Anonymous monk of
  Wearmouth-Jarrow, 42, 51, 73, 89, 139
  Whitby, 136
Antoninus, e., wall of, 24
Arian heresy, 48
Ashdown, 133
Ash Wednesday, 31
Asia Minor, Easter reckoning from, 32
Attila, k. Huns, 23, 26, 53
Augustine, abp. Canterbury, 18, 78–9, 95, 103–4, 140
  monastery, *see* Canterbury
Augustine, bp. Hippo, 52, 126
Augustus, e., 41
Avars, 112

Babylonia, *see* calendar
Badwulf, bp. Whithorn, 112
Barking, Essex, 71–2
Bath, *see* cartulary
Battersea, 71
Bearn, 111
Bede
  and Anglo-Saxon Chronicle, 134–5
  Continuation of, 101–114
  and heathenism, 3, 8, 68
  letter to Egbert, 98, 105
  works: *Chronica Minora*, 76; *Chronica Maiora*, 49, 73–4, 76–7, 93–4, 125, 139–40; Commentaries, 61; *De Natura Rerum*, 83; *De Temporibus*, 76; *De Temporum Ratione*, 3, 36–8, 40–43, 61, 66, 72–3, 76, 94–5, 138; *Historia Abbatum*, 42; *Historia Ecclesiastica*, (system of dates) 85–9, 95–6, (theme of), 17–19; Penitential, 8
Benedict Biscop, abbot, 63
Beonna, bp. Hereford, 114–15
Beornwulf, k. Mercia, 114–15
Beowulf, 132
Berhtwold, abp. Canterbury, 103
Bertana, abbess, 68
Bertha, q. Kent, 121–3, 125, 140
  chaplain of, *see* Liudhard
birds, mortality of, 133
Birinus, bp. Dorchester, 64, 134–5
Birr, 58
Bisi, bp. East Anglia, 103
Bode, law of, 148
Boniface
  abp. Mainz, 38, 45, 74
  archdeacon, 63
Bosa, 109
Bosel, bp. Hwicce, 103
Botwine, abbot, 110
Botwulf, 134
Brown, E. W., 58
Brussels, Royal Observatory, eclipse calculations, 93–4

Caedwalla, k. Wessex, 71, 74, 143–5
Caesar, Julius, 9, 18, 35
Caistor-by-Norwich, 16
calendar
  Anglo-Saxon, 3, 96
  Babylonian, 10, 30
  Egyptian, 2
  Greek, 2, 10
  Islamic, 12
  Julian, 1, 12, 30, 96
Canterbury abp., see Augustine, Berhtwold, Deusdedit, Honorius, Jaenberht, Justus, Laurentius, Mellitus, Nothelm, Tatwine, Theodore
  concurrent dating, 69–70
  St Augustine's (Peter-Paul), 93
  Scriptorium, 115
  see also cartulary
Carlisle, 27
Carloman, k. Franks, 108
cartulary
  Bath, 67
  Canterbury, 72
  London (Westminster), 72
  Winchester, 71
  Worcester (Hemming's), 67
Cassiodorus, 52
Ceawlin, k. Wessex, 131, 133
Celtic church, *see* Easter tables
Cenred (Coenred)
  k. Mercia, 70, 91, 134
  k. Northumbria, 88
Centwine, k. Wessex, 135
Cenwalh, k. Wessex, 129, 133, 135
Cenwulf (Coenwulf), k. Mercia, 115
Ceolfrith, abbot, 39, 42–3, 51, 63, 89, 100, 131
  life, *see* Anonymous monk of Wearmouth-Jarrow
Ceolred, k. Mercia, 70, 110
Ceolwulf I, k. Mercia, 115
Ceolwulf, k. Northumbria, 88, 104, 121
Cerdic, k. Wessex, 127–9, 131, 133
Cerdices ford, Charford, 128
Cerdicesleag, 128
Cerdicesora, 128
Charibert, k. Paris, 122
Charles the Great, e., 105, 108–110, 112, 114
charters
  dating clause, 67
  Kentish, 69, 142–5
Chartres, 99
Chelsea, Synod of, 110
Chertsey, 72, 146
Chester, 132
Chilperic, k. Franks, 122
Christmas, reckoning from, 9, 37–8, 105, 113, 116, 140
  see also Midwinter

chroniclers
  Aethelweard, 117, 120, 128–9, 133
  Eusebius, 37, 47–50, 54
  Fredegar, 48
  Gallic, 26–7, 29
  Hydatius, 25–6, 149
  Isidore, 51–2
  Jerome, 47–50, 54
  Marcellinus Comes, 26, 126
  Marius of Avenches, 49
  Orosius, 47
  Prosper, 27, 124–6, 149
  see also Anglo-Saxon Chronicle, annals, Bede
Circumcision, feast of, 37–8
Claudius, e., 18
Cleostratus, 2
Clofeshoh, see councils
Clonfert-Mulloe, 58
Clonmacnoise, 58
Clovis, k. Franks, 48, 125
Codex Amiatinus, 102
Colman, bp. Lindisfarne, 75
Cologne, 111
Columba, life of, 100, 136
Columbanus, abbot, 57
comets, 82–3, 85, 117
Concilium Germanicum, see councils
concurrent dating, 69–70
Condidan, k. Britons, 123, 133
Coniscliffe, 109–110
conjunction, 7
Conmail, k. Britons, 123, 133
Cornwall, conquest of, 27
consecration of bishops, 103–4
  of Ceolwulf I, 115
Constans, e., 24
Constantine I, e., 39
Constantine III, e., 24
Constantinople, *see* Indiction
Constantius of Lyon, 27, 50, 52
Constantius III, e., 24
Consularia Italica, see annals
consular lists, 33, 46–7, 124–5
Corvey, 45
councils
  Clofeshoh, 114–17
  Concilium Germanicum, 74
  Hatfield, 41, 80, 83–5, 94, 98
  Hertford, 84–5, 98, 143
  Nicaea, 30, 34, 53
  Orleans, 33, 48, 58
  Rome, 95
Creation, dates of the, 53–4, *see also Annus Mundi*
Crucifixion, 30, 32
Cumbria-Strathclyde, 32
Cummian, 58–62, 64–5
Cuthred, k. Wessex, 133–4
Cwichelm, k. Wessex, 133

cycle
  Great Paschal, 33, 39, 46, 138
  lunar, Islamic, 12
  luni-solar: 8-year, 2–5, 11, 31, 34, 130, 147; 19-year, 2, 11, 30, 33, 127–9; 84-year, 32, 44–5, 59–60, (at Rome) 33; 532-year, *see* Great Paschal above
Cynegils, k. Wessex, 135
Cynewulf, bp. Lindisfarne, 103, 109
Cynewulf, *dux*, 109–110
Cynric, k. Wessex, 128–9, 133
Cyril, bp. Alexandria, 34, 39, 63

Daniel, bp. Winchester, 103, 126–7, 135
Danube, r, 10
Darwin, C., 54
Defoe, D., 68
Degsastan, 95–6, 129, 132, 146
Deusdedit, abp. Canterbury, 40, 93–4
Devon, conquest of, 27
Diocletian, e., 34, 39, 97
Dionysius Exiguus, 34, 40–41, 63
  see Easter tables
Dionysius of Alexandria, 34
Dniestr, r, 10
Dorchester-on-Thames, 19, 64
  bp. *see* Agilbert, Birinus
double monasteries, 68
Driffield, 90
Drycthelm, 126
Dyrham, 123

Eadbald, k. Kent, 79, 95, 146–7, 150
Eadberht, k. Northumbria, 106
Eadric, k. Kent, 143
Eadwulf, usurper, 85
Ealdwulf, *dux*, 109–110
Ealhstan, bp. Sherborne, 118
Eanbald I, abp. York, 103, 108–111, 113
Eanbald II, abp. York, 112–13
Eanflaed, q. Northumbria, 63
Earnwine, 104
Easter
  battle at time of, 133
  controversy in Ireland, 58–61
  lunar limits of, 30–34, 61
  tables: Celtic, 31–2, 59, 62, 100, 137–8; Cyrillic, 34, 39; Dionysiac, 34 & *passim*; of Hippolytus, 31; Victorian, 33, 40, 46, 56–64, 123–5, 138
  see also equinox, Paschal controversy, Zeitz
East Saxons, heathenism, 68
Ebba, abbess, 69
Ebbsfleet, 140
Ecga, *dux*, 109–110
Ecgfrith, k. Northumbria, 84–5, 88, 145
Ecgric, 49
Echternach, 50

INDEX

eclipse
  lunar, 104–5, 112, 114, 116
  solar, 6, 93–7, 117, 134–5
Eddius Stephanus, 31, 50, 62, 72–4, 85, 90–92, 135
Edwin, k. Northumbria, 78–9, 86, 88, 92, 96
Egbert, abp. York, 8, 38, 101, 105, 107–108, 113
Egbert, k. Kent, 80, 83, 143–5
Egypt, *see* calendar
Elbe, r, 10, 20
Eider, r, 20
Elmham, Thomas, 69
Ely, 134
Ember Days, 115
Emly, 58
Eorcenberht, k. Kent, 95, 122, 146–8, 150
Eorcenwold. bp. London, 68–72
Eormenric, k. Kent, 124, 147
epacts, 35–6
episcopal lists, 96–7
episcopal sees, succession to, 103–4
equinox, 32, 34, 43
era, of Abraham, 48–9
  Christian, 34, 97–8
  of Diocletian, 34, 97
  Olympiads, 48, 53
  Passion, 33, 53
  Spanish, 51, 138
  of Rome (A.U.C.) 37, 53, 77, 98
Étaples, 28
Ethelbert, abp. York, 101, 103, 107–11
Ethelbert, bp. Whithorn, later Hexham, 108, 113
Ethelbert, k. Kent, 39, 51, 79, 94–5, 121–4, 131, 147, 150
Ethelred, k. Northumbria, 108–12
Eugenius II, Pope, 115
Euric, k. Visigoths, 52
Eusebius, bp. Caesarea, *see* chroniclers

Farinmail, k. Britons, 123, 133
Felix Gillitanus, 39, 63–4, 90
Finan, bp. Lindisfarne, 62
Fintan, *see* Munnu
Florence, 81
Fortunatus, Venantius, 122
Franks, Salian, 23
Fraomar, *dux*, 15
Fredegar, *see* chroniclers
Frigeridus, Renatus Profuturus, 24, 48, 124
Frisia, 20
Frithuberht, bp. Hexham, 104, 107–108
Frithuwald, monk, 67
Frithuwold, bp. Whithorn, 88, 104, 106–107
Fulda, 45
Fünen, 21

Fursa, 126

Gallic chroniclers, *see* chroniclers
Germanus, bp. Auxerre, 27–8, 50, 77
  see also Constantius of Lyon
Gibbon, Edward, 20
Gildas, 17, 21–5, 28, 126–7
Greece, *see* calendar
Gregory, bp. Tours, 21, 24, 26, 47, 53–4, 57, 121–22, 124–5, 140
Gregory I (the Great), Pope, 18, 39, 56, 78–9, 93, 95, 98, 122
  life of, 136
Gregory II, Pope, 40
Grendel, 132
Guthlac, 124, 132

Hadrian, abbot, 41, 70, 91–92
Hadrian, e., wall of, 24
Hadrian, Pope, 112
Haeddi, abbot, later bp. Winchester, 68–72
Hagona, abbot, 70–72
Hatfield, *see* councils
Heahmund, bp. Sherborne, 118
Healfdene, 28
Heardred, bp. Hexham, 113
Helathirnum, 109–110
Hemming, *see* cartulary
Hengest, 21, 77, 124, 130, 136, 140
Henry of Huntingdon, 102
Hereford, bp., *see* Beonna
Herodotus, 50
Hertford, *see* councils
Hesiod, 9
Hewald, 111
Hexham, 92
  bp., *see* Alhmund, Ethelbert, Frithuberht, Heardred, Tilberht
Higbald, bp. Lindisfarne, 8, 103
Hilarius, Pope, 103
Hippolytus, *see* Easter tables
Hlothere, k. Kent, 80, 83–4, 94, 118, 142–4
Hocca, Hooc, 71
Hodilred, *see* Oethelraed
Honorius, abp. Canterbury, 63, 93
Honorius, e., 17, 24
Honorius, Pope, 59–60, 86, 98
Horsa, 21, 77, 140
Hoveden, Roger de, 101–114
Hrothgar, 132
Hunfrith, bp. Winchester, 103
Hwicce, 18
  bp., *see* Worcester
  k., *see* Oshere, Osric
Hydatius, *see* chroniclers

Icanho, 65, 134
Ida, k. Northumbria, 21, 88

166

INDEX

In Derauuda, 103
Indiction, 13, 38–9, 41, 96, 113–14, 116
  Bedan, 41–44, 112–14, 116, 118–19
  Caesarean (Imperial), 42
  Greek (Constantinople), 41, 104
  Pontifical (Roman), 42
  primacy of, 66, 101, 118; and decline, 98, 118–19, 139
  rule for finding, 40, 83, 86
Ingeld, 9
Ingoberg, q. Franks, 121
intercalation, 4, 10, 32, 137
interregnum
  in Kent, 80, 143–5
  in Northumbria, 81, 85, 87, 92, 94
Iona, 32, 77, 99–100, 129, 138
  see also Segene, Slebhine
Ireland, Church in, 32–3, *see also* Paschal controversy
Isidore, bp. Seville, *see* chroniclers
Islam, *see* calendar, cycle

Jaenberht, abp. Canterbury, 107
James the Deacon, 56, 62, 64, 97
James of Nisibis, 125
James II, k. England, 87
Jarrow, *see* Wearmouth
  inscription at, 84–5
Jerome, *see* chroniclers
John IV, Pope, 60
John XIII, Pope, 139
John of Beverley, bp. York, 51, 103
Johnson, Samuel, 91
Jovinus, e., 24
Justinian, e., 39, 41
Justus, abp. Canterbury, 97
Jutes, 20–21
Jutland, 11, 20

Kalendae, pagan festival, 38
Kent
  devastation of, 70, 142
  Dionysiac tables in, 64
  Franks in, 16
  history of, 18
  k., *see* Eadbald, Eadric, Egbert, Eorcenberht, Eormenric, Ethelbert, Hlothere, Octa, Oisc, Oswine, Swaebheard
  literacy in, 122
  Vikings in, 28
king-list
  Northumbrian, 87–8, 124
  Wessex, 136
kingship, concept of, 87, 92, 130
Koran, 53

Langres, near Troyes, 42
Laurentius, abp. Canterbury, 103
law-speakers, 131

leap years, 148–50
Legatine Synod, 110, 112–14
Leicester, 27
Leire, 12
Leo I, Pope, 33, 53, 55
Leo IX, Pope, 139
Leutherius, bp. Winchester, 68
Le Verrier, U., 148
Libellus Responsionum, 78
Lindisfarne, bp., *see* Aidan, Colman, Cynewulf, Finan, Higbald, Tuda
Liudhard, bishop and chaplain to Bertha q. Kent, 122–3, 140
London, *see* cartulary
  bp., *see* Eorcenwold, Mellitus
Lothar, k. Franks, 121
lunation, 7, 94
Lupercalia, 9

Magh Lene, Synod at, 58
Maildubh, abbot, 134
Malmesbury, 134
Marcellinus Comes, *see* chroniclers
Marcian, e., 18–19, 76, 100, 125, 140
Marius of Avenches, *see* chroniclers
Markshall, Norfolk, 16
Marseilles, 26
Maserfeld (Oswestry), 81
Maurice, e., 39, 95, *see also* St Maurice
Maximus, bp. Trèves, 125
Mellitus, bp. London, later abp Canterbury, 97
Melrose, *see* annals
Mercedonius, month, 10
Mercia, k., *see* Aethelred, Beornwulf, Cenred, Cenwulf, Ceolred, Ceolwulf I, Penda, Wiglaf, Wulfhere
Meretun, 118
Messiah, 37
Meton, *see* cycle, 19-year
Midwinter, pagan festival, 3, 7, 137, *see also* Christmas
Minster-in-Thanet, 69
Mons Badonicus, 22
months, Anglo-Saxon, 3–4
  embolismic (intercalary), 4, 7–8
  lunar, 2, 6–8, 10
moon
  as a clock, 1–2, 10
  folklore, 11
  saltus lunae, 32
  see also conjunction, cycle, eclipses, lunation, months
Mosaic law, 9, 30
Mungret, 58
Munnu, abbot, 59
Murbach, *see* annals

Naiton (Nechtan), k. Picts, 39
Natanleag, Netley, 128

Natanleod, k. Britons, 128–9
Nativity, feast of, *see* Christmas, St Mary
Nennius, 11, 99, 126, 136
Nicaea, *see* councils
Nidd, Synod of, 90–91
Nile, r, 2
Nisan, 30
Northumbria, *see* annals
  k., accession, 87–8
  see also Aelfwold, Aethelfrith, Aethelwold Moll, Aldfrith, Alhred, Cenred, Ceolwulf, Eadberht, Ecgfrith, Edwin, Ethelred, Osred I, Osred II, Osric, Oswald, Oswiu, Oswulf
Nothelm, priest, later abp. Canterbury, 74
Nothelm, *praeco*, 115

obits, list of, 89
occulation, of 114 Taurus, 105
Octa, k. Kent, 124, 147
octaëteris, *see* cycle, 8-year
Oder, r, 10
Odoacer, k. Huns, 53
Oethelraed (Hodilred), 71
Offa, k. Mercia, 116
Oftfor, bp. Hwicce, 103
ogdoas, 5, 8, 11, 32
Oisc, k. Kent, 29, 124, 130, 133, 147
Oiscingas, 130
Olympiads, *see* era
Orleans, *see* councils
Orosius, *see* chroniclers
Oshere, k. Hwicce, 67
Osred I, k. Northumbria, 85, 88, 90–92
Osred II, k. of Northumbria, 110–112
Osric, k. Deira, 89
Osric, k. Hwicce, 68
Osric, k. Northumbria, 88–9, 91–2
Oswald, abp. York, 102
Oswald, k. Northumbria, 51, 62, 81, 86, 88–9, 92, 129, 135
Oswine, k. Kent, 142–4
Oswiu, k. Northumbria, 56, 75, 81, 84, 87–9, 92–3, 95, 99, 135, 145
Oswulf, k. Northumbria, 106
Otto the Great, e., 139
Oundle, 92

Parma, 111
Paschal controversy, 32–4, 137–8
  in Ireland, 58–62
Paschal epistles, 31
Paschale Campanum, *see* annals
Passover, 30
Pauli, R., 108
Paulinus, bp. York, 56, 65, 79, 86–7, 97
Pavia, 108
Peada, sub-k, Mercia, 80

Pecthelm, bp. Whithorn, 104, 134
Pehtwine, bp. Whithorn, 106–108, 110
Pelagian heresy, 18, 60–61
Pelagius II, Pope, 39
Penda, k. Mercia, 80, 132, 135
Penitential
  Bede, 8
  Egbert, 8, 38
  Theodore, 68
Peterborough, 121, 135
Phocas, e., 95, 146
Picts, 20, 22–5, 27, 78, 100, 126
Pincanheale, synod at, 49, 110
Pippin, k. Franks, 108
piracy, 27–8
Pirmin, abbot, 45
Pisa, 81
plague, 25–6, 93, 148
Pliny, 43
Poitiers, 121
Port, 127–9
Portchester, 16
Portsmouth, 127–8
Posentes byrig, 133
pottery, 20
Powys, 136
Prosper, *see* chroniclers
Provence, 81
Prudentius, 52
Purification, feast of, 9, 107

quartodecimanians, 31
Quentawic, 28

Raedwald, k. East Anglia, 146
Ramsey, *see* annals
Reccaswinth, k. Visigoths, 52
regnal list, *see* king-list
Reichenau, 45
Rhine, r, 9
Ripon, 74, 92–3, 135
  charter, 72–3
  date of *aduentus Saxonum*, 99–101, 125–6, 140
  see also Tatberct
Rochester, 70
Rogation days, 117
Romanitas, concept of, 52, 125
Rome
  Dionysiac tables at, 58–61, 134, 137, 139
  sack, by Alaric, 24
  siege, by Attila, 53
  see also councils, cycle, era, Paschal epistles
Romulus Augustulus, 53
Ronan, 62, 64
Rowena, 136

saga, 132
St Albans, 28

INDEX

St Augustine's, monastery, *see* Canterbury
St Bertin, *see* annals
St Évroul, *Annales Uticenses, see* annals
St Frideswide's, *see* double monasteries
St John Baptist, feast of, 9
St Mark, feast of, 107
St Mary
    Nativity of, 104, 113
    Purification of, 9, 107
St Maurice, 116
St Michael, feast of, 112
St Neots, *see* annals
saltus lunae, see moon
Sammland, 11
Sarmatian ornament, 11
Sawley, 101
Saxon Shore, 15, 25
Schleswig, 20
Scots (Irish), 22–5, 126
Seaxburh, q. Wessex, 135
Seaxwulf, bp. Lichfield, 68
Sebbi, k. East Saxons, 142, 144
Sedulius, 122
Segene, abbot, 58
Selsey, 89
Sens, 123
Septuagint, 65, 76
Seville, springs at, 53, 57
Sexagesima, 107
Sherborne, 117–18
    bp., *see* Aldhelm, Ealhstan, Heahmund
Sidonius Appolinaris, bp. Clermont, 52
Sighere, k. East Saxons, 143–4
Simeon of Durham, 101–114
Slebhine, abbot, 99–100
Slieve Margy, Synod at, 59
sol inuictus, 9, 114
Solstice, 9, 137
Spain, *see* era, Spanish
Squillace (*Vivarium*), 63
Stephen, k. England, 38
Stuf, 128
Sulpicius Alexander, 48
Swaebheard, k. Kent, 69, 142–5

tacencircol, 117
Tacitus, 9, 137
Taghmon, 60
tamga-signs, 11
Tatberct, abbot, 90
Tatwine, abp. Canterbury, 104
Thames, r, 16
Thanet, 69, 136
Theodore, abp. Canterbury, 41, 65, 68–70, 98, 138, 142, 144
Theophilus, bp. Alexandria, 63
Theodosius, e., 26, 63, 76
Thietmar, 12
Thucydides, 50

Tilberht, bp. Hexham, 110–112
trinoda necessitas, 66
Tuda, bp. Lindisfarne, 59
Twelfth night, 117
Twickenham, charter (*BCS* 111), 91
Tydlin, 71

Uertigernus, *see* Vortigern
Ulster, *see* annals, Irish
Utrecht, 50, 73

Valentinian III, e., 18–19, 23–4, 76–7, 100, 124–5, 140
Varro, 53
Venantius Fortunatus, *see* Fortunatus
Venice, 81
Verulamium, *see* St Albans
Victor, bp. Capua, 61
Victor of Tonnenna, 46
Victorius of Aquitaine, 33, 47, 53, 64, *see also* Easter tables
Vikings, 117–18
    in Kent, 28
Visigoths, law, 52
Vistula, r, 10
Vitalian, Pope, 41
Vortigern, 20, 22, 77, 99, 123, 133
Vulgate text, 54, 76

Wales, Church in, 32, 61
    Roman, 17
Wearmouth–Jarrow, 73, 85, 88–9, 94, 139, *see also* Anonymous monk, Ceolfrith
Werburh, abbess, 110
Weser, r, 20
Wessex, Easter tables in, 64, 72, 134–5
    k., *see* Aescwine, Alfred, Caedwalla, Ceawlin, Centwine, Cenwalh, Cerdic, Cuthred, Cwichelm, Cynegils, Cynric
    sub-k., 135
Whitby, Synod of, 49, 56, 62, 75, 92–3, 137
Whithorn, bp., *see* Badwulf, Ethelbert, Frithuwold, Pecthelm, Pehtwine
Wight, Isle of, 20, 128
Wiglaf, k. Mercia, 145
Wihtgar, 128
Wihtgarabyrig, 133
Wihtred, k. Kent, 122, 143–4
Wilfrid I, bp. York, 50, 56, 83–4, 99–100, 103, 131, 138
    and charters, 65–75, 97
    death of, 90–92, 94
    epitaph, 75, 91
    at Rome, 62–4
    see also Eddius Stephanus
Wilfrid II, bp. York, 103, 108
Willibrord, abp. Utrecht, 45, 50, 73–4, 89, 94, 103, 111–112, 138

INDEX

Winchester, 27
  bp., *see* Daniel, Haeddi, Hunfrith,
    Leutherius
  burials at, 16
Winwaed, r, 81, 89
Worcester, 18
  bp., *see* Bosel, Oftfor
  scriptorium, 115
  see also cartulary, Hwicce

Wulfhere, k. Mercia, 80, 145–6

Xanten, *see* annals

years
  Anglo-Saxon, length of, 3, 12–13, 124
  embolismic, 4–5
  Indictional, 39, 41–2
  post consulatum, 95
  regnal, drawback to, 92, 129
York, 19, 90, 101
  bp., abp., *see* Eanbald I, Eanbald II,
    Egbert, Ethelbert, John of Beverley,
    Paulinus, Wilfred I, Wilfrid II

Zacharias, Pope, 38
Zeitz, 44–5